Living Intentionally

Andrew H. Eschenfelder

WINEPRESS WP PUBLISHING

ISBN 1-57921-162-3
Library of Congress Catalog Card Number: 98-88568

Acknowledgments

Over the years it has been my habit, when listening to a sermon or reading a book, to write down concepts or ideas that seemed to me to be particularly worth remembering. It is now impossible for me to recall the exact sources of most of these concepts and ideas, many of which I have included in this book. I want to acknowledge that many of these ideas are not original with me, and I have tried to recognize the sources of those I could identify. I want to thank all of the preachers and authors whose wisdom has enriched my life and particularly those who gave me insights that I have included in this book.

Dr. Stanley M. Johnson has been a particularly rich source for me of both ideas and inspiration. Stan served as Senior Pastor of the Saratoga (California) Federated Church from 1975 to 1988, and our friendship and interaction on these issues has continued since then. I have learned a great deal both from the sermons he gave when a pastor at SFC and in our private conversations. Naturally I have included in this book many of the rich insights I have received from him.

Acknowledgments

I would not have written this book, nor adapted the material for use by groups, without the urging and assistance of Arvin Engelson. Arvin has been Pastor for Care & Family Ministries at Saratoga Federated Church since 1978 and has always been involved with pastoring the men of the church. It was he who persuaded me that other men would eagerly welcome mutual interaction on these issues, he who initially arranged for me to give my first talk at a men's breakfast, he who encouraged me to write the book, he who helped me with the first men's groups and guided me in finding better ways to lead men and also women in the discussion of this material. He is a true friend and mentor. (Arvin is twenty-three years younger than I am. We hope that we older men have something to teach the younger men, but it is clear that we also have a lot to learn from them).

I have revised this book several times after the courses I have led with groups of either men or women. In these courses, which extended over twelve or more weekly sessions, I gained important additional insight from the participants, and I want to thank those men and women for the thoughtful devotion they gave to those sessions, to me, and to each other. I am also indebted to the women who challenged me to explore the application of these ideas for women as well as for men. My first women's group was a wonderful and helpful experience.

I also want to thank my loving and patient wife, Jean, who must have felt at times that I was more devoted to this project than I am to her. In due course she became my projectionist, my proofreader, and my valuable consultant.

Contents

What's This Book About?
A Lifestyle for Everyone 7

SECTION 1: THE CHALLENGE

CHAPTER 1: Rafting the River of Life 17
CHAPTER 2: The Flow of Events 25
CHAPTER 3: Anticipating the Flow 37
CHAPTER 4: Living Intentionally 47
CHAPTER 5: Why Bother? 63

Synopsis and Reflection 71

SECTION 2: THE APPLICATION

CHAPTER 6: Coping with Forks
Which Path Am I Going to Choose? 79
CHAPTER 7: Coping with Dislocations
How Should I React to This Sudden Change in My Life? . . 111

CHAPTER 8: Realizing Our Resources
   Where Do I Find the Help I Need? 141
CHAPTER 9: Exploiting Our Occasions
   I Don't Want to Miss My Chance! 173
CHAPTER 10: Recognizing Our Givens
   Taking My Uniqueness into Account 187
CHAPTER 11: What Next?
   My First Steps on a New Road 203

SECTION 3: OUR UNIQUENESS

CHAPTER 12: Personal Characteristics 225
CHAPTER 13: Beliefs and Attitudes 243
CHAPTER 14: Personal History 277

Epilogue 313

APPENDIX A: Small Group Study Guide 315
APPENDIX B: Worksheets 325
APPENDIX C: Complementary Attributes Needing Balance 339
APPENDIX D: Growing in an Attribute 345

What's This Book About?

A Lifestyle for Everyone

Life is precious! Life is difficult! Life is joyous! Can you vigorously affirm all three of these exclamations?

Whether you hesitate to declare these as personal convictions, or can already claim them enthusiastically, I want to help you to treasure your life, to increase your joy and satisfaction in it, as well as to manage and minimize the difficulties. All by living *intentionally*.

Life is indeed precious. We cling to it unless joy has completely evaporated and difficulties overwhelm us. Most of us will sacrifice almost everything to preserve our own life or someone else's, for we only go around once here on Planet Earth. In this book we will consider ways to maximize our opportunities and live life to the hilt—*intentionally*.

Life is often difficult. None of us has mastered the art of living well. Fortunately, we usually get better at it as we mature. But for everyone it is a struggle. And sometimes we wonder if we can ever surmount the hurdles. So in this book, we'll look at better ways of dealing with difficulties.

Life is sometimes joyous. And most of us have tasted joy, even if we have difficulty describing it or making it happen. Joy is a deep contentment in our souls. It may be found in fulfilling a unique purpose; or basking in the love of another person; or standing in awe before the glorious splendors of nature. Life can be joyous even in the midst of its difficulties. In this book we will be thinking together about ways of experiencing joy more abundantly.

Our lives are stories written in chapters, or eras: childhood, youth, young adulthood, midlife, etc. In each era we are faced with a variety of opportunities and difficulties. *Living Intentionally* offers a lifestyle that enriches lives, whatever our era, our difficulties, our opportunities, our personal strengths or weaknesses. It can maximize our joy, while enabling us to manage our difficulties and make the most of our precious opportunities.

Many people have discovered new strength and joy from applying the principles of *Living Intentionally*, which are revealed in this book.

Steve had to decide whether to accept a new job. This would have advanced his career and provided a lot more money and perks; it would also have caused serious disruptions for the rest of his family. He made his decision *intentionally*.

Joan recently had to decide whether to marry Bob. Her first marriage had ended in divorce. Naturally, she was cautious about a second marriage. However, she felt she had learned a lot about what was necessary to make a marriage last and was optimistic. Moreover, the present romance with Bob seemed to have the ingredients for a wonderful marriage. Joan wanted to be sure that she considered all of the important factors and that her head influenced her decision as much as her heart. She made her decision *intentionally*.

Bruce had to decide whether to retire now or continue to work. There were so many factors to take into account, including the psychological impact of the drastic change in his lifestyle. Bruce made his decision *intentionally*.

Betsy and Fred had to decide what to do about their rebellious daughter. She had slipped into a destructive lifestyle and repudiated her parents. Betsy and Fred considered how best to rescue their daughter from the brink of disaster. Whatever they did, it was going to be tough. They dealt with this important issue *intentionally*.

In every era there are such branch points, or forks, in our path, times when we must decide which way to go. We want to make these decisions *intentionally*. Later in this book, we will talk about what we can do to make the best possible decisions at our forks.

Sometimes we don't have a choice of path, but only of response. Each era has its times when we are forced onto another path: a disabling illness or accident, death of a loved one, loss of a job, etc. Fran recently suffered the unexpected loss of her husband. He suddenly died of a heart attack. All at once her life was on a new course and she had to deal with unfamiliar issues. She found herself in need of substantial support and help. I call these disruptions our dislocations, because all of a sudden we find ourselves in a very different place. We'll talk about ways of dealing with our dislocations, including the resources that are available to help us cope.

Paul was getting into his later years and he began to think of the legacy he would leave behind him. How important were the things he had done? What were the most important things left for him to do? Was he having the impact that he wanted on his children and grandchildren? Paul wanted to be able to look back with confidence that his life had counted in the most significant way possible. He wanted to use every occasion to make the most of his remaining life. Paul used the insights he gained from this book to think through those issues and to decide what he wanted to emphasize in his remaining days.

Jim didn't like the way that circumstances were sweeping him along; he felt he was out of control. He wanted to stop and regain more control over the course of his life. We will talk about the process of taking stock of our current situation and reassessing where we want to go, whether we seem to be heading there, and new directions we should undertake.

Yes, life is difficult. We have many problems to deal with. The difficulty of dealing with our forks and dislocations can wear us down and rob our lives of joy. However, as we become more adept at dealing with our forks and dislocations, there is more room for joy. At the same time, whether in the midst of our difficulties or in easier times, there are things we can do to stimulate and nourish joy in our life. We also realize that each day presents new opportunities to move in the direction of our hopes and dreams. Even if we didn't make the most of yesterday, we still have a new chance today. We will talk about ways of making the most of every opportunity, thereby increasing our joy.

Each of our lives is unique. Your life is quite different from mine. But when we look beyond the differences in details, we see that we can all use the same wisdom. We all face decisions, albeit different ones, but we can use the same procedure in making those decisions. We all face dislocations, albeit different ones, but we can use the same principles in coping with whichever dislocations assail us. We can learn from each other, as well as from a careful review of our own experience. This book is a compendium of whatever wisdom I have been able to accumulate from my own experience and from what others have told me about their experiences.

Using our accumulated wisdom to deal effectively with the events of our lives constitutes a lifestyle I call *living intentionally*. This is a lifestyle for everyone, whatever our age or our circumstances. It stems from the conviction that in order to get where we want to go, we have to be intentional. We have to think about where we want to go and then take the steps that will get us there. We have to "set our sails" correctly. Ella Wheeler Wilcox understands the importance of the set of our sails. She wrote:

One ship drives east and another drives west
With the selfsame winds that blow;
Tis the set of the sails,
And not the gales,
Which determines which way we will go.

Yes, we are subject to conflicting winds. There is the wind of the culture pushing us one way. There is the wind of the Spirit pushing us a different way.

That poem reminds us that some people sail in the direction of whatever wind they feel the strongest (cultural pressure? short-term expedients?). Others set their sails aright and manage to go upstream to the full realization of their most noble long-term goals. We have to decide which way we want to go, and we can go that way even when the prevailing wind is adverse. But we do have to *set* our sails, as Oliver Wendell Holmes said:

> I find the great thing in this world is not so much where we stand,
> as in what direction we are moving:
> To reach the port of heaven,
> we must sail sometimes with the wind
> and sometimes against it—
> but we must sail, and not drift, nor lie at anchor.

If you want to understand what it is to sail, and not drift, to *live intentionally,* and also to learn how to do it, this book is designed for you.

This book is divided into three sections. In section 1 we will talk about *what* it means to *live intentionally* and *why* we want to *live intentionally.* Section 2 contains ideas about *how* to live more intentionally: how to deal with forks, dislocations, etc.; how to be alert to opportunities and make the most of them; how to recognize and utilize the resources that are available to us; how to accomplish the changes we want in our life. Section 3 helps us to enumerate and understand those unique and different characteristics of ourselves and our situations, which we must take into account in making decisions that are suitable and realistic for us. The appendix contains some supplementary material and optional worksheets, which will be referred to in the text.

As you read each chapter, you may decide that you want to come back to a particular section or idea and think more about it. There is space at the end of each chapter for you to note those places you want to revisit. Also, at the end of the first section, and at the end of each chapter thereafter, there is a synopsis of the important points of the text to make it easy for you to review. There are also a few questions you can answer if you want to try to apply the material of the chapter to your own particular situation.

Many readers will read the text without taking time to answer the personal application questions, perhaps just noting their content and relevance. On the other hand, some readers will want to do a deeper personal exercise, in preparation for trying to live more intentionally. In that case, it is recommended that you use the personal application questions and a journal. The journal is for you to record your responses to the PA (personal application) questions, as well as other ideas, reflections, and issues that you want to think about later. There are quite a few PA questions. You may want to select a few particular questions before going on to the next chapter and come back to other questions later.

It certainly helps to have a companion with whom you can discuss these concepts and your reactions to them. A particularly fruitful way of using this book is as the text for a small group study. This material has been tested in groups of men and in groups of women. Those who have participated in such groups have felt that they received a much greater benefit from their time together than from studying alone. This is because of what they learned about the issues from the other participants, and also because of the close relationships they established with each other.

I have found that all men and women really want to have a few close comrades with whom they can discuss the important issues in their lives. If they didn't realize it before, they are sure of it once they have participated in one of these groups. They find that this type of material fosters a strong supportive bond between the participants of a group much faster than other approaches they have experienced. In our groups we quickly developed a trust in each other to the point where we could be genuine, candid, and vulnerable. We came to realize that we have such common ground in our daily struggles that, as we share our stories, we are accepted as we are, and do not have to pretend. We discover wisdom and new encouragement for our lives from the stories that are recounted by the others. The small group approach is the best way to reflect on this material and is highly recommended.

Our study groups have been of various sizes: as small as four, usually eight, sometimes twelve or more. Typically the groups meet weekly for an hour and a half on each topic. It is easier to explore each person's experiences and insights when the group is small. Larger groups have an advantage and a disadvantage. The advantage is that the greater diversity in a larger group introduces a broader range of personal experiences to learn from. The disadvantage is that longer sessions or additional sessions are necessary, or each person's involvement in the conversation must be severely limited. Interestingly, our most recent group of four spent more time on the material than our typical groups of eight. They became really involved with each other and wanted to go into greater depth. We recommend at least four in a group and not more than eight.

Those small groups have been of either men or women. An intergenerational group, where everyone is over the age of thirty-five, is particularly interesting, especially as the older ones are able to share what they have experienced and learned in similar circumstances to what the younger ones are now confronting. We have found that men or women under thirty-five are interested in discovering the kinds of experiences they have yet to encounter, but the whole process doesn't mean as much to them as it does after they have lived through their twenties and are well launched on their careers and families. This material has also been taught in larger classes of men and women together. Recently an interactive class of young couples has been a great joy. Those couples were eager to discuss those particular issues with other young couples. They also formed valuable bonds with other couples of kindred spirit. In any group, some time must be left in each session for questions and discussion. The discussion is particularly rich in the small, intimate, same-sex groups.

I hope that this book is a resource that can accelerate the establishment of such groups for men and for women. Some advice on using the material in small group studies is included in appendix A.

Even if you are not a member of a group, you can benefit from individual study of this book. People who have been exposed to these concepts have said that their lives have been blessed by it. It is my hope and prayer that yours will be also. Let us begin, in section 1, by trying to understand what it is to live intentionally so that you can discover whether it seems to be something that you would like to pursue further.

The Challenge

Chapter 1

Rafting the River of Life

What pure bliss! Jim was lying back in a sturdy rubber raft, letting the sun warm his body. He slowly drifted down the American River. It was one of those wonderful days in Northern California, about ninety degrees, with a cooling breeze, and the water itself was quite cool. Jim had that delicious feeling that comes when you pause to rest after a good physical workout. You see, Jim had just finished shooting the rapids. He and his raft had been propelled through a gorge by turbulent water. The water had accelerated dramatically as the channel narrowed. It dashed over and around the boulders, which had fallen into the gorge. Jim had struggled to keep the raft from being swamped. He had to use his paddle both to steer and to fend off the rocks. What exhilaration! What exhaustion! What contentment! . . . as he now lay on the raft, letting his heart slow down and his muscles relax, as the cold water evaporated from his skin and clothes.

As Jim relaxed, he reflected that the experience was an allegory for the course of his life. He can't do anything to control the flow of the water in his course. Time rushes on and he has to take it as it comes. Sometimes his life just moves along smoothly and peacefully; at other times he can barely fend off the catastrophes. He struggles to keep up with the pace of events and is swept from one threatening scenario to another. Of course, he isn't completely helpless, even in the rough water. And life is pretty thrilling as he shoots the rapids, using his skill to try to adapt to the circumstances as they rush by.

He used to enjoy this adventure. However, Jim realizes that he is not as content in his present life as he wants to be. One reason for that is the intrusion of too much chaos and uncertainty into his daily life. He doesn't know just where he is trying to go, and he is relatively powerless to influence where he will wind up. Too often he comes perilously close to being swamped. His lifestyle is almost entirely reactive. All of a sudden he was struck with the awareness that the times when he feels peaceful and in control have been getting more infrequent. He spends most of his time in the rapids.

The River of Life

Jim's analogy of his rafting experience for his overall life experience is a good one. It reminds us of the onrushing flow of time and circumstances with which we have to contend. It depicts the many changes in the quality of our circumstances, which can happen quite suddenly and can either exhilarate us or overwhelm us. It also illustrates the importance of the kind of preparation we have made for our journey and how we have equipped our boat. And it vividly portrays the limited control we have over what will happen to us. Let us reflect on these factors for a minute.

As we move down the river of life, the conditions change appreciably and sometimes very suddenly, from tranquil to hectic or even turbulent. At times our life can be very tranquil, serene, placid, like the quiet spots in the river. More often, there are at least modest disturbances, which require us to make some corrections to get back on the course we have intended. Those times can be *hectic*. The dictionary defines *hectic* as "characterized by confusion, rush, excitement." We certainly get excitement and things do seem confused as we rush through the intermediate rapids that occasionally interrupt our normally well-ordered course. Sometimes those periods can be very extended.

Then come the deepest and stormiest rapids. We describe them as turbulent, chaotic, tumultuous. Seemingly we are just tossed to and fro at the mercy of forces we cannot control. We have to give up on trying to steer and are incapable of fending off the rocks. We just have to hold on for dear life and ride it out, hoping that somehow the raft will stay upright until it comes into calmer water. We have absolutely no control.

A lot of people today feel overstimulated and overextended. Their lives seem to be confused, unraveling, coming apart at the seams. They are buffeted by a succession of things that catch them unawares, especially at a time when they are most unprepared. Some are quite undone by the chaotic nature of their lives. Other people, however, have found a way to see useful patterns in the midst of the chaos, and they have discovered techniques that enable them to live fruitfully in spite of the chaos.

How Much Control Should We Have?

In a sense we want to live on the edge between too much and too little control. Too much control leads to stagnation. We don't want things to be so controlled in our lives that life is a bore. Every person wants some exhilaration and mystery in his or her life. A reasonable lack of control is invigorating. On the other hand, we also don't want to be overwhelmed. Too little control leads to chaos. When it comes to the crucial things, we all want to have enough control to prevent disaster or pain and to essentially go where we want to go. As on the river, we want to live at the edge between too much calm and too much excitement. We want a reasonable amount of control.

So we all try to have a reasonable amount of control over our lives. And there are a lot of simple things we can control. But just when we begin to think we are managing our affairs pretty well, some unforeseen event vividly demonstrates how little control we really have. Our car breaks down at an inconvenient time.

19

Someone drives through a red light and strikes us when we least expect it. We are suddenly attacked by serious illness. The house begins to shake with the violent tremors of an earthquake. The income we thought was pretty secure suddenly disappears when our job evaporates during a corporate restructuring. Some close friend or loved one seriously disappoints us or even betrays us.

To some extent each of our lives has an element of chaos in it. Something is chaotic when it is so complicated and seemingly so erratic that it is futile to try to predict or control the outcome. Can you predict with any assurance what your life situation will be even a year from now? Can you so control yourself and your environment that you can make happen what you want to happen? We know the answer to both of those questions is no.

On the other hand, even in chaos there are patterns that repeat themselves, and there are things we can do to manage the chaos. The definition of *chaos* used to be "extreme confusion or disorder." However, Webster's newest definition is "a pattern or state of order existing within apparent disorder." That definition has emerged from recent discoveries by mathematicians and physicists that a whole range of phenomena, which appear disordered, actually have patterns or states of order. There is a surprising amount of pattern and order in things that seem completely disordered, just as there is often considerable disorder and randomness in some things which we tend to think of as perfectly ordered.

An example of a chaotic phenomenon is weather. The behavior of the atmosphere obeys the cause-and-effect laws of physics and chemistry. Even so, it will never be possible to precisely predict the weather at a given place and time, even with the most powerful computers. That is because weather is so complicated and so sensitive to slight variations in environment. However, in spite of that unpredictability, given certain weather conditions, it is possible to statistically state the percentage of the days that will be clear, and the percentage that will be rainy, as well as what the range of rainfall and temperature is likely to be. And that is helpful.

Similarly, we cannot predict the details of our lives. Even if we start from similar backgrounds, with about the same aptitudes, in a comparable environment, our lives may take quite different courses. The opportunities which are presented to each of us are quite different. The particular decisions we each face are quite different. We don't know what particular catastrophe will assail us, but we can be almost certain that one or more will. Not many people go through life without some catastrophic loss of health (either physical, mental, or spiritual), or some loss of possessions due to an uncontrollable event (such as a hurricane, earthquake, fire, accident, etc.), or the premature death of a loved one (spouse, child, etc.).

But, the more important similarity is that in the midst of the seeming chaos of our lives, there are patterns that are useful and allow us to manage within the chaos. Even though we don't know what catastrophe will befall us, there are things we can do to anticipate such catastrophes. As a result we may be able to reduce the likelihood of their occurrence. We are better able to cope with them when they do occur, and to recover from them after they have occurred. Even though we don't know exactly what decisions we may be called on to make, we can learn from others a pattern of decision making that enables us to make a better decision every time. Even though our lives differ in details, there is a pattern in the evolution of all lives. As we pass through adolescence, marriage and childbearing, emptying of the nest, midlife crisis, retirement, etc., we can anticipate those phases and make our transitions more gracefully. There are things we can learn and do to manage the chaos.

This book is intended to help us live with the uncertainties of life and to make the most of this life experience, in spite of its unpredictable and uncontrollable nature.

What Then Should Be Our Attitude?

Faced with the reality of turbulence and unpredictability in our lives, we can have one of several attitudes. I will refer to them as *going with the flow; reacting to the flow;* or *anticipating the flow.* Let us refer to Jim's rafting experiences in order to sort out these three attitudes.

Jim could just launch his raft without bothering to look at a diagram of the river, or seeking to understand the kinds of turbulence he might face as he proceeds downstream, or giving a thought to how he would cope with that turbulence when it confronted him. If Jim put his paddle away and just let the water take him where it would, he would be *going with the flow*. He might decide to go with the flow because he is a firm believer in fate and feels that he should acquiesce to his fate. He might go with the flow because he is a firm believer in God and feels that God wants to manage his life and that he should let him do so. He might go with the flow because he doesn't feel he can do otherwise; he doesn't even realize there is a paddle in his boat!

When Jim used his paddle to propel his raft into the mainstream, to steer around protruding boulders, and to fend off the rocks in the rapids to the best of his ability, he was *reacting to the flow*. He might be as firm a believer in God as the one who goes with the flow, but he believes that God expects him to do what he can for himself, while he trusts God for his ultimate well-being and for those things that are beyond Jim's competence.

Anticipating the flow involves studying the terrain, talking to those who have already gone down the river and have traversed the rapids, profiting from their experience. It also involves preparing a map for ourselves and perhaps even equipping ourselves with a small motor. With the map we have some knowledge of how to get where we want to go and which branch we should take at each fork in the river. With the motor we can move in the direction we want to go, even if the current isn't going in that direction. Of course, we don't have to use the motor and can drift along when the weather and course are nice, but we can also make corrections when we perceive that things are not going the way we want them to. Our lifestyle can be more proactive.

A reactive lifestyle is the choice of many in today's world. But there is a realistic alternative: a style of living we call *living intentionally*. Living intentionally involves anticipating the flow, having a map and a motor for our raft. In this book we will describe what it means to live intentionally and try to help the reader make those changes that will help him/her to live intentionally.

Living intentionally is based on the following two important facts. As rational human beings we have two very important advantages:

- We can imagine the future and we can prepare for it.
- We can remember the past and we can learn from it.

We can anticipate some of the important decisions and events that we will face in the future. We can learn from our own past and also from the wisdom that others have accumulated as they have lived their lives. There are things we can do ahead of time that help us to make the most of the opportunities that lie before us and that will ameliorate the potential catastrophes.

Let us think further, in the next chapter, about the likely flow of events that we want to anticipate and prepare for.

Points I Want to Come Back To

Later, when I have more time, I want to think more about the following sections, questions, or ideas associated with this chapter:

_____

_____

_____

_____

_____

_____

_____

_____

_____

_____

CHAPTER 2

The Flow of Events

If I try to write a history of my life, I first tend to list a sequence of events I have experienced: graduating from school, taking a particular job, marriage, etc. I immediately recognize that my story is different from someone else's because of the circumstances that surrounded me at the time and the choices I made. The course of our lives is determined by the choices we make in the flow of events.

Sometimes it seems that no sooner have we made one choice and moved off on our path than another choice confronts us. At other times we rush along our path as if we didn't have an option. We can forget that we have choices and overlook important choices available to us. We should recognize that we do, in fact, have choices in almost everything we do. If we are going to live intentionally we need to think clearly about our choices and then make deliberate and wise decisions.

In order to make wise choices and to make the most of the events and opportunities of our lives, we have to anticipate them with a sufficient lead time to be able to decide how to take advantage of them. What events are we talking about?

The "Events" of Our Lives

The events of our lives are of four basic types, which I designate *forks*, *dislocations*, *changes of season*, and *occasions*.

FORKS

Suppose that you or your spouse has received an offer of another job, and you are struggling to decide whether to accept it or stay in the present job. You are trying to balance the impact on professional advancement, the financial well-being of the family, the advantages of a house move vs. a much longer commute, the effects of a change in school for the children, and many other factors. You are confronting a major *fork*. Forks are those branch points that occur in our path which involve decisions that must be made as to which direction to take. Every day we face a variety of forks, but every once in a while we face a fork that is especially crucial. The decision we make at that fork has a profound impact on our lives. Such forks include choices in our career, our personal relationships, and our lifestyle. They involve our health, personal priorities, financial prosperity, etc.

DISLOCATIONS

Now, suppose you are laid off and must live with substantially less income while finding other employment. When such a thing happens, I call it a *dislocation,* because suddenly we find ourselves in a totally different place in our lives, and our lives will never be the same as they were. Dislocations are different from forks in that the change in direction is forced upon us, and the decisions involve how to cope and respond, rather than which direction to take. As with forks, the dislocations are of varying degrees of consequence. There are also two kinds of dislocations. Some represent changes of season in our lives and are predictable dislocations. The other kind of dislocations may or may not come to us, but if they do they are grievous. They come when least expected, and they are very traumatic, e.g., cancer, heart attack, earthquake, financial disaster, etc. We will not face all of these, but we will face our portion. We don't know for sure which will afflict us, but we know we can't escape all of them. These are unpredictable in that we can't be sure which of them will befall us, but the fact that we will experience some of them *is* predictable. Our difficulty is to know how much to try to prepare for any of these and in what ways to prepare. We know that there are things we can and should do to try to prevent a house fire, to make it possible for us to cope with one if it occurs, to help us to recover afterwards. What steps should we take in anticipation of a sudden, unexpected loss of physical health, or one of the other dislocations?

Changes of Season

Changes of season are the predictable dislocations in our lives. Those come to almost everybody. We can be sure we will experience them, e.g., adolescence, marriage, childbirth, midlife crisis, job disruption, emptying of the nest, retirement, death of a mate, etc. They are dislocations in that the circumstances of our lives become forever changed. Some are very traumatic. They all require major readjustment. We obviously should anticipate the predictable changes in season and make some preparations for them.

Occasions

The names of the categories above (forks, dislocations, changes of season) almost immediately convey the nature of the events of that type. The implications of the fourth category, *occasions,* are not as apparent. I have searched for a particularly apt, descriptive title, and *occasion* is the best I have so far discovered. Consider the dictionary* connotations of *occasion*: 1) a favorable time, an opportune time, a convenient time. An example of this connotation is: "The trip to Disneyland was the perfect occasion to become acquainted with the children"; 2) a particular time or happening. An example of this is: "On the occasion of our last meeting, you said . . ."; 3) a fact, event or state of affairs that makes something

---

* *Webster's New World Dictionary*, Third College Edition, 1994, Prentice Hall.

else possible, like "a chance meeting was the occasion of the renewal of their friendship"; 4) a special time or event suitable for celebration. An example of this is: "Their 10th anniversary was a real occasion; everyone had a wonderful time."

By *occasions*, I mean those times and events in our lives when everything is just right to accomplish an important objective if only we "seize the day" (*carpe diem*). We can make good things happen if we are alert to those opportunities, and we can create a result or a memory that will have continuing benefits. If we live intentionally, we want to anticipate such times and events and make the most of them.

We recognize that various examples of these events are more or less likely at particular stages of our lives, which we might describe as eras.

Eras

In talking about eras, some people just refer to the decades of our lives: the teens, twenties, thirties, etc. But, I have found it most convenient to think of life in terms of thirteen-year eras. These are briefly characterized as follows:

- *Childhood*—from birth through age thirteen. That is the time when we are introduced to such important concepts as family and society, and when we learn the rules of the game of life. We are fortunate if our parents and teachers have a sound understanding of those concepts, rules, and principles, as well as a good ability to teach and model them. Alas, many of us learn the wrong things and have to spend a lot of our lives correcting those early patterns. During childhood we also first experience the emotions of life: love, joy, pain, shame, guilt, etc.
- *Youth*—the ages of thirteen to twenty-six. I believe our personalities and attitudes are most strongly shaped by our experiences in these years. It is the era in which we build our minds and our bodies. It is the time when we face the great temptations in our society and a time when most rebel

in some form. In our youth, we also make some of the most crucial decisions of our lives, such as our choice of mate and career. Those decisions shape the rest of our lives in a profound way. Even if we change careers or even mates later on, those early decisions shape our lives. It is during that era that we often lose someone who is close to us and experience grief. We also bleed in other ways and learn about the processes of healing. Youth is one of the most formative eras in our lives.

- *Young Adult*—the ages of twenty-six to thirty-nine. In those years we are busy establishing a career and a family. We are facing entirely new challenges and having to learn completely new skills. We realize that the responsibilities we have undertaken both in the workplace and in the home are pretty awesome and wish we had the benefit of a lot more experience.

- *Striving Adult*—from thirty-nine to fifty-two. During this period we are usually making maximum progress in our careers and probably realizing the greatest pace of advancement. We are also probably experiencing the greatest stress in our careers. This comes at the time when our children are in those hazardous teenage years, and it is a time when we are so busy with our careers that we may not spend as much time with them as we ought to. It is also during this time that we may have second thoughts about many things, including mates and career. It usually is the time of the infamous *midlife crisis*, and has the seeds of potential catastrophe. That crisis may come a little later or a little earlier, depending on the pace of our life development. But it surely comes as our trajectory begins to level out.

- *Midlife*—from fifty-two to sixty-five. When we look back later, we often realize midlife is when we began to go over the top, and we have to come to terms with our limitations. It may be a time when we choose to change careers. Midlife is also the time when we see the blooming of the second generation. Our children get married and have their own children (our grandchildren). We may also find that we have a new responsibility for our parents, who have aged to the point where they can't be as self-sufficient as they once were.

- *Elder*—from sixty-five to seventy-eight. Now we have to come to terms with declining vigor and declining productivity. However, we can still be very active and it can be the best time of our lives. It is a time when we rediscover simple joys and think more seriously about passing important things on to the younger ones following behind us.
- *Venerable*—from seventy-eight to ninety-one. Some might call that old age, but I have assigned the title Venerable. A few people, as they grow older, turn into crotchety ogres, but most grow wise and mellow. We love our venerable seniors, probably mostly because they show such a capacity to love us. However, this era is really a time of living in earthquake country. There is the Sword of Damocles hanging over our heads. We know that any moment might bring disabling illness or death. But somehow it is in this period also that we can really appropriate the deep peace that God wants us to have and that passes all understanding—it can't be understood in view of the circumstances.

Now, let us make some comments about events we might anticipate in the four categories, recognizing that some of them are more likely to occur in particular eras of our life.

Comments on Future Events

Forks

Examples of forks include the following:

- Is it time for me to seek a different employer or a different business opportunity?
- Should I rescue my child from his current situation or let him fend for himself?

- Should I submit myself to a course of chemotherapy?
- Should I sue them or continue trying to negotiate?
- Should I speak up and risk incurring the displeasure of my boss, or my neighbor?
- Should I make a commitment of my time and energy to serve in that capacity?
- Are we really in a position to buy that house?

Thus we encounter forks in every arena of life: career, family life, health, personal priorities, financial prosperity, etc.

We quickly realize that we face different forks in different eras of our lives. In our earlier years we will have to decide whether to marry a certain person. In our middle years it may be which course to follow in dealing with a rebellious child. In our later years the fork might involve whether to sell the family home and move into a residence designed to accommodate seniors.

What we may not realize is that there is a learnable methodology for dealing with forks. We can learn how to prepare for and decide forks in a way that is a lot better than we might have done in our earlier years. We can also profit from each other's experience as well as from our own. A lot can be learned by discussing our fork experiences and paying attention to how other people have decided their forks.

CHANGES OF SEASON

We can all recognize the following as belonging in this category:

- *Adolescence.* As we think back, probably the first obvious change of season in our life is our transition from childhood into youth, commonly called adolescence. Of course, we are so young at this stage that we don't really anticipate and prepare for the profound changes that occur at that change of season. Our bodies are changing in ways we don't understand. Our relations with kids of the opposite sex become very different. We also have to start becoming more self-sufficient, learning how to protect ourselves, taking responsibility for younger ones, etc. There is usually a certain amount of trauma involved, both for us and for those who have to live with us. Most of us rebel in some ways. Some who are not properly nurtured rebel in violent ways. But this season is a very important aspect of our development and is a threshold to even more wonderful stages of life.

- *Marriage.* Certainly the course of our lives is never the same after marriage. Of course, that is what we hoped for. However, substantial readjustment is needed on the parts of both partners in order to make a success of a marriage. And the adjustments don't just happen once; they are continually needed as the marriage and the partners evolve.
- *Having children or learning that you can't have children.* Either result has a profound effect on the course of our lives and requires a substantial readjustment.
- *Disruption of employment.* This, too, is more and more common, even at a relatively young age. The question now is not so much whether it will strike, but when and in what form.
- *Loss of mate.* Even young people are not immune to this. A young friend of mine lost her husband very unexpectedly when the car he was working on fell on him. We probably all know young people who have lost their spouses through accident or disease. This can come during any of the eras.
- *Midlife crisis.* Everyone faces a form of this just as they do the adolescent crisis. Like the adolescent crisis, it is a natural phase in the normal development of a person. It, too, should not be dreaded nor denied, because going through it produces necessary changes and prepares us for the next stage of life. The midlife crisis occurs when we begin to suspect that our best days are behind us and that we are not going to realize our fondest dreams and expectations for our lives.

We think that if we do something drastic, we can perhaps break out of the rut we seem to have dug for ourselves.

- *Children leaving the nest.* This also occurs in a later era. For some people it is a time when they feel lost, because they have been so absorbed in raising the children. For other people it is the exciting beginning of a whole new phase of life. It depends on how they prepare for it.

- *Retirement.* This may be far away for you, but it needs advance preparation. It is clearly a big factor for midlife people. An important thing to remember is that people are living longer and are having very long retirements. The average retirement now is over twenty years. That's a long period to prepare for with regard to income as well as life conditions and activities.

- *Dependent parents.* Yes, people are living longer than ever before. But as they live longer, they are less able to completely fend for themselves. More and more younger people find themselves restricting their mobility, either to care for aging parents or to remain near to them. Here are some facts: In 1995 Atlas Van Lines surveyed employees to find out why they turned down a relocation. Sixty-four percent of the respondents cited "family ties." Previously, as more women entered the workforce, "spousal employment" had become the primary reason for turning down a relocation. Their spouse had a good job and it didn't make sense to abandon that. But by the mid-1990s, "family ties" edged out "spousal employment." There are estimates that by the year 2000, thirty percent to forty percent of the work force will have to provide care for an elderly parent.

Clearly we need to think about preparing for all of these predictable dislocations. We certainly can learn from others who have already passed through these changes of season.

It is less clear how much we should prepare and in what way for the next category of events.

Dislocations

People in my discussion groups, have confronted 1) loss of their possessions by an uncontrollable event (such as a failed investment, an accident, a fire or earthquake); 2) catastrophic loss of health, (perhaps physical health, such as cancer or a heart attack; mental health such as a nervous breakdown; or spiritual health, such as severe depression or loss of hope); 3) abandonment by a spouse; 4) physical abuse in the marriage relationship; 5) rejection by a child; 6) death of a child; 7) a child succumbing to addiction—there are so many possibilities!

We may think that the likelihood of being confronted with some of these is pretty remote, but we all know other people to whom they have happened. When I was thirteen, my six-year-old brother drowned. My mother couldn't save him. She suffered terrible guilt and was hospitalized for years as a result. That event had a dreadful impact not only on my mother, but also on my father, my sister, and me. There are also people in my church who had felt that they were doing a good job of parenting. All of a sudden one of their children rejected them, repudiated all the values the parents held dear, and ran off into some form of self-destructive behavior. We need to recognize our exposure to dislocations and decide what we should do to be equipped to deal with them should they befall us—some will!

Occasions

Consider the case of Paul, now retired. He once looked forward to retirement, and worked long hours to amass enough capital to sustain a good retirement. So now he can play golf every day . . . and he is miserable! First of all, he finds that the golf, which was once a rare treat, is too much as a steady diet. But he didn't develop any other activities to absorb his interest after retirement. Furthermore, he was so used to managing activities and people that he gets too involved in trying to manage his wife, his church, his golf club. He also misses the regular schedule of activities and the constant interaction with the people at work. Worst of all, he now has time to sit back and reflect on his life. The result is that instead of enjoying the reflections, he has nagging regrets about things he did or didn't do. He wishes he had made better use of the opportunities he had.

Paul worked so hard that he missed opportunities to be with his children. He missed opportunities to take trips and vacations that would have given both him and his children those precious memories that can be the source of so much continuing joy. He also feels he missed some career opportunities, that would have given him a chance to do some other interesting things, and might have allowed the family to enjoy life more. He knows he missed some financial opportunities when he could have better secured his retirement by a timely investment. He could have accepted opportunities to become involved with activities that would have enriched his life and his retirement. He passed up occasions when he could have been a positive influence on the younger men he was working with. He is very aware of the great hopes and expectations his parents had for him, and indeed those he had for himself, and he feels he has not done a very good job of fulfilling the destiny that was laid before him, and the legacy he inherited. He fervently wishes that he had lived more intentionally.

Paul obviously missed some of his *occasions*. We want to be more careful to be alert to ours, and to make the most of them. We don't want to look back and regret our missed opportunities. Some of these opportunities come naturally, such as graduations, marriages, etc., when we can celebrate life with our families and make memories that our children will hold precious in future years. It is also important to create other memories which is possible when the *occasion* is just right.

In the next chapter we want to think more about how we can anticipate the coming flow of forks, changes in season, dislocations, and latent occasions.

Points I Want to Come Back To

Later, when I have more time, I want to think more about the following sections, questions, or ideas associated with this chapter:

_____

_____

_____

_____

_____

_____

_____

_____

_____

_____

CHAPTER 3

Anticipating the Flow

We have seen in the last chapter that there is a multiplicity of events in our flow. We have said that we can live better if we prepare for some of these events before we are suddenly confronted with them. Obviously we can't prepare for every event that might come our way: forks, dislocations, changes of season, unrepeatable family opportunities, and other *occasions*. Therefore we are next faced with the questions: a) how do we identify the particular events to prepare for? and b) can we really prepare for them?

The way for us to identify the events to which we ought to give our current attention is suggested by thinking about life as an *interactive maze*.

Living in an Interactive Maze

We have all enjoyed trying to solve a maze puzzle in a newspaper or magazine. There is a *starting point* and a *goal*. Moving our pencil from the *starting point* through the printed pattern, we encounter branch points (where we have to decide which path to take) and sharp corners (where our direction is abruptly changed). As we traverse the maze, we try to make choices at each branch point in order to reach the *goal* without being blocked by a deadend or taking a long detour. To solve the maze it is important that we be able to see the whole maze—the location of the goal with respect to the starting point and the general layout of the alternative paths—so we can choose the paths wisely. It is not too difficult to do that if we are looking at a printed page.

I have also seen mazes constructed in a field where you have to find your way along paths defined by hedges. The hedges are tall enough that you cannot see the whole maze, and finding your way is infinitely more difficult—unless you have a tall ladder. If you carry a tall ladder you can get up above the hedges and see the whole scope of the maze. Keeping that scope in your mind's eye, you can make intelligent choices when you come down from the ladder.

Now, I said that life is like an *interactive* maze. What is different about an *interactive* maze? I visualize a maze where the pattern of hedges is not fixed, but it changes as we go along, depending on our choices as well as on the strange growth habits of the hedges. Aren't these the characteristics of life? We do not deal with a static situation in life, but one in which circumstances are always changing and we try to adapt to those changes.

What we realize, then, is that it is essential for us to stop periodically in order to rise above our current circumstances. We want to get high enough that we can look forward and back over the maze of our life and get the total scope in perspective.

1. I need to climb the ladder. This involves setting aside some time for keenly looking at my situation and reflecting on it. It also means that I have to get myself into a position where I can look at my life with objectivity and perspective. I may need a partner to help me do that.
2. Once up the ladder, I first look forward. Even high on the ladder I can't see distant points clearly. I certainly can't see the conditions at the end of my path, and even some parts of the near future are obscure. But I can identify some changes that lie before me, see some likely forks and even spot some dislocations which are out there, even if I can't

tell whether my path intersects them. I want to fix these things in my mind so that when I get down I can make some preparations and some wise moves.

3. While I am still on the ladder, I also look carefully around the vicinity. I want to clearly identify the circumstances that limit my mobility, that constrain what I am realistically able to do. I may see a path a little way out in the maze that heads straight toward my goal, but there might be a significant barrier between me and that path. A detour may be necessary.

4. I also want to look back. If I have come a long way, it may be hard to recognize how my path twisted far back. I can see enough of the recent path, however, to realize the complexity of what I have traversed, to appreciate what has sustained me through it, and to recall what was helpful to me as I made my decisions at previous forks. I may see helpful things about these forks that I can discern only from the vantage point of being beyond them.

5. Finally, after I have the clearest possible perspective on the future, the present, and the parts of the past that can help me deal with the future, I get down from the ladder, back into the maze, and try to make the most intelligent choices I can for a while.

6. Of course, I can't take in the whole maze at once, so I will have to stop again after I have carried my ladder further in the maze, put it up again, and take another look to get a fresh vision. We have to make *periodic assessments* in which we get a renewed vision, make some crucial decisions about directions and tactics, and then go forward intentionally.

My hope is to encourage you to resolve to make periodic assessments, and to show you how to do that.

Anticipating Future Events

So climb up on a ladder and look out over the maze of your life. Your purpose is to identify changes you want to make in your life and to anticipate some of the events that might be forthcoming, so you can prepare somewhat for them. What do you see?

Of course you can't see all the details of the actual path. Those details depend somewhat on what happens as you walk the path, because this is, after all, an *interactive* maze. But you *can* see some features out there. The most obvious are the inevitable changes of season that occur in everyone's life, such as *midlife crisis,* the several stages of *retirement,* and *death of mate.* If you have already passed through some of these, you know they happen to us all. If you have not yet been confronted with one, you may think you can avoid it. Be assured, each one lies somewhere along your path. Be further assured that there are important things you can do ahead of time so that you can pass from one season to another with more ease and grace.

Somewhere along the line we suffer such severe frustrations in one or more of our roles (as a worker, family provider, mate, parent, etc.) that we become severely depressed and conclude that the only relief is to escape. The present circumstances are intolerable and there doesn't seem to be any hope for improvement. This is the infamous *midlife crisis.* We may make some catastrophic choices, or we can weather the crisis and move on to better times. The difference is usually in how well we have anticipated and prepared for such a crisis, and in the kind of personal support we receive at that time. It really helps to understand the signs that such a crisis is approaching, the phases of the crisis, the dead-end roads some people choose in order to escape, the areas we need to work on to triumph over the crisis, and the resources that are available to help us. There are good books in our libraries and bookstores which were written to help us anticipate and prepare for this change of season.

Eventually we all have to cease productive work and just enjoy life as much as we can. This is mandated by our age and infirmities. To pass suddenly from a fulltime job to full retirement is a very traumatic leap. Fortunately, most of us pass through one or two intermediate stages that ease us into full retirement. For most of us, our career involves a consuming job that absorbs fifty to sixty hours a week, dominates our schedule, and usually requires us to satisfy someone else's expectations for us. If we are fortunate, as the first stage of retirement, we find a way to gradually move into a variety of part-time, productive activities that allow more personal freedom, even though they still require some concession of schedule, some satisfaction of others' expectations, and doing some things that we would just as soon not have to do, but are necessary to get the job done. Later we make a transition to the next phase: complete control of our own schedule with the freedom to do whatever appeals to us as the most satisfying activity of the moment, meeting only our own expectations of performance and productivity. In all of these stages we are still physically able to be active and productive. It is easier to evolve through these levels to complete retirement.

It seems obvious that we can make such transitions smoothly only if we have prepared to do so. Of course we need to develop plans to support ourselves financially, as income from our labor gradually diminishes. We also need to prepare ourselves to cope emotionally and to plan a satisfying lifestyle. We need to be aware of some of the potential dangers of retirement, the inherent sources of distress, the balances that must be maintained in retirement and things we can do to grow old gracefully. I am now in my second stage of retirement. I have had to be intentional in order to move smoothly into those two stages. I am sure that I can continue to make significant impacts with my talents, time, and energy for many years, but there are things I should do now to facilitate that. Our life can be much more satisfying if we anticipate those retirement transitions and prepare for them. There are also good books available to help us anticipate and prepare for retirement.

The transition I most hate to think about is death of mate. But my refusal to think about it is not going to lessen its likelihood. My refusal to think about it and prepare for it is only going to make the actual event even worse. I fully realize Jean and I are not likely to die at the same time. That implies one of us will someday have to face the necessity of getting along without the other. And if you are young, I am sorry to say that you can't be sure it will be a long time before that happens to you. Surely you know of someone your age who has already lost a mate. What a frightening prospect! Are there things we should do now to prepare for that event? The answer is yes. We have to think about what we can do to keep such a thing from happening before its time, and do those things that will help us cope with the event and recover from it. I have purchased insurance to provide financial support for my wife and also to provide medical and physical care for her if she can no longer care for herself. I have also purchased long-term care insurance for myself so that my disability will not wipe out her resources. I have made a will. I maintain a notebook for her in my desk drawer that contains copies of important records and procedures. I have tried to simplify our investments and to automate the deposit of proceeds. I have taught her to handle our finances the same way I do. I have avoided making long-term financial commitments that she might not be able to continue. As much as I hate doing it, I just have to think about what would be necessary for each of us to get along without the other and prepare for that.

One of the things I see looming on our horizon is a move from our home to a seniors' residence. Fortunately, I am still physically capable and mentally strong. I think my golf game is still getting better and I haven't noticed any deterioration of my mind yet. I am able to take care of the yard and manage repairs to our home, but they are becoming more cumbersome every year. I know my capabilities will eventually deteriorate. Already I can tell that I am going downhill physically. I can't lift things as I used to and can't do anything without aches and pains for the next couple of days. I have to face the reality that a time is coming when we should move out of our house into a living situation where Jean and I are both relieved of housework. I know there are things I ought to do now to prepare for that event.

I know that I should also prepare for some of the changes of season in the lives of my children and grandchildren. From the vantage point of my ladder, I can see the point when my grandchildren are graduating from high school and going on to college, marriage, careers, etc. It reminds me that my times to enjoy their childhood and youth are rapidly passing. So are my opportunities to play whatever role I can in influencing their character, their personalities, their ability to cope with the hazards that they will face. I want to take advantage of the opportunities I have to help them develop into wonderful human beings and to pass on to them precious family history and values. I want to plan events so that we can create some precious family memories. I can also see that they will need more money than their parents can afford in order to go to college. There are things I am doing now so that we will be able to help them with that.

We have been talking about changes of season. We know they are going to happen. We just don't know the details yet. And I know there are things I can and should do to prepare for them. I also see other features ahead that may or may not interrupt my path—the *unpredictable, traumatic dislocations*. These are categories of events that I have to expect will lie in my path, but I won't know the specific nature of the event until I come to that juncture and discover what particular form that category will take for me. In some ways it is like a board game. I can see that the path leads through a category of events, but what the particular event will be I won't know till I land on that spot and find out what is on the top of the stack of game cards.

Our first such category is *catastrophic loss of physical, mental, or spiritual health*. So many friends have suffered from heart attack, cancer, stroke, Alzheimer's, or a violent accident. Can I realistically expect to go through the rest of my life without encountering one or more of these events? It's not likely. Are there things I can do now to prepare for an event in this category, even though I don't yet know exactly what card I will draw? There are.

Then there is *loss of possessions by an uncontrollable event*. People in different parts of the country experience different kinds of uncontrollable events. They may be natural events, like tornadoes, hurricanes, or earthquakes. We in California all know that an earthquake can suddenly devastate us. We personally experienced the earthquake of 1989, and have pictures and scars on our furniture to remind us of the way our belongings were scattered and broken. We witnessed the destruction from an even worse earthquake in Kobe, Japan, both on TV and in our newspapers.

We heard how the situation there parallels ours here in the Bay area and know that an earthquake like that could hit us at any time. We also experienced the rain and wind of the winter of 1995. We had some tall pines on the hill overhanging our bedroom, and there was a night in the winter of 1995 when we didn't dare sleep in our bed for fear those trees would crush us in it, as happened to some others. You may have lost property in other natural catastrophes. Furthermore, we can suffer a loss of possessions from other uncontrollable events—such diverse things as accidents, changes in law, or even shifts in the economy. We've experienced a substantial devaluation of some investments due to a change in government policy, and we've seen a significant reduction in our retirement income caused by a drop in interest rates.

There are things I should do now to prepare for such events. We've taken out trees that could threaten our safety. We have secured furniture to the walls. We have purchased earthquake insurance. We maintain reserves of fuel and water. We have adjusted investments with an eye to the kinds of economic changes that might occur. We know we can't insure ourselves against all perils and damage, but we can do some things to minimize impact and help us to recover.

We don't want to overwhelm ourselves by dwelling on perils, nor discourage ourselves with the magnitude of trying to protect against them. But we do need to recognize the variety of things that can happen and realize that there are some steps we can and should take to help us cope with those which will befall us. Too often we decide it is too painful or difficult to anticipate them, and just hope that we will be immune. Indeed, we can be just as negligent about planning for the joyful things in life.

As you look forward from your ladder, what future events do you foresee? What forks can you anticipate in the reasonably near future? Are there significant changes in your family situation to be expected at a particular time: children leaving home? parents becoming infirm? inadequacy of your present house? retirement?

Identifying Possible Changes

After you come down from your ladder, the next step is to identify the changes you would like to see in your life and the particular events you want to prepare for. What specific changes would you like to see in the person you are; in what you are likely to accomplish in the coming years; in the relationships of your life; in your lifestyle? What issues do you want to resolve? What projects do you want to complete? What preparations for future events do you want to begin? In what ways do you want to attempt to adjust your surroundings to better suit yourself; or in what ways do you feel that you have to adjust yourself to those elements of your environment that you can't change? Who are the people to whom you want to pay more attention?

How Much Should You Prepare?

We each need to evaluate the extent to which we should try to prepare ourselves for these events that may well lie before us. Obviously it makes a difference whether they are certain events, which we are sure are coming, or uncertain events, which may or may not. We know that it is impossible to prepare for all future events. It is also impossible to *completely* prepare for *any* future event. It would be foolish to devote too much time and energy to trying to prepare for future events that might never occur. Nevertheless, it is prudent, and part of living intentionally, to take certain basic steps that will better equip us to anticipate and deal with some future events.

We can try to think of steps that can help either in a) decreasing the likelihood of the occurrence of some traumatic future events; or b) increasing our ability to cope with such a future event when we are in the midst of it; or c) increasing our ability to be restored and to recover after the event. A very common and simple example is the possibility of a house fire. Taking well-known steps of fire prevention can decrease the likelihood of a fire. Planning escape routes, locating fire extinguishers, and installing smoke alarms can help us cope with the occurrence of a fire. Documentation of house contents, purchase of insurance, and storage of important documents in a bank vault can help us to recover after a fire.

There are also steps similar to those that we can take for the unspeakable possibility of the premature death of our mate: steps that can decrease the likelihood of such a premature death; steps that would increase our ability to cope with such an event while we are in the midst of it; and steps that would increase our ability to be restored and to recover after that event. Similarly there are steps for other traumatic, unpredictable dislocations that might befall us. Some of those steps apply to the whole class of dislocations: steps such as building our spiritual strength and the circle of close friends who would provide needed support.

Making a periodic assessment is an important element of *living intentionally*. We want to take time to rise above our circumstances, identify changes in our lives that would be beneficial, as well as events for which we want to prepare, and then decide on specific steps to take next.

Intentional living can really make a difference in our lives. I think everyone would prefer to live intentionally. To some it could sound like too much work, but it isn't when we are convinced of the importance of living intentionally. Perhaps a person doesn't know how to live intentionally, or perhaps he/she just hasn't taken the time to do the necessary homework. One of the purposes of this book is to guide the reader's thinking through some of the homework that makes intentional living possible.

Points I Want to Come Back To

Later, when I have more time, I want to think more about the following sections, questions, or ideas associated with this chapter.

_____

_____

_____

_____

_____

_____

_____

_____

_____

CHAPTER 4

Living Intentionally

So far we have talked about making the most of some of the events in our lives. We do that by anticipating such events so that we can prepare for them as wisely as possible. We recognized that we all face some of the same kinds of events, sometimes even similar situations. That is helpful, in that we can learn from each other's experiences.

We can all approach these events in a similar way. On the other hand, the distinct way you should react to the events in your life is perhaps quite different from the way I should react to mine. That is because we are all different individuals with our own personal circumstances. It is obviously very important that we each understand the things that are true and unique about ourselves. I call these things our individual *givens*.

When we were given a problem to solve in school, there were always certain givens that set the circumstances of the problem. And the solution to the problem had to be consistent with the givens. So, also, there are givens in our lives: our unique personalities, our preferences and aversions (what we like and what we want to avoid), our skills and our dependencies (what we can and what we can't do for ourselves), the constraints of the people to whom we are connected, the situations in which we are involved, and certainly our financial limitations.

In order to make plans, that really suit me and are realistic in terms of what I can accomplish, it is essential that I clearly understand my *givens*. We will talk more about the process of taking an inventory of our *givens* later in section 3 of this book.

While I refer to these things as my *givens*, I have to realize that they are not necessarily rigid. An important aspect of assessing our *givens* is to understand how "given" they really are! Our situations can and do change, and as individuals we can and do change. To what extent can these *givens* be changed? and what would it take to change them? I need to think about *adapting*.

Adapting

When my son graduated from college, a neighbor got him a job in his company. Tom was doing all right, but he soon concluded that he was not presently suited to corporate life. Either he was going to have to adapt himself to that industrial lifestyle, or he was going to have to change his job situation to be more compatible with his interests, inclinations, etc. His conclusion was to leave industry and go back to school for another four years. He then took a job as a high school teacher. Tom recognized that his work had to change or he had to change, and actually it was some of both.

I have friends who concluded that they needed to adapt themselves to living in a big city or get a new job in a more rural location. Another concluded that he was going to have to change himself, adapting more to the idiosyncrasies of his wife, or his wife was going to change herself, or he would need to get a new wife. Fortunately, they each adapted somewhat.

I can live life more enjoyably, as well as more effectively, if I can increase the compatibility between myself and my environment. I may need to take steps to mold my environment to be more compatible with my personality, or I may try to reshape myself somewhat to better fit into my environment. If I can't change my environment, I will have to try to accommodate myself to the realities of that environment. I may have to do a little of each.

I don't want to just make life easier for myself—certainly not if it means sacrificing some of my values or goals. But, it does make sense to adapt if it helps to advance my goals, in keeping with my values. Therefore, I want to consider what changes would be appropriate in myself or my environment so that I can live life more enjoyably as well as more effectively. Thoughtful *adapting* is another aspect of *living intentionally*.

Living Intentionally

In a real sense, living intentionally involves *assessing, adapting, anticipating,* and *applying*. We need to do a careful *assessment* of ourselves and our situation (assessing our givens). Then we want to do what we can to *adapt* our environment to be as compatible as possible with ourselves, or adapt ourselves to our environment. We also want to *anticipate* the flow of events that are likely to occur in our future (anticipation includes not only identifying the events as likely, but also preparing to cope with them to the best of our ability). And, finally, we need to *apply* to our particular situation the principles that have been developed for *Living Intentionally*. In section 2 we will review some of these principles and techniques. And in section 3 we will provide a framework for describing the *person that I am*, identifying our individual idiosyncrasies, evaluating our situation, and assessing our givens.

Why Do We Call This Living Intentionally?

Living intentionally involves having a purpose and living each day thoughtfully in the ways that will best achieve that purpose. The reason I chose the word *intentionally* is that this word includes both of these elements. The word *intentional* comes from the same root as words *intend, intense, tendency, tendon, tendril,* and *tendron*. Think about those words. Think of the way a tendril stretches forth from a plant with the firm purpose of providing support for that plant. A tendron is a young shoot or sprout of a plant that stretches forth for the purpose of acquiring energy from the sun. These are not passive words! We recognize that there is a sense of *purpose* in these words, but also a sense of *stretching* to achieve the purpose. The Latin root of those words is the verb *tendere,* which means "to stretch." Adding the *in* implies "forth" or "toward." So we call the lifestyle in which we are interested *living intentionally* because it involves living with a sense of purpose and living in a way in which we stretch forth to accomplish that purpose.

I believe living intentionally means to live *with intent* and to live *according to that intent, intently*. Living *with intent* means having a purpose, design, and plan—we have a purpose we want to achieve and a goal we want to reach, as well as a design and plan for getting there. To live *according to that intent* means that everything we do and all the decisions we make are calculated to move us closer to our intention. To do it *intently* means to do it eagerly; with determination; unwaveringly; with our minds and hearts devoted to the purpose; equipping ourselves for the journey.

Our Purpose

We have said that the word *intentional* implies living with a sense of purpose and with a sense of stretching to achieve that purpose. But we have not yet talked about what the purpose is toward which we are stretching. Can you say what *purpose* shapes your actions and decisions?

We also talked about *living intentionally* being somewhat analogous to working our way through a tall maze of hedges that are higher than our heads. We have to do a periodic assessment of our lives: that is, purposely stop to rise above our current circumstances, take a good look to assess whether we are in fact moving toward our *goal*, and then get down and make some course corrections, if they are necessary. But we didn't talk about what our *goal* is. Can you say what *goal* you are striving to reach?

Recently, I have had some strange dreams. In one dream, I am in a countryside that is unfamiliar to me. I don't really belong there except that I am passing through. I know that I have a home, but my problem is that I don't know how to find my way home. I have to ask other people to show me the way. In another dream, I am a manager and the boss obviously expects me to do something. But I am confused about what I am supposed to be doing. I am also very conscious that I have limited abilities to get it done, whatever it is that I am supposed to be doing. The boss keeps telling me what I am supposed to be doing, but I can't understand him. I am embarrassed to have to keep asking him to repeat what he has said. These two dreams leave me with two big questions: Where am I? and What am I supposed to be doing?

My dreams stimulate my thinking in the wee hours of the morning. I wake up and think; *Is there any wisdom allegorically contained in this dream?* Here is what I have thought as I reflected on the dreams:

- God is continually trying to tell me something and sometimes I just can't figure out what he is trying to tell me.
- We don't really belong in this world except on the way to our true home. We know that things in this world are *not* the way they are supposed to be, and we believe we are headed to our real home where God has all things the way they are supposed to be.
- I do have a job to do here. I need to understand what God wants me to do and then try to do it, even though I am conscious that I don't have all the knowledge or smarts the job really calls for.

That raises a question. If this isn't our true home, why did God put us on this planet anyway? I think the answer is in the story of the Prodigal Son (Luke 15:11–32). God wants us to come to him out of our own free will. But he knows that with our free choice and fallen nature, we will insist on taking the inheritance he has for us and going to squander it in lavish living. So he lets us do that in a foreign land (like the Prodigal Son). He also knows that we have to discover for ourselves the meaninglessness of such a lifestyle, and then come to our senses and voluntarily find our way home again. There and then he will kill the fatted calf and welcome us with a huge party. But first, we have to learn our lessons! So, that's why we're here—to learn our lessons and to choose our Father's eager arms of welcome.

Now our question was this: What is the *goal* toward which we are working our way through the maze? My conclusion is that our *goal* is the home God has prepared for us. We are moving through this maze with all the skill we can develop in order to reach that home.

Now, what about our *purpose*?

I believe that our *purpose* is complex, in that it has multiple parts. Our first purpose is to find our way to the home that God has prepared for us. So we want to measure the things that we do, and evaluate them in terms of whether they move us closer to our ultimate home. But I think we need another *purpose*, which has more to do with the job that God has for us to do while we are here.

If I ask you to state the major *purpose* that motivates all your effort, what would you say? Of course, I can't hear your response to that question. But I have observed a lot of people, and I would guess that your answer might well be on the following list:

- *To provide the best life I can for my family.* Many people act as if that is their *purpose*. And that's a reasonable *purpose*, if we are fortunate enough to have a family. God has given us that family and no one else is in the position that we are to see to its welfare. That is our privilege and our responsibility. We readily accept our responsibility for the economic and material well-being of our families, but we are also responsible to nurture their emotional, spiritual, and community life.

- *To be as productive as possible with the time, energy, and talents I have been given.* We could call that being fruitful. Being fruitful is a reasonable *purpose*. After all, Jesus said in John 15, "I am the true vine; you are the branches. This is to my Father's glory, that you bear much fruit, showing yourselves to be my disciples. My Father is the vine-dresser. He cuts off every branch that bears no fruit, while every branch that does bear fruit, he prunes so that it will be even more fruitful." It is clear from this that we are expected and charged to be fruitful. Fruitfulness is expected of Jesus' disciples, and fruitfulness is a major way in which we glorify God. In fact, if we aren't fruitful we should expect to be discarded. Yet even as we bear fruit we can expect to be pruned. We can rely on God to whittle away at the excesses of our lives so that we can marshal all of our strength in being fruitful in the right way. Yes, being fruitful is a reasonable *purpose.*

- *To enjoy this precious gift of life to the utmost.* God has given us this life to be enjoyed. Jesus said He wants us to have joy. Some people have no purpose other than to enjoy the life they have been given. I know I get joy from being fruitful, but there are other important joys he has prepared for us as well. I am not making the most of my life if I have turned it into drudgery, no matter how fruitful and successful the result.

- *To be as much of a blessing as possible to those who surround me.* Surely part of the joy of life is to realize that I have increased the joy and well-being of those who are close to me. They are an important source of my joy and I want to be a source of theirs.

- *To get to know the Lord and his truth and learn to live accordingly.* After all, if our *goal* is the home that the Lord has prepared, this life is our opportunity to get ready for it and learn how to be a proper citizen of it.

- *To learn as much as I can and become mature.* We are all still under construction. We haven't yet achieved full maturity. What does it mean to be fully mature? The Oxford dictionary says, "complete in natural development or growth; fully developed in body and mind." Maturity carries with it the implication of completeness, wholeness, having achieved the fulfillment of the original design, fully adequate for that for which it was designed. For what were we designed? Are we fully adequate for that yet? The Bible holds out the goal for each of us to become fully mature (e.g., Eph. 4:13).

Other purposes that some people obviously stretch to achieve include the following:

- To accumulate as much money and possessions as possible
- To get to the point where they don't have to be concerned about money
- To rise to the top of their professions, to become #1
- To live their life in a way that would make their parents proud
- To leave as rich a legacy as they can to their heirs

Is your *purpose* on this list or is it something else?

What we see is that there are a number of good candidates to be the *major purpose* of our lives. I think the ones on my first list are prime candidates and worthy of deep consideration. I think we can justify each one of them biblically, and at one time or another I would have declared each one of them my choice. At present, however, I think of my *purpose* as being to live my earthly life with *creative stewardship*.

Now what do I mean by creative stewardship?

Creative Stewardship

We all know that a *steward* is one who is entrusted with managing a household or estate. He is not the owner, but he is the agent of the owner. He is accountable to the owner for the progress of the estate under his management. Richard B. Cunningham has written a book called *Creative Stewardship*.* I particularly like the portrayal of the concept of stewardship provided by Cunningham

---

* *Creative Stewardship*, Richard B. Cunningham (Abingdon Press: Nashville, TN) 1979.

in the second chapter of that book. I have pulled out a number of quotes just to quickly give you a picture:

> Life is a drama of creation and redemption. "Christian Steward-ship" is the title. God and man are the chief actors, and the world is the stage. God is the author, director, and lead actor of the drama. He also owns the theater and will drop the final cur-tain. And yet He allows man, as actor, to make his own innova-tive contributions to the script, so that Christian stewardship becomes a creative collaboration of God and man, a divine-human venture into God's future. All the drama's action revolves around these important elements: that God is owner of the world, man is the Steward, and the world is the estate for which man is responsible. The drama's plot hinges on the pur-pose of God, the nature and role of man, the nature and purpose of the world, and the meaning of life and how it is to be lived. The pivotal event on which the story turns is God's mighty act of redemption and revelation in Jesus Christ. . . .
>
> The universe exists as a theater for the glory of God. No matter how spectacular and dazzling this universe of God's, with-out man there is still an emptiness in the theater. The universe is complete and the glory of God fulfilled only when the human actor walks upon the stage. As the crowning achievement of God's creative work, man can witness to the glory of God and enter into personal relationships with his Creator. The vastness and grandeur of the universe also spotlights the paradox of man—his insignificance when measured against the universe and his greatness when standing before God. Man is meant for God. But man must freely and responsibly choose to love and serve God. Man's role in life is to glorify God by loving God and man, and by exercising dominion in God's world, by acting as God's representative in the created order, living creatively in the authority delegated from God, and finally by being responsible to God for the actions of his life. . . .
>
> God places the world under man's management. Man's stew-ardship over the earth involves him in a creative collaboration with God in God's own creative process. Stewardship is not merely the individual's responsibility for his own life. It includes his social responsibility for the resources and created values of the whole world as he participates at every level of society.

Man's whole life is properly and joyfully lived as a steward. We hold no title to anything. Our time, health, and what we call our "possessions" are only loaned to us by God, who will someday ask for an accounting of how we used them. We are given an opportunity by God to do some wonderful things in collaboration with Him and to participate creatively in the accomplishment of His purposes. We trust God for those things which are in His province as our Lord and Master, and gain satisfaction from performing *our* role as trusted steward. We look forward to hearing Him say someday, as he is quoted as saying in chapter 25 of Matthew (v. 21), "Well done, thou good and faithful steward! You have been faithful with a few things; I will put you in charge of many things. Come and share your master's happiness."

This raises an interesting question. Is the drama that Cunningham talks about *our* story or *God's* story? Who is the primary author of this story? Cunningham says that the basic plot is God's, but He allows us and wants us to participate in His creative work by "making innovative contributions to the script." The basic plot involves our discovery of God, our response to His invitation, our wanderings away from Him, and our reconciliation with Him. The details of how that happens depend not only on Him, but also on what *we* do in response to our circumstances. We each have our own river and have to sail our own raft: going with the flow, reacting to the flow, or anticipating and managing the flow. We each have our own maze and have to find our own way to the *goal*. We each have our own set of *givens,* and God expects us to do what we can with that set of *givens.*

If we accept the notion that our *purpose* is *creative stewardship*, what are the implications? The first question I ask myself is, *In what realms do we exercise our stewardship*?

The Realms in Which We Exercise Our Stewardship

We exercise our stewardship in a variety of realms, including the world as we find it; our use of the time allotted to us by God; our physical and mental abilities; our personal relationships; our material possessions; and our role as leaders. I have named six realms in which we exercise our stewardship. Are there other realms that I have left out? You may well be able to name another. But, let us think a little about the ramifications of those we have already identified. There are things that may come immediately to your minds as you think of your role as a *steward* in those six realms. But let me prompt you with a few of my own thoughts.

The World as We Find It

God does not intend for us to separate ourselves from the world as we find it, but to work creatively within that world. It is the testing-ground for our personal growth. It is the stage for the life drama of stewardship that Cunningham refers to.

I immediately recognize that I need to think of the world in several parts. There is the immediate circle of family, friends, and church; there is the broader community in the geographical area in which I live; then, the whole of the United States; and finally there is the entire world. What are my responsibilities as God's *steward* in each of these spheres? What are my responsibilities for the relief of suffering in the greater spheres, overseas as well as in my local community and the rest of the United States? What are my responsibilities to work for the reconciliation of races, ethnic groups, and religions? What are my responsibilities to work for the reformation of our culture? We also are the stewards of the resources and environment God has provided. As a good farmer, we do not want to consume the natural resources we have been given, but to cultivate, replenish, nurture, and build them up. What are my responsibilities toward the environment?

Many questions come to mind as soon as I begin thinking of my role as one of God's Stewards over this world.

Our Use of the Time Allotted to Us by God

Time is a precious resource that we can waste or use creatively. God relies on us to be a steward of our use of time and to use it well.

None of us knows how much time we will have. I can testify that as we get older, time goes faster and faster. It seems to me that no sooner do I finish brushing my teeth in the morning than it is time to do it again before I go to bed. One of the things we want to think about is how we distribute the use of the precious time we have between those several realms: what portion to our work in the world, what portion to our personal relationships, etc.

Even as we try to use our time wisely, we have to remember that God also gave us the gift of Sabbath rest. We are also stewards of our work/rest rhythm and must be sure that we use the right amount of time to rest as well as to be productive.

Our Physical and Mental Capabilities

We have all been given some unique talents and abilities as well as the general capabilities of physical activity, speech, etc.

Am I using the physical and mental capabilities that God has given me vigorously and effectively? Am I continuing to develop these capabilities? Is my speech used to edify and uplift? Am I conscientious in teaching others what I know and what I have learned to do, passing it on? Do I practice good mental and physical hygiene?

Am I using my unique talents to good effect? Am I developing my capabilities as I could?

Our Personal Relationships

There are persons who have been placed close to us, in our families and otherwise, for whom we have a unique opportunity to be an extraordinary blessing. Others aren't in a postion to do what we can in these particular situations. This is a God-given opportunity that we don't want to neglect.

The most precious of the many gifts that God has given to us are Himself and those people He has entrusted to us in a very special role (spouse, children, parents, siblings, close friends). The greatest calling in life is to live in loving, trusting relationships with God and with these special people. The health of these relationships can bring us our greatest joys. The deterioration of these relationships can bring us our worst torment.

When these relationships do deteriorate, it is usually due to our neglect of them and our failure to follow the principles God has provided for good stewardship of such relationships. We want to ask ourselves: Are we being good stewards of these relationships? are we devoting the time and creativity we should to our relationship with God? with our spouse? with our children?

Our Material Possessions

Material possessions can be a tremendous blessing or a hazard to our Christian health. Sometimes we invest too much of ourselves in acquiring and protecting possessions and, as a result, neglect relationships and development of character. Thus we sacrifice investments that have permanent value for those which are transient.

We can use our material possessions creatively in our roles as stewards. They too have been entrusted to us by God. For what purposes should we use them? To what extent should we conserve them and to what extent should we consume them? We need to be concerned with our stewardship in the acquisition of material possessions as well as in our use of them.

Our Role as Leaders

All of us are given roles of leadership. For some the domain of leadership is large; for some it may be more modest. But we all have responsibilities to lead in some area—in the family, at work, at church, in the community. If we are given positions of leadership, the Bible makes it clear that in all areas we are to lead as stewards.

Many people accept leadership roles because they want to make things happen. That's fine, but in order to achieve outcomes they desire or believe to be necessary or right, they may seek power and control in order to manipulate people, situations, and events. Some people lead because they feel they want to fulfill their potential. That's fine, but to some that means accomplishing the most earth-shaking results, and they think they can only do that in the most important positions and in the most essential organizations. Some people lead in order to satisfy other ego-related drives (for recognition, for appreciation, for applause). The Bible tells us that we have been given the privilege of power and leadership, not to indulge ourselves, but to serve one another (Gal. 5:13–14). We are to be servant-leaders; stewards of the well-being of those whom we lead; making sure that we are not exploiting them to satisfy our own needs, but seeing to it that the highest priority needs of those being led are being served.

We are privileged to exercise our stewardship in many realms. I suggest that you think through what living in creative steward-ship in each of these realms implies for you.

Hierarchy of Goals

In section 2, we will talk about establishing goals for our-selves in the various arenas of our life—our personal relation-ships, our lifestyle, etc. We can already see that goals exist in a hierarchy at several levels. If we have an overriding purpose, such as living in creative stewardship, we see that we will exercise that stewardship in at least six realms, and we could establish goals for ourselves in each of those realms. Then, each goal requires subgoals. For instance, if one of my goals in the realm of per-sonal relationships is to increase my participation in the lives of my children, one subgoal might be to attend more of their school events. Another might be to establish times when we talk to-gether about what's going on in their lives. But this discussion of goals is a subject for a later chapter.

Conclusion

What a thrill it is to think that God allows us to participate in His creative endeavor, and that He allows us to even write our part of the story. We have a noble purpose: to be good stewards of the part of the world in which God has placed us. We remember that the job of a steward is to cultivate, to nourish, to preserve, to pro-tect, to repair, to replenish, and to produce a harvest. As we do these things in the several realms we have discussed, we can have a joy of fulfillment as we stretch to accomplish our purpose. All of this moves us closer to our final *goal*: our reunion with our Father and our other relatives who will welcome us as we enter our true *home*, which He has prepared for us.

Points I Want to Come Back To

Later, when I have more time, I want to think more about the following sections, questions, or ideas associated with this chapter:

_____

_____

_____

_____

_____

_____

_____

_____

_____

CHAPTER 5

Why Bother?

Why Do We Want to Live Intentionally?

Living intentionally obviously takes effort and determination. Why do we want to be so determined and expend the effort that is necessary? There are at least four very important reasons:

- We want to live intentionally for our present contentment.
- We also want to live intentionally for our future contentment.
- We want to live intentionally in order to keep faith with our ancestors and with our descendants, most especially our children and grandchildren.
- We want to live intentionally because that is the way that we are intended to live.

Let us look at the first of these reasons, *for our present contentment*. Most people are more content in their present life when they have a map and motor than when just living reactively with obscure purposes. Living reactively makes us feel helpless and insignificant. Knowing that we have a purpose and are making progress toward that purpose gives us a sense of vitality and fulfillment. We need to feel we are gaining ground, not just holding our own; we are accomplishing, not just coping. There was an article in the *San Jose* (California) *Mercury News* early in 1995 saying that the first babyboomers were entering their fifties and were asking, "Is this how I really want to spend my valuable time?" Then it proceeded to discuss the cause of this reaction and the likely consequences of this trend. The babyboomers are realizing they need to be more intentional for their present contentment.

We also want to live intentionally *for our future contentment.* Most things will go a lot better when there has been some advance preparation. If I anticipate them and prepare for them, I will enjoy them more and they will have a better result. Furthermore, as we grow older we can't help but look back and reflect on how well we have taken advantage of this one chance at living that we have been given. We know we only go around once. If I let my current behavior patterns prevail and just follow the path I am on, will I be able to rejoice when I look back, or will I have bitter regrets for not having been more intentional with what I did with my life?

We also want to live intentionally in order to *keep faith with our ancestors and with our descendants,* most especially our children and grandchildren. Keeping faith with my ancestors and descendants means living in a way that does honor to my ancestors and provides the best possible encouragement to my descendants. Am I keeping the faith with my ancestors? I can feel so clearly the influence of my mother and father. And I know they were strongly influenced by their parents and their grandparents before them. I know the Bible is right when it says that we influence at least the next four generations. Just from the last four generations, I am the culmination of thirty different ancestors! Those people invested in me, and I want to make the most of their investment. (Of course, some people have an unfortunate heritage and have to intentionally disconnect from the lifestyle of their ancestors, taking a new course.)

Am I keeping faith with my descendants? Just as I have been strongly influenced *by* numerous ancestors, *I* will strongly influence numerous descendants. I influence my grandchildren directly as I interact with them, and also indirectly, as their parents (my children) reflect the influence I have had on them. Then my grandchildren will have their own children and my influence will be compounded, for good or for ill. My life is important. The world today is different because of me. I not only influence my children and my grandchildren, but also all the other people with whom I interact.

So I feel it is my responsibility to live in a way that not only does honor to my ancestors, but also provides the best possible encouragement to my descendants. I want to live intentionally for the sake of my children and grandchildren, for the sake of the legacy I leave behind.

Finally, I want to live intentionally because I am convinced that *this is the way that we are intended to live.*

As We Are Intended to Live

Logic tells us this is the way we are intended to live; intuition tells us this is the way we are intended to live; religions tell us this is the way we are intended to live.

When we think about the way we have been designed, logic tells us we are intended to live intentionally. We were designed with minds that can remember and that can imagine. Why do we have minds with such capabilities? We must have been given the minds we have so that we can anticipate and prepare. We can imagine the future and plan for it, and we can remember the past and learn from it. It is a tragic waste of our powers, and of the way we have been blessed, to not live intentionally.

We all have an internal concept of how we are intended to live—a concept built into us, which we might call intuition. This is reflected in the people whom we admire, whom we naturally want to emulate. We call such people our heroes, recognizing that there are huge heroes and more moderate heroes. We have huge biblical heroes (Jesus, Paul, Joshua) and we have huge secular heroes (Abraham Lincoln, Martin Luther King). Our more moderate heroes are people we see in our current society who also live in a way that we would like to emulate. All of our heroes live intentionally. In fact, we observe that if they don't live intentionally, we usually don't consider them heroes. They have a clear purpose and stretch themselves to achieve their purpose, intently. Think of one of your heroes and see if he/she doesn't live intentionally.

Paul encouraged first-century Christians to live intentionally. In his letter to the Ephesians, he exhorted, "Live life with a due sense of responsibility, not as persons who do not know the meaning and purpose of life, but as those who do. Make the best use of your time, despite all the difficulties of these days. Don't be vague, but firmly grasp what you know to be the will of the Lord" (Eph. 5:15–17).

During a talk at a men's retreat, Lewis Smedes reminded his audience that when we get to heaven we will all have to recount our stories. And the Lord will say to some of us, "That's not *your* story! You didn't write that story; you just went with the flow!" Even if we didn't just *go with* the flow, we may have just *reacted to* the flow. That isn't enough. More than going with the flow, or reacting to the flow, we are intended to do what we can to *anticipate* and *determine* the flow. That is what we call living intentionally.

We realize that living intentionally is more than just living according to our intent; it is also living according to God's intent for us.

In trying to live intentionally, we know we will not achieve all that we would like. But we have to realize we are not intended to be perfect, only to do the best we can with what we have. Paul knew he should live intentionally, and he was remarkably diligent in doing so, first as a persecutor of Christians and then as one of Jesus' strongest advocates. But he also was disappointed in the degree to which he lived up to his goal for himself. He said that, try as hard as he might, at times he did not live up to what he intended. Nevertheless, when he reached the end of his life, he was able to say in his letter to Timothy, "I have fought the good fight; I have finished the course; I have kept the faith" (2 Tim. 4:7). We would like to be able to look back and say the same thing. Living as we are intended to live is *keeping the faith*. Let us reflect just for a minute about *finishing the course* and *fighting the good fight*.

When I was in college I ran cross-country. Our course was laid out through some city streets and also through one of the town parks. Sometimes we ran on hard pavement, sometimes on the soft earth of the woods. Sometimes it was an easy run along the flat, often a torturous run up grueling hills. It was in cross-country that I learned that it is almost as hard to run downhill as uphill. The key to cross-country is stamina and endurance. Sometimes you can just barely bring yourself to put one foot in front of the other. But what a joy when you come across the finish line having successfully run the course! And, even though I would concentrate on my own performance during the race, it was really a team score that counted. So I was aware of my teammates. One time we all joined hands as we neared the finish line and came across together. That picture made the sports page. Running cross-country is a lot like living this life.

I remember my friend Stan Johnson describing the finish of the Hawaiian Triathlon. It is nighttime when they finish, but the finish line is illuminated with floodlights. As each runner comes into the bright light, near the finish, all his friends and family run out to take his hands and to cross the finish with him. Stan has a great picture of himself coming across the line hand in hand with his son, Doug. We speculate on what kind of an afterlife awaits us when we have completed the running of our life course here on earth. We can hope that our friends and relatives will similarly greet us as we cross that finish line. I have to ask myself, *What do I want to do so I can cross that finish line with satisfaction?*

Paul desperately wanted to finish the course satisfied that he ran the race to the best of his ability, but also thought of it as having "fought the good fight."

We know the course is a struggle and that we have to battle to live well. We have to contend with our natural inclinations, with the elements in our culture that would push us in the wrong direction, and with actual evil ones out there who will bring us down if we don't have the whole armor of God. We recognize that our greatest struggle is spiritual. We need to remember that our greatest resource is also spiritual. But we will say more about that in chapter 8 of this book, including the whole armor of God.

Well then, I have concluded that I want to *live intentionally* so that I can be more *content* in my present life and my future life; so that I can look back in my old age and feel that I have *kept the faith*, especially with my ancestors and my descendants; and so that I can rejoice in having *finished* a good course, having *fought* a good fight, and having *lived* according to the way I was *intended* to live by my Maker.

How much longer do we have to live? A few decades? A few years? A few months? Those who are younger may expect many more years and feel they can wait a while before getting serious about their life. Those who are older may feel their remaining years are numbered, and sense that it is urgent for them to make the most of every day. In fact, whatever our age, we may have few or many months or years ahead. But, in any case, what time we have is precious, and, if we think seriously at all, we know we should make the most of whatever remaining time is allotted to us. So, mindful of my goal, mindful of the nature of the course, I prepare myself to write the future chapters of my story, to run the next segments of the course. And I want to do this *intentionally*.

Can I Do It?

This sounds like a lot of work—it may sound overwhelming. We do recognize that life is difficult. Why add to the difficulty by encouraging people to undertake the discipline that is necessary to live intentionally? The only justification is the benefit that results. A modest amount of effort to apply the principles contained in this book can make a tremendous difference in the course of our lives. And life is even more difficult when we live reactively than when we live intentionally, even taking into account the work involved in living intentionally.

But we have to recognize the following truths:

- Living intentionally is easier for some persons than for others. Some people will be naturally inclined to live intentionally. It will be quite foreign and difficult for others.

- The same principles described in this book apply for everyone, no matter what their proficiency in living intentionally; no matter that each person has a very different situation in detail, or that their particular forks and dislocations may be quite different.
- We need to first put our toes in the water, then try to wade, finally learn to swim. The important thing is to try to live a little *more* intentionally, not necessarily to become a master at it.
- Whatever effort we apply to this, even if only a little or at an elementary level, will enhance our lives.
- Every person is capable of doing enough of this type of introspection, with the help of suggestions contained in this book, to substantially benefit his or her life.

Some of the people who have used this material successfully had previously lived entirely reactively. But they learned the concepts and tried to apply them to their own lives as best they could. They demonstrated that people's lives will be blessed if they make a reasonable effort and apply these principles to the degree that is right for them. You too can do it–in the way that is right for you.

Living intentionally is a lifestyle that can benefit everyone— men and women, single and married–and all generations, including young people who are just beginning their careers and marriages, striving adults with growing children who are struggling to balance the demands of career and family, those in midlife who are wondering if they have already seen the best of their lives, those contemplating retirement, and active seniors who want to make the most of their remaining years.

If you have decided that you want to live more intentionally, we have help for you in the next section. You will find there wisdom and techniques that have been discovered by other people as they have lived their lives. And even though your particular situation is different in detail from that of every other person, that wisdom and those techniques can help you.

Points I Want to Come Back To

Later, when I have more time, I want to think more about the following sections, questions, or ideas associated with this chapter:

_____

_____

_____

_____

_____

_____

_____

_____

_____

_____

Synopsis and Reflection

(CHAPTERS 1–5)

By way of review, we will list some of the key points of the preceding chapters and then list some questions, which the reader might consider before going on to section 2.

SYNOPSIS

- Our present life is precious—it is the only one we will ever have. We are intended to enjoy this precious life. Yet living this life well is very difficult. It is beset with problems, hazards, and some calamities. At the same time, every day provides opportunities to make our lives better and more enjoyable. *Living intentionally* enables us to manage our difficulties, capitalize on our elusive opportunities, and increase the joy in our lives.
- Life is somewhat like rafting down a river: We are swept along with the tide; we have slight influence on the flow of events; we can't call an intermission; our circumstances can change very suddenly, sometimes exhilarating us and often

threatening to overwhelm us. How we fare depends on how we have prepared for our journey.

- As time and circumstances rush along, each person has to decide whether he/she wants to just "go with the flow," "react to the flow," or "anticipate the flow." The most common lifestyle is one of "reacting to the flow," especially when we are young. We experience a steady stream of events and circumstances and do our best to react to each in a way that will produce the best result. We're not sure what will happen next and feel like amateurs, with too little experience and all too little preparation to cope with these new challenges.

- As we grow older, gain more experience, and talk to others about how they live their lives, we come to realize that there is an alternative lifestyle, which does a better job of "anticipating the flow" and preparing for it in a way that allows us to deal more effectively with the problems that beset us and to take better advantage of our opportunities. We call this lifestyle *living intentionally*.

- There are principles and techniques for living intentionally, which we can learn from each other. Even though our lives do differ substantially in the details, they all contain some of the same ingredients: forks, where we have to decide which direction to take; dislocations, where we have to decide how to cope with a sudden change in circumstances; changes in season, where we progress from one stage of our lives to the next; and special occasions, which we can turn into moments of joy and accomplishment if we are alert and prepared. In addition, we all have the common problem of improving the compatibility between ourselves and our environment.

- The course of our lives is determined by the choices we make. We can overlook some choices that are available to us, and we can also make sloppy, unfortunate choices. Making the most of our lives requires that we be alert to the choices available to us, think clearly about our alternatives, and then make deliberate and wise choices.

- It is important for us to stop periodically and rise above our current circumstances to a point where we can get a perspective on the maze of our lives. We need to review our overall purpose, our short term goals, the constraints, which seem to be limiting us, and evaluate whether some course corrections are needed. What new steps do we want to take in our personal relationships, in our careers, in our lifestyle, for our family prosperity and happiness?

- Living intentionally involves living with a sense of purpose and living in a way in which we stretch forth to accomplish that purpose. It involves *assessing, adapting, anticipating,* and *applying*: assessing ourselves and our situation; either adapting our environment to be as compatible as possible with ourselves or adapting ourselves to our environment; anticipating (including preparing for) the flow of events that is likely to occur in our future and, finally, applying to our particular situation the principles that have been developed for living intentionally.

- We want to live intentionally so that we can be more content in our present life; so that we can be more content with the future events in our life; so that we can look back in our old age and feel that we have kept the faith, especially with our ancestors and our descendants; and because we are convinced that this is the way that we are intended to live.

- Living intentionally is a lifestyle that can benefit everyone— men and women, single and married—and all generations, including young people who are just beginning their careers and marriages; striving adults with growing children who are struggling to balance the demands of career and family; those in midlife who are wondering if they have already seen the best of their lives; those contemplating retirement; and active seniors who want to make the most of their remaining years.

- The principles described in this book apply for everyone, no matter what their proficiency in living intentionally; no matter that each person has a very different situation in detail, or that their particular forks and dislocations may be quite different.
- Whatever effort we apply to this, even if only a little or at an elementary level, will enhance our life. We need to first put our toes in the water, then try to wade, finally learn to swim. The important thing is to try to live a little *more* intentionally, not necessarily to become a master at it.
- Every person is capable of doing enough of this type of introspection, with the help of suggestions contained in this book, to substantially benefit his or her life.

PERSONAL REFLECTION

- What changes have you intentionally made in your life situation as a result of thoughtfully analyzing what would make your life more pleasurable, satisfying, and productive?
- What are some of the decisions you have had to make in your life so far, where, if you had decided otherwise, your life might have been quite a different story? Are you satisfied with the way you went about making those decisions? Are you interested in what other people have learned about making such decisions?
- Have there been times in your life so far when your situation was suddenly and irrevocably changed due to some drastic happening (death, accident, job loss, etc.)? What were the things that sustained you during those difficult times? Do you feel you were reasonably prepared for such events?
- Can you identify a time in your life when you were at your wits' end—there was no way to go and the problems were insurmountable? Was God there when you called on him, or was he absent, as in Psalm 77?

- Can you identify some "modern miracles" in your life so far? *Modern miracles* are things that have happened to us that are hard to explain by natural causes. The probability of them happening without some divine intervention is very low. It might be an imminent accident from which you were spared; an opportunity presented that was just what you needed; a person who provided just the right clue, etc.
- Have you thought about the events (forks, predictable dislocations, important family experiences) that are likely to intersect your path in the reasonably near future? Have you thought about the ways in which you could increase your preparation for these events?
- Do you manage to find the time to do the things you most want to do?
- How much control over your life do you feel you have: almost none? not enough? as much as you can reasonably expect to have, considering the degree to which life is unpredictable and uncontrollable? Do the lives of other people seem more or less well ordered than yours? In what aspect of your life do you wish you had more control?
- To what extent do you think that you already live intentionally? Are you more likely to go with the flow, react to the flow, or anticipate and manage the flow?
- How do you feel about your ability to live more intentionally? Do you feel that it probably involves so much work that it would take all the fun out of life, or do you realize that living intentionally would probably put more fun into your life?
- What aspect of this book, as it is described, currently intrigues you the most?

The Application

CHAPTER 6

Coping with Forks

Which Path Am I Going to Choose?

Forks come in all shapes and sizes. Have you yet had to confront any of the following situations?

- You have recieved a diagnosis of cancer and have to decide whether to submit your body to surgery, radiation, or chemotherapy
- Your beloved child has succumbed to peer pressure and fallen into drugs and other self-destructive behaviors. Should you take the drastic action that has been recommended and commit her to a treatment center, an action that she views as abandoning her to a prison?
- Business is going steadily downhill in spite of all your valiant efforts. Your financial situation is deteriorating rapidly. Should you bite the bullet and move to a lower-cost region, disrupting the friendships and comfortable routines of the whole family?

These are major forks, where the decision as to which path you take has enormous consequences. Life is full of other forks that may not be quite so dramatic, but where the decisions we make also have an important effect on the course of our life. Sometimes we understand the impact of a fork only by hindsight. As I have talked with men and women about the forks they have previously faced, a common reaction has been, "I never realized the profound influence that particular fork would have on my life." Some have even reacted, "If only I had thought through that fork in the way this book advocates, I believe my whole life would have been different."

Thinking about Forks

In facing new forks we need to apply all the wisdom we have accumulated about making such decisions. It is valuable both to review what we have learned from our own previous forks and to talk to others about how they dealt with theirs. This is how we learn to cope with the forks that are either imminent or likely in the future.

I asked men and women to talk about a key fork of their life. I first asked each of them to think about a few questions regarding their experience with that fork. Then we went around the table and took turns telling each other the results of our mental reflection. As we proceeded, each person became more and more interested, and discovered more that he or she wanted to relate to the others. In the process we discovered a lot about forks. Most obvious was that our forks arise in a wide variety of situations, and they vary in the intensity of impact they have on our lives. Then we discovered the many factors we have to take into account as we deal with forks. We came to appreciate the variety of sources from which we can gain insight as to how to cope. Furthermore, it became obvious that people use somewhat different patterns in handling their forks, and each person has to adapt the common wisdom to his own situation and his own personality.

The wonderful truth, however, is that even with all that variability about forks, we have to master only one method for deciding our forks, and that method will serve us well with every fork. Our individual task is to develop the technique that works for us. Let us first think briefly about the variety of situations in which our forks arise.

Variety of Situations

In our younger years we face a variety of minor forks: Shall I take a commercial course or college prep? Shall I go steady with x or continue going out with a variety of girls/boys? Should I get a job this summer or go to summer school? But our first major forks are usually about our careers.

Our first career decision usually involves selecting the type of training and education that we will seek. Our son Tom always had a great love for music and decided to become a drummer. He played for two years on a rubber pad before his teacher said he had shown the persistence that justified buying him a drum set. He became an expert in all forms of percussion. He played in all the musical groups, jazz to symphony, was drum major of the band in high school, and was in the national champion drum and bugle corps. Then it came time to go to college. He had to decide whether he would make a career out of music, which he loved, or something else that would provide more income.

In fact, he decided to go to college and study biology, thinking to become a doctor. However, he soon discovered that biology was not for him, and so he switched to psychology. He reasoned that an understanding of how people think and behave would be good in any undertaking. He continued his interest in music during college and went on the road with a band for a year before accepting a job in industry. After a year or so of that he decided he wanted to teach music even if that didn't earn him very much money. That decision involved going back to college to get another four-year degree. He now delights in being a music teacher. Deciding which career to prepare for is a major fork and may involve more than one fork. Then this is followed by other career forks: Should I accept this job, or that one? Should I accept a transfer to another location or stay where I am? Is it time for me to seek a different employer altogether or a different business opportunity? Should I finally give it all up and retire?

The next arena of major forks is marriage and family. We are confronted with decisions: Should I marry this person? Should we have another child? Should I rescue my child from his current situation or let him fend for himself?

The choice of career and the choice to marry are the most crucial decisions we make. By *crucial* we mean the ones having the most profound effect on the total scope of our lives and succeeding options and choices. But there are also important forks other than those of career and family. These have to do with matters of faith; of moral, ethical, or health choices; and what I will call personal business.

In the arena of faith we have decisions such as these: am I ready to accept Jesus as my Lord and Savior? Is it time for me to join this church? Is it now time for me to rely on the Lord to work out this situation or should I still try to do more myself?

In the arena of moral, ethical, or health choices, we have these and other decisions: Should I sue them or continue trying to negotiate? Shall I finally give up smoking for good? Should I submit myself to a course of chemotherapy? Should I personally support this particular social cause? Should I speak up and risk incurring the displeasure of my boss? or my neighbor?

In the arena of personal business, I include questions like these: Should I make a commitment of my time and energy to serve in that capacity? Are we really in a position to buy that house? Should we sell our house and move into a seniors' residence? If so, when and where?

Very significant forks abound in every arena of our lives. But as we said before, forks vary quite a bit in the intensity of impact they have on our lives.

Variations in Intensity of Impact

Forks range in consequence all the way from the almost trivial decisions we make every day to momentous decisions that produce a profound change in our life. When we are thinking about past forks and forks that we are about to confront, we need to evaluate the intensity of their impact. Some career decisions, for instance, may involve only doing similar work in a different arena, perhaps a different department of the same company. The family may feel little impact from the change, except that their financial situation may be somewhat improved and perhaps a parent is working longer hours for a while. On the other hand, the career change at other forks would produce substantial changes in the circumstances of all of our family members. It can involve moving across the country with a complete change in friends, schools, and church, and separation from historical roots and relatives.

With other forks, there may even be a profound impact on personal relationships within the family, even more serious than impacts on geographic or economic family circumstances. For instance, consider the case of so-called tough love. If one of our children is completely out of control, we may have to lay down the law and tell him he is going to have to abide by our rules if he is going to continue living in our home. Or we may have to decide to send him to a school where his education will be continued, but where he will also get the discipline that we find it difficult to apply in our homes. That can be tough on the father, the mother, the siblings, and the relationships between them. The other children may not understand why the parents are being so "hard-hearted."

In some extreme forks we may even have to change ourselves. I think of the case of some redeemed marriages, where, in order to make the marriage work, each person has to make some changes in personal attitudes and behavior. They essentially have to become new persons! How difficult that is, but what an impact!

In our groups, our discussions revealed forks that involved impacts across this whole range of severity. We want to concentrate our attention on the most consequential forks. If we develop a useful technique there, it will also serve well for the lesser forks.

We also discovered that most forks have many features in common. Let me recount the story of one of my own forks to show how such a review can illustrate the common features as well as principles that apply to dealing with all of them.

My Story

I worked for IBM for thirty years. In 1967 we were living in New York and I was working in our research headquarters in Yorktown Heights, which is in the Westchester County countryside, north of New York City. I was asked to go to California because it had been decided to substantially expand research in San Jose and build a new laboratory there. In spite of the fact that we had grown up in the East and that's where our families were, we moved. I became director of the research program in San Jose, and before long we designed and built the new laboratory and added many new researchers. For six years I enjoyed directing that program, but finally was beginning to feel like I was falling into a routine.

In June, beginning the seventh year, I was at a conference at Stanford University when I got a message to call my boss in New York right away. He told me to meet him in his office the next morning. As I made the long trip to New York I kept wondering: *What's up, that he would summon me so suddenly, all the way across the country?* In his office he told me I was being transferred back to New York to run the research lab in Yorktown Heights. Another man had already been told he was going to San Jose as my replacement. Wasn't that wonderful? Wouldn't you go for a promotion that involved a return to your family roots? However, the decision wasn't that obvious, and this presented me with a fork of the first magnitude.

It was assumed that I would quickly agree and move the family. One of the interpretations of the initials IBM was "I've Been Moved." This was especially true in the sales force. It was less true in the technical divisions, but we also were moved. IBM had locations all over the country. They wanted their people to gain experience in different parts of the business and in different geographic locations. And, indeed, there were a lot of reasons for me to accept the promotion. But, there were also a lot of reasons for me to refuse it.

This is typical of all of our tough forks: the reasons for choosing one path are about as compelling as the reasons for choosing the other. If the advantages of one far exceed those of the other, our decision is trivial. We want to talk about making the difficult decisions, where there are a lot of factors to be taken into account in the decision, and both paths have important pros and cons.

I grouped the factors that I needed to consider into six categories: impact on career, finances, family, ego, personal goals and convenience, and moral and ethical principles. Of course, career and finances are related, but by *career* I mean professional growth, and there can be financial factors quite independent of career. We will almost always have to consider a combination of almost all of these factors. The decisions we make at forks are never just about finances, or just about our families. Decisions that seem to be about finances also have important ramifications for the family, and family decisions often have significant financial implications. And there are usually factors involving ego, personal convenience, and moral and ethical principles. Let us consider these six categories, both as to their typical presence in our forks and also as factors in the particular fork that I faced.

1. *Career*. The progress of our careers impacts every other aspect of our lives. Therefore we always need to take into account whether the effect of our decision on our careers will be beneficial or detrimental. We may decide to take the path that is less favorable from a career point of view, because other reasons are more important, but we always want to evaluate this factor.

What about the impact of my decision on my career? The executives of IBM wanted me to move. The new job was back at the corporate hub, where I would interact with corporate issues and with corporate officers more than I had previously. It had the potential for significant future career advancement. In addition, my replacement in San Jose had already been appointed—what career path in IBM was open to me if I refused to go? My current career path clearly would be advanced by moving, but did I really want to go where that career was taking me? Might I actually be forced to embark on a better, albeit different, career if I refused to go?

2. *Finances*. We always have to take into account the effect of any decision on the accomplishment of our financial goals and on the financial well-being of our families. That means,

of course, that we need to be aware of our financial goals and think about these in conjunction with the other circumstances of a particular fork.

In my case, our financial well-being clearly would be served by the move. This promotion offered the largest salary increase I had ever had, as well as other intriguing perks. If we didn't go, it would be a long time before I got a salary increase, even if IBM would let me stay and keep the salary I already had. The cost of living was about the same in both places. It was probably a good time to sell our California house and a good time to buy in New York. What about the costs of cross-country travel in either case: to visit relatives if we didn't move or to see our children if we moved and they didn't?

3. *Family*. Most of us are very aware of our responsibilities as spouse and parent. At each fork we want to evaluate the branches for their implication on the lives of our mates and of our children. Career moves often involve relocation, which can be very hard on the family. Of course, such a move might eventually turn out to be a blessing for them. All of our fork decisions have an important impact on the family because our families share our lives so intimately. We always want to carefully consider this aspect.

Our move to New York would certainly have a large impact on our family. I had uprooted my family six years earlier to go to California, and the move was not likely to be popular with them. Our son, Tom, was at the University of California and would definitely remain in California. Our daughter, Sue, was going to be a senior at Saratoga High School and then go on to college. A particular concern was the impact on Sue if she left one set of established friends, and preparation for a western college, to become a stranger in an eastern senior class. There the other girls already had strong relationships and were preparing for a different set of colleges. If we moved we would be far removed from Tom and Sue, or they would have to disrupt their schooling. Jean also had many important attachments in Saratoga. In addition, we had enjoyed putting down roots in California; we had a very enjoyable life there. We had a home in Saratoga, a comfortable suburb of San Jose, that was ideally suited to us.

On the other hand, all of our other relatives were back East, including our aging parents and our cousins. If we were in New York we would be better able to help our parents as needed. The larger Eschenfelder clan had always been a close family and we used to get together frequently, but that had obviously suffered since we moved to California. Indeed, there were pros and cons for either choice regarding family impact. In addition, some of the things I considered under category five, personal convenience, certainly had family impact.

4. *Ego.* Sometimes, especially at career forks, a man will decide to take another job, even though he already has enough money and the new job might be a significant inconvenience to his family. It seems to be a matter of ego. Acting in his manly role as conqueror, he just can't turn away from a new, exciting mountain to climb and prove to himself as well as others that he can do it. Similarly, a woman may be impelled by ego at her branch points. One, who has devoted years to raising a family, will want to try another career in the public domain just to prove to herself she can also be successful in that arena. We need to be explicit as to how much our ego is inclining us into a particular branch of a fork.

My fork also had ego implications. The work would be challenging professionally and I was eager to show that I could do it. There was also a lot of prestige in the new position, and I would relish the perks. What would turning my back on it do to my ego? What would other people think of me in either case?

5. *Personal goals and convenience.* As individuals, we have personal priorities in addition to those of career, finance, and family. Perhaps we want a certain amount of leisure to pursue a hobby, or want to further our education, or want to live in an area where we have certain amenities. We may have an aversion to commuting. We may have a love of boating and very much want to have such opportunities available. These issues of personal convenience will also be affected by the decisions we make at our forks, and we need to take them into account even when other factors are the primary ingredients.

In the area of personal goals, I have a great desire to be fruitful and productive, to use well the talents the Lord has given me. In which place would I be best able to do that? More on the side of personal convenience, we had now experienced living in Saratoga as well as near Yorktown Heights, and we much preferred Saratoga. We particularly liked the climate and lifestyle. Furthermore, we had other community involvements that we wanted to continue. I anticipated retiring in California and didn't relish another move back. If our children continued in California, as well might be in their best interest, we would not be able to see them anywhere near as often as if we also were in Saratoga. Furthermore, I knew the kind of political environment that existed in the headquarters of research and the company, and much preferred the more natural, congenial relationships that I would be leaving.

On the other hand, Jean and I both had our roots at Rutgers, in New Jersey, and we would be able to go to the football games and reunions if we moved back there. We had missed that. The children grew up in Westchester County and had fond memories of the area and their friends and the seasons with a white Christmas, ice skating, sleigh riding, etc. Our favorite vacation spot was Lake Winnepesauke in New Hampshire. Here we're talking about a huge lake full of islands. And warm water with sandy beaches. There isn't any lake like that in California, and that was our greatest regret about living in California. It was inconvenient, as well as expensive, to have to fly across the country every time we wanted to visit our favorite vacation spots or see relatives. So there were factors of personal goals and convenience on both sides of the fork.

6. *Moral and ethical principles.* Even forks that are not primarily within this realm often have important moral or ethical implications, and we have to measure them against our principles. In addition, some branches may make it harder for us to find the time or environment in which to pursue development of our spiritual life, or the exercise and enjoyment of it.

As I thought about moral and ethical principles, I recalled that IBM had been very good to me and my family, and I felt to some extent I ought to help them achieve their objectives. On the other hand, they were used to moving people for the convenience of the company and hadn't considered the impact on my family when they decided to move me. An even larger factor for me was our involvement with the Saratoga Federated Church. We had both grown spiritually in that church as in no other. We didn't know of any church back in New York that could approach the one we so enjoyed in California. In addition, we had just reorganized the church. I had been the leader of the goals committee, and I had just been elected as the president of the first new council of elders. I had a lot invested in the well-being of that church and was eager to help bring about its transformation and launch it on its new direction. I also did not want to walk out on my new position there.

I think my story illustrates the diversity of factors that usually have to be taken into consideration in every fork. As you think about your previous forks, I expect you to see that they involved important factors in all six categories. So also will your future forks.

Now let us continue with the story. How did I go about making my decision? Perhaps I took a different approach than you would. I took out my pencil and paper and analyzed the following things:

- Impact on Sue: I talked with school officials in both Saratoga and where we would move to in New York as to their experience with girls transferring in their senior years. We also evaluated the possibilities for leaving Sue behind with friends or neighbors so she could complete her senior year in Saratoga.

- Possible job alternatives: I explored alternative assignments if I turned down the promotion. I also explored the possibility of a delay in moving for a year to allow Sue to complete her senior year.

- Personal characteristics: I reviewed my own personal skills, traits, and activities that I liked the most and the least and then compared them with the likely situation if I went or stayed.

- Personal goals and priorities: I tried to be explicit about what I really wanted out of my life and the payoff from either course of action.

- Sense of personal urging: I tried to get in touch with my inner spirit and sense what was working within me.

- Previous experience: I tried to understand what I had learned from other past forks in my path that would shed light on this case. I thought of how other forks had gone when I had done what IBM wanted. I especially realized how God had honored my previous decisions and had led me into good things when I earnestly tried to do the right thing, even when it was not the most natural or popularly expected decision.

- Pros and cons of each alternative: Armed with all of this, I tried to balance the two courses of action, even though there were significant uncertainties. For instance, I couldn't know what I would be allowed to do within IBM if I decided not to go.

This illustrates another important principle for dealing with forks. There are issues involved in every fork that are extremely important, and other issues that are less important. We need to identify all of the issues, and then decide which matter the most to us. In addition, there are a number of questions that have to be researched and answered before we can make a sensible decision. We need to identify those questions, and then search out the answers to them. In my case, I had to find out what other career opportunities were available to me; what was the experience of girls who had changed their school in the midst of their senior year; whether there were ways to leave Sue in California to finish her schooling; whether there was a way to delay my transfer until Sue had finished her schooling, etc.

After identifying what was important and obtaining the best answers I could to the questions that were relevant to the decision, I just had to decide what seemed the most sensible course to follow, considering my values, preferences, and overall objectives.

What did I conclude? I decided not to go. The management was surprised at my response, but they were unusually adaptive. They offered me a substantial delay in reporting east, but I still decided not to go. To my great relief, I was allowed to stay in the San Jose laboratory as a base of operations. There were some of the expected negative consequences. However, soon I got the opportunity to coordinate IBM's nationwide work in a new technology. Eventually I was invited to teach that technology in the graduate school at the University of California at Berkeley and to write the prime textbook on the technology. These were experiences I would not have had if I had agreed to move, but they were unforeseeable at the time of the *fork* decision. I mention these to demonstrate that God is faithful. He provided great blessings for us on this new path. I am sure he would have also on the other path. We have continued to live in Saratoga, and have our children and grandchildren near us. Of course, I also retired from IBM at fifty-six, probably earlier than I would have, and what some would call prematurely. But I am well satisfied with the choice I made.

Dealing with Forks

We are constantly making choices, and whether they are the little forks or the life-altering forks, we apply to all of them the same background of values, preferences, and overall objectives. What we each need is a process for dealing with the many factors involved in our forks. That process should be the one that suits us the best. We need to observe how others deal with their forks, decide on a process that seems right for us, and then gradually refine that process as we observe how it works when we apply it to our own situations.

We can learn from our own past experiences, and we can learn from the experience of others.

Learning from Our Previous Forks

We have seen that we can discover important principles, which can be applied to all of our forks, by examining how we have handled previous forks and how they turned out. I have included in appendix B a form on which the reader can do a little analysis of a previous fork. That form contains the following questions, but there is more space on the sheet to put down your answers.

1. Name a fork that is already behind you, which may have yielded significant insight about dealing with forks.
2. With respect to this fork, list some of the factors that complicated your decision.
3. To what extent were the following factors involved in the issue? career; finances; family; ego; moral/ethical/principles; personal goals and convenience.
4. To what extent did this fork imply changes in family circumstances; changes in close personal relationships or changes in your personal behavior/attitudes?
5. How did you go about making the decision you did?
6. Who did you have available to help you? Who or what influenced you most?
7. In retrospect, what did you learn about the process by which you can best face a major fork? What recipe would you prescribe?

I encourage you to think about some of your previous forks in this way.

Learning from the Experience of Others

My groups of men and women have found that they profited greatly from discussing their previous forks with each other. As I said before, the more they got into it, the more time and energy they wanted to devote to it—because they found it so illuminating. They used that same basic form outlined above to make notes on one of their typical forks. Then they verbally shared key elements of these notes with each other. Important observations and guidelines emerged from those discussions, which I will review shortly.

But before we do that, let us be aware that we can also learn by reflecting on how other people have handled their forks: our parents and other relatives (this makes a very interesting and important dialogue), historical characters (from what they have written or what has been written about them), and biblical characters. Perhaps the biblical characters are least obvious. Let me illustrate by telling you what I observed from reflecting on the stories in the Bible of Jesus making decisions at His forks.

Jesus Confronts a Major Fork

Jesus confronted major forks in His path. Perhaps the two most crucial ones for Him were the one at the beginning of His ministry and the one just before His trial and crucifixion. In the first one He had to decide how He was going to go about that ministry and the establishment of His kingdom. He agonized over that alone during forty days in the wilderness (Matt. 4). In the last one He had to decide whether to willingly go to the cross, and agonized over that alone in the Garden of Gethsemane (Matt. 26:36–46). Let us reflect on how He dealt with the first of these two forks.

There were many ways Jesus could go about building His kingdom. He had just been baptized and had received God's blessing and commission (Matt. 3:13–17). How should He go about it? The people were expecting Him to use force and overthrow the existing powers. He ruled that out. To what extent should He use the miraculous? Should He allow himself to be exalted, or go among the people as a humble servant? How should He reach out to all of the people? Should He appoint deputies and teams of evangelists? We could think of a myriad of questions that would confront Him as He wrestled with the approach to His task. The Bible tells us that He went off into the wilderness for forty days and wrestled with temptation. As we interpret what the Bible relates about that, we can discern some of the major questions: the method to use—the easy way, or the hard way, God's way, or the way that men use and understand? (Matt. 4:8); how to satisfy His material needs (food, clothing, etc.) (v. 3); how to face inevitable physical threats (v. 6); who He would get to help Him and how to prepare them (v. 18–22).

Let us observe the process Jesus used in making His decisions. When confronted with a major fork, Jesus went out into the wilderness and fasted. He eliminated all comforts and distractions that might hinder Him in thinking and praying about the issues. Jesus was tempted, by half truths and even portions of Scripture taken out of context, to achieve quick solutions and expedient satisfaction of His human needs. Jesus made sure that He used the complete truth of Scripture, "every word that proceeds out of the mouth of God" (v. 4). Jesus did not compromise God's way, as best He could understand it, even when that way led to danger, suffering, and even death. His process involved isolation, temptation, use of Scripture, and following God's leading.

What then are the principles we can learn from the specifics of this story?

- When confronted with a vital issue, eliminate comforts and distractions, which might hinder clear thinking or the perception of God's leading.
- We can expect to be tempted when we are most vulnerable, particularly in terms of our basic needs. The time of forks is a time to be on our guard against being led astray, and to hold fast to our principles.

- Even Scripture can be used to put us on the wrong track. We should make sure we know the whole truth, and not let some partial truth lead us astray.
- Nourishment by the Word of God is even more important than the nourishment of our bodies, especially in trying situations—remember this and seek that nourishment as a top priority.
- We may need to sacrifice the opportunity to improve our material well-being in order to go in the right direction.
- We should not succumb to the temptation to "test God," but have faith that He will sustain us and lead us in the midst of our difficulties.
- There are shortcuts to power and accomplishing purposes (even God's purposes), which we may have to consciously avoid, because the price of using them is too high.
- We may have to restrain the use of some of the strengths and powers God has given us in order to accomplish things in the way He wants us to.
- We may have to be personally humiliated or debased, or at least take the path away from personal exaltation, in order to do what is best and what God is leading us to do.

These are principles that apply to our own decision-making today. We might not have expected to discover so much that is useful today from an ancient Bible story.

As we study the ways in which we and other people deal with their forks, we learn some important things from each case and we discover that there are different patterns for coping with forks; people use somewhat different processes in making their decisions.

Variations in the Process of Making a Decision

As we look at the ways that different people go about making decisions, we discover that they do it in somewhat different ways. Two major variations in these approaches include analysis versus intuition, and solitude versus community.

In coping with forks and deciding which path to take, some of us are immediately inclined to get out paper and pencil and analyze the alternatives. That's what I did. Others are more inclined to listen to their intuition, and want to decide on the basis of what feels right to them. In fact, we each ought to use a combination of analysis and gut feeling or intuition, but each individual is inclined to use one or the other as the dominant mode. It is clear that we can either overanalyze or underanalyze. Sometimes we need to let our will shove our emotions back in a box, and sometimes vice versa. Eventually both types of people, whether we are primarily analytical or intuitive, develop an internal leaning and have to take a leap of faith based on gut feeling.

In addition, we are each inclined more toward being an introvert or an extrovert. An introvert will tend to go off alone for a combination of analysis and feeling assessment, while the extrovert will tend to want to talk it out with someone else. Somewhere along the line we all need to talk to someone to check out our analysis and intuition. We can talk to someone meanfully only if we have already established a deep personal relationship with them. It is therefore important to have established such relationships before the fact. We can make the following observations on the need to talk to someone:

- The greatest mistakes are usually made alone and out of fear. We should be sure to talk to someone.
- We can't talk to just anyone. We need the right person, previously cultivated.
- Even with a deep personal relationship with another person, we hold on to a private area. As a result, no one else can know everything we know and feel just the way we feel. We inevitably have to deal with some parts by ourselves.
- Often the best ones to ask are Mom or Dad, even when we've grown up. Many of our critical decisions are made at a young enough age that our parents are still available, and they have an important perspective. They may give us in-

put that causes us to be more cautious, or they may stimulate us to move more rapidly. Some have found it useful to ask someone else who has previously been very close to them—even an old girlfriend or boyfriend!

- It is important when discussing forks with others (especially in a group) to listen particularly for the similarities to yourself and your situation rather than the differences. If we listen to the differences, we may tend to feel that the situation is too different from ours for us to profit from it. If we concentrate on the similarities, we begin to see how we can really learn something relevant from the exchange, and it helps us to perceive the most useful insights. The differences are much less relevant, but they may be significant. So we have to note them. However, too much emphasis on the differences can blind us to the helpful insights.

Whether we are inclined to analysis or intuition, solitude or community, we all need to establish our own pattern of decision-making, which is gradually developed and refined over the years. We need to be exposed to the patterns that others find useful while shaping our own, but we should not expect one pattern to be appropriate for everyone.

I have tried to accumulate some observations about forks and some guidelines that seemed to emerge from the experience of myself and other men and women. Let me just tell you some of the observations we have made and suggest some guidelines for dealing with forks.

Observations about Forks

- If we are not careful, we can breeze through a fork without realizing there is an alternative path open and available to us. We have to be alert to the choices available to us.
- We never get beyond some forks; we continue to have to face that fork day after day. A very simple example is that of

an alcoholic who chooses to quit drinking. That person has to make that choice every day and never really gets that fork completely behind him. Also, we don't just say we are going to lose weight, and then watch it happen. We have to face little forks every day about what we are going to eat, what exercise we are going to get, etc.

- Sometimes we forget that they are *our* forks. A man may decide how the family will respond to a fork, and that fork then becomes more of a dislocation for his wife rather than her fork as well. Her question becomes how she will respond, not which branch she wants to take. It is also true that while men may sometimes be inclined to deal with their forks with minimum involvement of their mate, a woman more often *has* to deal with her forks without her mate (because he has predeceased her, or otherwise left her).

- We have to be careful not to think one branch of a fork is necessarily the *right* branch and the other is the *wrong* one. It may be that they both are fruitful directions, and that they are merely different. It is true that they are not equivalent. One might yield a different kind of result, and it is worth considering both and making a choice. But the choice is not a matter of life and death, right and wrong, God's will and not God's will. We can wrongly agonize too much over which to choose, believing that only one would be God's choice. He might, in fact, not care so much which we choose and would bless us in either choice. On the other hand, there might be a right and wrong choice, and God might want us to choose a particular one. We have to be discerning and sensitive to what's at stake.

- Life is like a chess game: we can make a good move every individual time and still wind up in an untenable position. We need to gradually develop the knack of making an optimum set of moves, not a set of individually optimum moves.

- We can't automatically assume that what worked in the past will work in the current situation. Someone may make all the right moves for a particular stage in life, but then things change, and different moves may be better for their current circumstances.

- It is important that I face my fork as early as possible. I shouldn't wait until the situation reaches a crisis to do my analysis and make a decision. In a crisis, options are reduced and mistakes are more likely. I should try to anticipate forks.

- Other people have important input to give, but we have to make the decision that seems best for us—we have to live with it. After you give it your best consideration, go with your gut feeling no matter what others say.

- The influence of parents on decisions may be very subtle, e.g., inclining us toward or away from a career or a mate implicitly, even though not overtly. I mentioned that our son Tom had to decide whether to go into music or pick another career in which he could make a better living. After working for a company for a while and also spending a year on the road with a band, he went back to college again for four more years, got his degree in music, and is now very happy as a high school music teacher. He said he always wanted to go into music, but that the reason he didn't from the first was because he *perceived* that we didn't think it was an acceptable way of making a living! We must be discerning as parents lest we inadvertently encourage our children in a direction we did not intend, and as children lest we succumb to an inappropriate or misperceived pressure.

- Even when we are trying to reason logically, we are all likely to take a few intuitive shortcuts that are erroneous. Massimo Piattelli-Palmarini has identified a variety of "mental illusions" to which we are all likely to succumb (identified and explained in his book *Inevitable Illusions*).* Those mental illusions have been likened to optical illusions. We know that

---

Inevitable Illusions, Massimo Piattelli-Palmarini (John Wiley and Sons: New York, ISBN 0-471-58126-7) 1994.

our brains will play optical tricks on us: we think we see something one way, but, when measured, we see that it is really something else. Just so, our minds also sometimes play tricks on us when we think we are being rational. Sometimes what seems to be an obvious intuitive conclusion, is clearly seen as wrong when examined logically, step by step. We need to be aware of these mental illusions, and take care not to fall into their trap. There is no substitute for precise, logical reasoning. This is another reason for having a confidant with whom to review our fork reasoning. This may be a spouse, friend or mentor, but it should be someone who thinks logically and can spot our mental illusions.

- Each decision involves a lot of uncertainty. We cannot just plug known facts into an algorithm and let a computer decide the optimum decision. Factors that play a role in our decision can change in the midst of our decision and cause us to doubt that we are doing the right thing. Sometimes we are assailed by doubt and fears during the transition, and then we find that everything works out fine. The decision was the right one, even though we had a lot of grief in the process. On the other hand, sometimes we find that we are sort of euphoric in the process of change, and only later find that the end result wasn't what we had hoped. We wish that we had made the decision differently.

- Perhaps we should shy away from an alternative that involves substantial uncertainty and risk. On the other hand, that might be the most fruitful course. In any case, we have to think seriously about the uncertainties and the risks. We often tend to neglect them and assume that the factors we are taking into account are stable. Some are bound to change. As a consequence, we have to expect emotional ups and downs. We have to be prepared for periods of conviction and periods of doubt, periods when we are swamped with fear, and periods when we are basking in confidence. In the midst of those unsettling uncertainties, we need something to hang on to, to anchor and stabilize us in the storm. We will talk more about this in chapter 8.

- Sometimes individuals feel they had abundant choices when young, but now their path is narrowing and they have fewer and fewer choices. They are being driven by momentum, like cattle being herded into a chute from which they can't escape. We need to remember that we still have choices, and failure to see and make a choice is itself a choice.

- An important part of our responsibility as fathers and mothers is to communicate whatever wisdom we have accumulated to our children. But while we should teach them as much as we can about the techniques of decision-making, we need to be careful about going too far in making the analysis for them or telling them what their conclusion should be. If they are reasonably mature, there are times when we need to step back and let them make their own mistakes. Only in that way will they truly learn.

Now then, let us pull together all of our observations about how we and other people handle forks into a set of guidelines for facing forks, to which we can refer when confronted with a fork.

Guidelines for Facing Forks

From all of our discussions, the following emerge as sensible guidelines for coping with forks:

1. Don't panic! and Don't swing too far! Be patient while sorting things out. Take time to absorb the situation. Suppress the tendency to act too quickly. Try to sort out both the facts and your feelings. What is it and what is it not? How are you feeling about it?
2. Evaluate whether it is in reality a fork or a dislocation. Is the direction really a decision for you to make (is it truly open and therefore a *fork*), or is the direction essentially inevitable, so that the issue is not which way to go, but how you should cope with it (a dislocation)?

3. Go off alone and take stock (in case of a fork or a dislocation):

   a) Eliminate comforts and distractions. (When Jesus faced serious forks in His path, He went off into the wilderness and fasted.)

   b) Take it to God in prayer. (God wants to be our Lord and a key partner in our decisive moments, and he promises to lead us: "I will instruct you and teach you in the way you should go; I will counsel you and watch over you" (Ps. 32:8).

   c) Identify the key issues and put aside those issues which might at first appear key, but are quite subordinate. Key issues would include the various motivating factors involved (career, financial, family, ego, moral/ethical, personal goals, and convenience). After we have listed the issues, we need to assign weights to them according to their relative importance to us. A man in one of my classes said that he had found it valuable to also list the worst that could happen for each direction and whether there was a back door, an escape, in case his choice was wrong.

   d) Review your list of personal influences (priorities, goals, likes, skills, traits). After all, what we decide has to satisfy those aspects of our person. It is obviously good to establish such a list before forks occur:

      • I want to choose the path that will optimize the future, get me where I want to go. This means that I need to have an explicit definition of my personal *goals*—goals for myself, for my family, and for the institutions in which I am personally invested (such as my church).
      • I want to choose the path that is truly worthwhile, to do the right thing. That means that I need to clearly understand my *values*—my ideals, the things

that I esteem, that I want to be known for, and that I want to honor.

- I want to choose the path in which I can be truly productive, to accomplish something significant. This means that I need to know my *skills*—my abilities, the things that I can do particularly well and better than many other people.
- I want to choose the path that I can enjoy, that satisfies my inner drives. That means that I need to be aware of my *traits*—which include the things that satisfy me and the things that annoy me.

So in facing my forks and dislocations, I really need to understand my goals, values, skills, and traits. (We will see how we can assess these for ourselves in chapter 10.)

  e) Identify key questions that should be researched and answered.
  f) Identify the best sources for insight (own previous experiences, other people who have had similar experiences, professional counselors, God).
  g) Pray for openness and guidance.

4. Decide to decide. It is important to decide when we will make a decision. We can make decisions too quickly, but we can also keep putting off a decision. What kind of decision is needed, and at what time will we make it? Define the question, the decision process, the timetable. It is important to make the best decision I can, and then be satisfied that I did what I could with what I had. Future regrets are futile. Waiting until I have all the answers is also futile. I can't assume that I can have a perfect result. We have to decide when we are going to decide!

5. Research the key questions, including interacting with other people. Certainly we need to explore the needs and the ideas of all of the affected parties in these considerations, espe-

cially our family members. When I am overwhelmed by the magnitude of a fork, I find that it pays to deal with the smaller parts of the issue. If I pray about very specific details, I find that I get answers about those details. Eventually the big picture is settled as well.

6. Evaluate your assumptions. We consider a variety of assumptions in making each decision. For instance, I may let the fact that my daughter and her family live here play a large role in deciding to stay here, rather than move to a new opportunity somewhere else. But those assumptions all have some degree of uncertainty. I need to think through how my decision would be influenced if each assumption changed. Suppose my daughter's husband got a job offer somewhere else, and they moved away. Would that change the decision I would make?

7. Review what is already known from previous decisive experiences. What was learned from and during them that is relevant to the present situation?

8. Be sure that we have thought about the long-term implications of the decision. We are quick to perceive short-range pressures, and we have a tendency to want to relieve those short-term pressures. As a result we give them undue weight. A couple I know bought a house for their divorced daughter and burdened themselves with the responsibility for the mortgage payments. They thought that was a wise move to help her in her situation. Now they are retired with limited means, and the house needs major refurbishment. Those costs are a major burden that is cramping their retirement life, and they don't see any way out of their dilemma. If they had thought about such long-term possibilities, they probably would have made a different decision.

9. Beware of faulty reasoning. We briefly discussed the problem of *mental illusions* earlier in this chapter. This can be a greater problem when we are more inclined to be intuitive in our reasoning. It is a good thing to have someone who is a good logical thinker go over our reasoning and affirm

that our conclusions follow logically from our circumstances and goals.

10. Take everything to God in prayer in all phases of the process. First of all, we want to go to Him in the right attitude: attentive, trusting, eager to find his righteous path. Look how the Bible urges us to seek God's counsel:

Consider it pure joy, my brothers, whenever you face trials of many kinds, because you know that the testing of your faith develops perseverance. Perseverance must finish its work so that you may be mature and complete, not lacking anything. *If any of you lacks wisdom, he should ask God*, who gives generously to all without finding fault, and it will be given to him. But when he asks, he must believe and not doubt, because he who doubts is like a wave of the sea, blown and tossed by the wind. (James 1:2–6)

My son, if you accept my words and store up my commands within you, turning your ear to wisdom and applying your heart to understanding, and if you call out for insight and cry aloud for understanding, and if you look for it as for silver and search for it as for hidden treasure, then you will understand the fear of the Lord and find the knowledge of God. *For the Lord gives wisdom* and from his mouth come knowledge and understanding. He holds victory in store for the upright, He is a shield to those whose walk is blameless, for He guards the course of the just and protects the way of his faithful ones. *Then you will understand* what is right and just and fair—every good path. For wisdom will enter your heart and knowledge will be pleasant to your soul. Discretion will protect you, and understanding will guard you. (Prov. 2:1–11)

Show me your ways, O Lord, teach me your paths; guide me in your truth and teach me, for you are God my Savior, and my hope is in you all day long. . . . Who, then, is the man that fears the Lord? *He will instruct him* in the way chosen for him. He will spend his days in prosperity and his descendants will inherit the land. The Lord confides in those who fear him; He makes his covenant known to them. My eyes are ever on the Lord, for only He will release my feet from the snare. (Ps. 25:4–5, 12–15)

He guides me in paths of righteousness for his name's sake. Even though I walk through the valley of the shadow of death, I will fear no evil, for you are with me. (Ps. 23:3–4; He will not guide us into paths contradictory to his righteousness).

11. Then we want to note the manifestation of God's leading. God's answers are given by

    a) The people, ideas and information that He interjects into our path. (So we should pay attention to doors that appear to open or close, and to suggestive interventions in our thoughts or daily events.)
    b) His interjections into our prayerful, daydreaming ruminations. (So we should let our minds pause in our prayers to listen for His answers, let our minds be flexible and open to His influence, and let our minds be attentive to what occurs to us while in prayer.)
    c) His influence on our analysis and His influence on our leanings. (So we should pay careful attention to ideas that occur in our analysis and to our internal urgings.)

12. Make a decision. Finally we have to take the *leap of faith*. We review all of our analysis (pros/cons) and our intuition (internal urgings). After all the analysis and intuition, everything comes down to a leap of faith. It is essential to "choose and go!"
13. What about after we have made the decision? I have to keep alert for evidences of God's redirection. Suppose I made the wrong decision. Is it all right to go back and revisit it? Even if it was the right one, the situation can change.

    a) Hindsight is often a costly indulgence. We usually cannot go back exactly to the same branch point. It is like those plates of spikes at a parking lot exit, where you can't back up without damaging your tires.

b) On the other hand, God honors our honest mistakes, and we need to be alert for His indications that we have made a mistake and His opportunities to rectify those mistakes and get on the right track.

c) In any event, surely we should look back and see what we have learned.

In Conclusion

The decisions we make at the forks in our path obviously have a profound effect on the course of our lives. As we grow older it is amusing to speculate on what our lives would have been like if we had taken the alternate route. It might almost be fun to live another lifetime discovering what the other path-choices would lead to. But we are given just this one great adventure. So it is important to realize how significant are the choices we make. At the same time, we want to remember that God honors our choices and will help us to make the most of them, as well as helping us to recover from our mistakes.

I encourage you to spend some time thinking about some of the forks you have dealt with in the past, perhaps using the analysis sheets. Also, if you can, talk to some others who are doing the same thing. It is very interesting and profitable.

Once again, let us remember that:

- God will direct us at our forks. "I am the Lord your God, who teaches you what is best for you, who directs you in the way you should go" (Isa. 48:17).
- We need to pray, be quiet before Him, and listen for that voice saying, "This is the way; walk in it." "Whether you turn to the right or to the left, your ears will hear a voice behind you, saying, 'This is the way; walk in it'" (Isa. 30:21).
- God knows we have little strength for this, but He will provide for us. "See, I have placed before you an open door that

no one can shut. I know that you have little strength. . . ."
(Rev. 3:8).
- Even though we are not strong in this, we go boldly forward through our forks, "for God did not give us a spirit of timidity or fear, but a spirit of power, love, and self-discipline" (2 Tim. 1:7).

In this chapter we have thought about how we go about facing the forks in our path. It does take a spirit of self-discipline and a confidence that, with God's help and our accumulated wisdom, we have the power to make good decisions. In the next chapter we will talk about facing our dislocations, in a similar spirit.

Synopsis

- In facing our forks, we need to apply all the wisdom we have accumulated about how to cope with them effectively. It is valuable both to review what we have learned from our own previous forks, and also to talk to others about how they have coped with their forks.
- As we share our fork experiences, we can accumulate some guidelines for dealing with forks that are useful for everyone (see text).
- All of our fork decisions usually involve a combination of considerations: career, finances, family, ego, personal goals/convenience, and moral/ethical principles.
- There are issues involved in every fork that are extremely important, and other issues that are less important. We need to identify all of the issues and then decide which matter the most to us.
- In coping with forks and deciding which path to take, some of us are immediately inclined to get out paper and pencil and analyze the alternatives. Others are more inclined to listen to their intuition, and want to decide on the basis of what feels right to them. In fact, we each ought to use a combination of analysis and gut feeling or intuition.

- We are each inclined more toward being an introvert or an extrovert. An introvert will tend to go off alone for a combination of analysis and feeling assessment, while the extrovert will tend to want to talk it out with someone else. Somewhere along the line, we all need to talk to someone to check out our analysis and intuition.
- Whether we are inclined to analysis or intuition, solitude or community, we all need to establish our own pattern of decision-making, which is gradually developed and refined over the years. We need to be exposed to the patterns others find useful while shaping our own, but we should not expect one pattern to be appropriate for everyone.
- We seem to get more analytical as we grow older and more experienced. While we analyze some important factors in the choice of our initial careers and our mates, there is usually a large degree of going with the flow. However, we are more inclined to be analytical in later life, especially when we try to cope with forks involving change in employment or disruption of a marriage.
- The Lord has promised to direct us in our forks as we seek His counsel.

Personal Reflection

- Use the outline given on page 92 (there is a blank worksheet for this in appendix B) to review one of the forks you have already experienced in your history, and see what you learn from such an exercise. Do you feel that the process you used was adequate? Has this chapter given you any ideas of how you could improve that process?
- Are you facing a fork right now? Or can you anticipate a fork you should face in the near future?
- What are the most crucial issues involved in that fork?
- What are your present thoughts as to how you should evaluate the alternatives and go about reaching a decision in this

fork? How does the material in this chapter of the text apply to this specific case?

- Which things discussed in this chapter most obviously apply to your current situation?
- Who do you have to help you consider this fork, and how do you think you might involve him/her?
- Do you know of a fork that your children might soon face? What advice do you think you ought to give them as they face such a fork?
- Which of the observations about forks (p. 97) seems most important for you to remember?
- Which of the guidelines for facing forks (p. 101) seems most important for you to remember?

Points I Want to Come Back To

Later, when I have more time, I want to think more about the following sections, questions, or ideas associated with this chapter:

_____

_____

_____

_____

_____

_____

_____

_____

_____

_____

CHAPTER 7

Coping with Dislocations

How Should I React to This Sudden Change in My Life?

I was introduced to tragedy at a very impressionable age. In July 1938, just after I had turned thirteen, my brother drowned. At that point, the life of our family went off on an abruptly different course.

I do not remember tragedy before that time. Our family life had been very pleasant. Oh, I had had some traumatic moments, like the time when I accidentally hit my sister in the head with a sledgehammer. We were trying to put a tent up in the backyard. Grace was holding a stake for me while I pounded it with the hammer. I slipped! I was banished to my room with the shades drawn, not knowing how much damage I had done to her. But we all survived that incident, and I don't remember any real disasters before 1938.

We went on vacations together as a family before 1938. Usually we all went to Manasquan, an oceanfront town in New Jersey. Sometimes we stayed at the same small hotel with our aunts, uncles, and cousins; sometimes we rented a cottage by ourselves. The fathers would often leave their families there while they worked during the week, and then they would come down by train for the weekends. We had memorable times. But after I was ten, I went to boys camp each summer. In the summer of 1938 I went to Boy Scouts camp in July.

One day my counselor came to me to tell me that my father had come to see me. It was very unusual for a parent to be there in the middle of the session, and I couldn't imagine why he had come. I can vividly see him even now. He was waiting for me in the middle of the dirt road, with my uncle standing just behind him and to the side. I can't remember how soon I knew something was very wrong. He told me that my six-year-old brother had fallen into the Manasquan River and drowned. Jackie had been walking with my mother along the bank, and before she could stop him, he tried to climb into a boat. I discovered later that my mother had tried valiantly to save him, although she couldn't swim. As it happened, my sister passed the accident in a car with her cousins on the way to the beach. She was unaware that the excitement at the riverbank involved her mother and her brother until they came to get her.

This was what I call a real tragedy:

- It certainly was a tragedy for my mother. My mother never recovered from the shock of that event. She spent years in a mental institution and died young. I am sure that she was wracked with guilt. She realized that she exposed Jackie to the hazard, and she was unable to save her child when he needed her. What a tragedy!
- It was a tragedy for my father. He lost his son and, in a very real sense, his wife also. I often wonder what blame he may have felt for himself, for my mother, and whether he ever said anything to her he later regretted. My dad now had to be both parents to me and my sister, even while he was struggling with his own loss and trying to be successful at his career. What a tragedy!
- It was a tragedy for my sister Grace. She lost the companionship of her mother during very formative years. She was

ten at the time. She should have had her mother to nurture her as she made her way through her teens. I have never been sure in just what ways those events distorted her life, but I know they had lasting effects. Grace may have lost a brother and a half, as well. I haven't been the brother to her that I could have been. I think it may have inclined me to avoid the kind of intimacy that can hurt so when we lose it. What a tragedy!

- It was a tragedy for me. I lost the companionship of a brother—I often speculate on what it would be like to have a brother. I lost the nurturing of my mother and, in particular, the sweet side of my parenting. My dad was great with us, but he couldn't replace our mother. I probably also felt increased pressure to live up to my father's hopes, because I realized that all of his hopes for his sons were now focused in me. Who knows what total effect the tragedy has had on me?

- Was it a tragedy for my brother, Jackie? It is true that he graduated early to that perfect home the Lord has prepared for us. In that sense we rejoice for him. On the other hand, I believe that God has put us here to gain experience living this earthly life and to learn our lessons before we pass on. Jackie died when he was only six. He missed the opportunity to enjoy the relationships of family, marriage, and children, to fulfill the inherent potential that God gave to him, to accomplish who knows what. That seems tragic to me, but only God knows for sure.

Jackie's drowning was a compound tragedy, and such a tragedy is an example of the *dislocations* that come, unexpectedly, into our lives.

Why Dislocations?

Why do I call this type of an event a *dislocation*? Dislocation literally means an abrupt change in location, or place, or position. In the sudden drowning of my brother, we all found ourselves abruptly in a new place in our lives. We were all precipitated onto a new course; our lives were never to be the same. In a *fork* we find ourselves moving in a new direction, but there is a smoother transition, and we have a choice as to which direction we want to take. There was no choice on our part; we were just jolted into an entirely different situation. In a dislocation the only choices we have are how to cope and how to respond.

Dislocations may be minor, but the ones we want to think about are the more serious ones, where the consequences to our lives are momentous. Such dislocations are often tragedies, either actual or perceived. At first, I titled this chapter "Coping with Tragedies," rather than "Coping with Dislocations." However, in my first women's group, the ladies pointed out to me that having children is a real dislocation. The parents' lives are drastically and permanently changed. It may even be the single biggest change of circumstance and direction in their lives. However, that is not a tragedy. So not all dislocations are tragedies.

One woman also pointed out that not all calamities are tragedies. She said that the death of my brother was a horrible calamity, but not a tragedy, until it was transformed into one by my mother's "unsuccessful" way of grieving. So I looked up the words in my Oxford dictionary. Oxford said that *calamity* describes deep distress arising from some adverse circumstance or event; a *tragedy* is a calamity with "a fatal or disastrous conclusion." We can say that deaths, accidents, illnesses, and other losses are calamities. What we do about them makes them tragedies, or not. In that sense, calamities are universal, tragedies are not.

So while this chapter helps us to deal with all dislocations, I am trying to relate particularly to calamities that bring pain, suffering, perhaps death, and where it is almost impossible to discern any good in the situation. These may not turn out to be actual tragedies, after we finally discover how to survive them. But at the time, they appear to be tragedies in that their occurrence seems to portend "a fatal or disastrous conclusion." The violent death of a loved one is such a tragedy. We may survive it, but someone has experienced a fatal and disastrous conclusion, and, at the time, we're not sure we can endure it ourselves. Sudden layoff from a long-standing employment is perceived as a tragedy, and can be considered a tragedy for the purposes of this chapter, even though it may turn out to ultimately lead to a better situation for us. Actually, we realize that good can eventually emerge from the ashes of any tragedy, but it is hard to realize that in the midst of our pain and suffering.

Types of Dislocations

We can think of several categories of calamities: calamities of physical, mental, and spiritual health; calamities of relationship; calamities of career; and others.

PHYSICAL, MENTAL, AND SPIRITUAL HEALTH

First there are calamities that afflict our bodies, minds, or spirits. They are the consequence of injury, illness, or a traumatic experience. They may result in permanent disablement, if not death. Or the disablement might be temporary and we may ultimately recover, but that recovery comes only after long and arduous treatment and recuperation (and we are left with scars).

We tend to think first of physical calamities. An example of that type would be an accident which resulted in the loss of one or more limbs. My brother's drowning is in this category. Then there are mental disablements. They are even worse than the physical ones. I think most of us would say that we fear loss of our mental capacity even more than loss of physical capacity. A nervous breakdown or a stroke can be in that category. But the worst of all is spiritual injury or death, because our spirit underlies our physical and mental well-being. We can cope with either of these if we have spiritual health, but we are lost if our spirit is destroyed, such as when we lose all hope. Some tragedies combine all three dimensions. A sexual molestation, for instance, can result in physical incapacitation, mental aberration, and intense spiritual depression. Recovery from any of those tragedies requires long treatment, patience, and loving relationships.

RELATIONSHIPS

We may also experience disablement of a personal relationship, or even death of that relationship. There too, recovery may be achieved after the traumatic injury, but that recovery comes only after long and arduous treatment and recuperation.

Suppose your best friend's sociable relationship with your wife evolves into playful flirtation and eventually into a serious affair that destroys the integrity of your marriage. That is a tragedy of relationship! Suppose your beloved child, who has been the apple of your eye and for whom you have anticipated a great future, suddenly takes up with people who are an evil influence, turns against you, and rejects all that you value and hold dear. How could you have failed so miserably as a parent? What can you do to save this child? That is a tragedy of relationship! Suppose your spouse, who once seemed so tender and caring, begins to abuse you with increasing ferocity. What have you done to deserve that? What could you do to turn it around? How should you protect yourself? That is a tragedy of relationship!

CAREER

Many men and women have invested their lives in particular careers only to be laid off after many years, with uncertain prospects of finding suitable employment. Or they have built up businesses only to have the business climate change so that serious illness or death befalls their business. A person may have as much at stake in career as in health and relationships, and that calamity can be grievous. Ultimate recovery may be possible, but, there too, only after long and arduous treatment and recuperation.

OTHER MAJOR DISLOCATIONS

What of the midlife crisis (for men and for women)? What of the sudden emptying of the nest when the children leave? What of retirement? What of aging parents suddenly becoming incapacitated and dependent on us? Those also can be very serious dislocations in a person's life. They may not be calamities, but the decisions we make as to how to cope and to respond to these dislocations have profound consequences.

Preparing for Dislocations

Having recognized the wide range of dislocations that can befall us, the natural question is *To what extent should we try to prepare for dislocations?* We know that it is impossible to prepare for all of them. It is also impossible to completely prepare for any one of them. It would indeed be foolish to devote too much time and energy to trying to prepare for dislocations that might never occur. Nevertheless, it is prudent, and part of living intentionally, to take basic steps that will better equip us to anticipate and cope with some dislocations.

Our big problem is that instead of preparing for dislocations, we tend to ignore them. We don't want to waste our time, and we persuade ourselves that the likelihood of occurrence is really quite small. What is the likelihood of a major earthquake in the San Francisco Bay Area (where I live)? Is it large enough that we should prepare for it? The horror of the Kobe earthquake filled the pages of the local *San Jose Mercury News.* Alongside those articles were others, showing the similarities of the Bay Area configuration to Kobe and predicting similar results. There were also articles describing how Bay Area residents *could* prepare, *should* prepare, and of some saying that they *intend* to prepare—someday! The headline screamed, "All Talk and No Action on Preparedness."

For dislocations, at least we can do the following:

1. Identify the ones that are amenable to modest preparation, and do what is prudent to get ready for them.
2. Recognize the nature of traumatic dislocations, so we are not stunned by the experience of dislocation when it does come.
3. Build relationships and spiritual strength, which will sustain us during and after dislocations.
4. Draw on the experience of others who have experienced the same dislocation.

Let us consider each of these in turn.

Dislocations Amenable to Modest Preparation

Clearly we should prepare somewhat for all of the changes in season and predictable dislocations that we know we will have to face. Some of those are

- *Loss of mate.* We have already mentioned this and some of you may have had to pass through it already. We can think of things we can do to increase our ability to cope with such a dislocation while we are in the midst of it; and others that increase our ability to be restored and to recover after such a calamity. There are even steps we can take to guard health and practice safety which might delay the onset of such an event. We will come back to this shortly.

- *Midlife crisis.* Everyone faces a form of this, just as they do the adolescent crisis. Like the adolescent crisis, it is a natural phase in the normal development of a person. It should not be dreaded nor denied, because going through it produces necessary changes and prepares us for the next stage of life. The midlife crisis occurs when it finally hits us that we have achieved the bulk of what we can realistically expect to achieve, or that we are not going to achieve what we had dreamed or expected: "Is this all there is?"

- *Retirement.* Many of you are undoubtedly confronted with some aspect of this: either worrying about how you can prepare for it, emotionally and financially; or wondering how to make the transition to retirement; or wondering how to make the most of the time you now have in retirement.

- *Having children or learning that you can't have children.* Either result has a profound effect on the course of our lives and requires a substantial readjustment. We should prepare for either eventuality. I read an article the other day that told of the increasing number of women who have put off having their children for one reason or another. Now they were discovering they waited too long; they had left behind their childbearing opportunities. Do you see how someone could prepare for that?

- *Children leaving the nest.* This event can leave people high and dry, with a lack of purpose in their lives, or it can represent a wonderful new opportunity. They can apply their time and energy to a whole new realm of activity and discover valuable new personal relationships. The transition is much easier if there has been some anticipation and preparation.

- *Parenting our parents.* I have a friend whose children, one by one, graduated from school, were married, and moved into their own homes. That friend was offered a wonderfully challenging and rewarding career opportunity. She accepted it eagerly and was doing very well at it. Soon after, her mother got to the point where she could no longer live independently. Then she really wanted and expected to move in with her daughter. My friend was beside herself. Should she give up this career she had just launched and take care of her mother? Or should she find a good care facility for her mother even though her mother didn't want that? Most of us get to a point where our parenting of children is replaced by a need for parenting our parents. My father always told me, "Andrew, I don't want you to ever move me into your home. If I can no longer take care of myself, I want you to put me in a good care facility." Actually, he died while his wife was still alive and he could fend for himself. Would he still have felt the same way if that hadn't been the case, and he came to the time when he was helpless? Clearly, most of us have to eventually face such a situation.

- *Disruption of employment.* This is more and more common. The question now seems to be not so much whether it will strike, but when and in what form.

Clearly we need to think about preparing for these predictable dislocations. In each of these cases, can you think of things that could help to (a) decrease the likelihood of the occurrence of the dislocation; (b) increase your ability to cope with such a dislocation while you are in the midst of it; and (c) increase your ability to be restored and to recover after the dislocation?

Sporadic Dislocations

It is less clear how much we should prepare, and in what way, for the sporadic traumatic dislocations. In addition to the loss of possessions by an uncontrollable event such as we have already mentioned (earthquake, stock market crash, failed investment), some examples that have confronted friends of mine include the following:

- various physical and mental illnesses, including cancer, heart attack, nervous breakdown, severe and unexplainable depression, and despair;
- abandonment by a spouse;
- rejection by a child;
- a child succumbing to addiction and
- physical abuse in the marriage relationship.

We may think that the likelihood of being confronted with these last four is pretty remote, but we all know other people to whom these have happened. I have a friend who had delighted in her daughter. Even though she had been enjoying success in a career, she gave that all up in order to devote herself to the upbringing of that daughter. There came a time when that daughter utterly repudiated her mother. She told her mother that she hated her, that she never wanted to be like her mother in any way, and that she did not want to ever see her mother again, let alone talk with her. That mother was devastated! She couldn't imagine how she had failed so utterly. In her own words, it was as if her personhood had been stolen from her and she was a total failure. I am glad to say that eventually, through much prayer and patience, that daughter came around and a wonderful relationship was reestablished. Praise God!

Yes, these things can happen to all of us. We need to accept our exposure to such events. We need to talk about preparing for them. Which ones should we prepare for and in what way? As we said above, at least we can recognize the nature of traumatic dislocations so we are not stunned by the experience of dislocation when it does come. We can also build relationships and spiritual strength, which will sustain us during and after dislocations.

Recognizing the Nature of Dislocations

When we think about the traumatic dislocations, we notice that they all have a number of similar features. We want to enumerate some of those features, for we realize that we are better able to cope with the dislocations if we know what to expect. Of course, we can only learn so much from reading about these or witnessing someone else go through them. Unfortunately, we fully understand only by going through such an experience ourselves. But it is helpful to be aware of these typical characteristics of traumatic dislocations:

- *Sudden disruption of our lives.* They send us on a different course. Our previous course is lost forever.
- *Shock and unreality.* At first we can't believe it is happening to us, and we find ourselves operating on nerve, numb to the actuality of what is occurring.
- *Stark reality and depression.* It really is happening! Why me? "O God, why hast thou forsaken me?"
- *Lonely pain and suffering.* Others who have been through similar tragedies can help, but to a large extent we have to endure our pain and suffering alone—no one can take it for us and no one can see it exactly as we do.
- *Strong medicine and tender care.* Some of the required treatments are strong medicine indeed, and, as a compensation, we need very tender care from those friends and professionals who minister to us.
- *Slow, tedious mending with oscillations.* The recuperation is usually long and seemingly endless. There are also setbacks when we wonder if we are going forward or backward.
- *Gradual healing leading to scars.* Eventually the wounds heal over and scar tissue forms. The scars contribute an

interesting ingredient: the scar tissue is hard enough to provide some additional protection in that area against additional wounding. However, the scars are there for our lifetime. They may not be readily apparent to others, or even to ourselves, but they influence our behavior subtly, if not obviously.

- *Perplexing allergies.* Paradoxically, while the hard scars that develop might be expected to reduce our sensitivity, we may also acquire an *allergy*, wherein we develop an exaggerated sensitivity. We find that our systems have been so sensitized by our exposure to the trauma of a situation that forever after we react to any additional exposure to similar things with behavior or attitudes that are perplexing to us. We may find that we have mysterious reactions to particular situations or types of people that we don't like and don't understand. In the case of poison ivy, we know what produces the rash, and we can't prevent our reaction to it, but we can apply soothing calamine lotion. So, too, with these allergies, with care we may be able to discover what things produce these troublesome reactions in us. There may not be a cure for that allergy. Even so, we may learn to anticipate the reaction and may be able to find a soothing antidote to apply when it occurs. As a last resort, we may have to condition ourselves to avoid that which stimulates it.

- *Guilt and forgiveness.* In some dislocations we will also have to deal with a load of guilt. I can well imagine the way that my mother must have blamed herself for the death of my brother and the load of guilt that she carried for the rest of her life. There was no way she could shake off that guilt. That is probably the reason that she had to spend so many years in a mental institution. And, then, I also wonder what my father may have said to her. I don't know that he did, but wouldn't it have been human for him to say things like "Why did you ever take Jackie to the river? You knew how dangerous that is!" That would have compounded my mother's guilt and then loaded my father with guilt as well, as he realized that he had added to her burden and perhaps caused her institutionalization. Or think of the time when a driver is careless for just a moment and causes the death or maiming of another person. How often we might say, "Oh, if only I could live that moment over again." Our lives will never be the same; and that's a dislocation! Surely, blame and guilt are a part of many dislocations. Lewis Smedes said that one of our problems is that "we can remember the past, but we can't forget it." He pointed out that this is the reason we carry guilt and are so in need of forgiveness. Without forgiveness, of ourselves and each other, and by our Heavenly Father, we are doomed to carry a heavy burden of guilt.

- *Disabilities, but compensating strengths.* To some degree we are disabled by the tragedy. We may never be able to look at things the same way, or even act in the same way, but we tend to develop compensating strengths. The man who loses his legs in an accident usually builds much stronger arms so that he can function. The person who survives a relational tragedy also builds some compensating strengths.

- *A new life.* It is true that after a dislocation our lives will never be the same as before the dislocation. But sooner or later, if we deal with the dislocation in the right way, we discover and learn to enjoy our new life. My mother never quite came to the point of enjoying her new life, but even that was possible. My father, and we children, survived the trauma and found joy in our lives after the tragedy. It may seem that we can never find joy again after the death of a dearly loved spouse or child. But I rejoice that the good news of the gospel is that God promises resurrection for the survivors as well as for the departed. Whether it is death of a loved one, sudden loss of a job, disabling illness, or other dislocation, a joyful new life is possible beyond the dislocation.

It really helps to know what to expect in dislocations. It helps us to have confidence that our situation really is going to get better, even though at the time, the end of the tunnel is completely invisible. It helps to know that is not a unique ordeal, but that others have also walked that path and survived. It helps to understand about the scars, the allergies, the possible need to deal with guilt, the new life afterwards.

As I have thought back to the big dislocations of my life, like the drowning of my brother and the loss of my mother, I have been able to identify scars and allergies that I have developed. I have thought about ways in which I was disabled by those tragedies and compensating strengths I have acquired. That awareness has helped me to make more sense of my present condition and to live more successfully now. I encourage you to think about your various dislocations and ask yourself:

- What scars have resulted?
- What allergies?
- In what ways have you been disabled?
- What compensating strengths have you developed?
- Are you still carrying a burden of guilt?

Perhaps the most common ingredient of all in our tragedy is the presence of suffering and pain. There are a few things I want to remember about suffering, pain, and tragedy.

Suffering and Pain in Tragedy

We can agree that suffering and pain are realities of this life, falling on the good and the bad. I cannot eliminate them completely and the fact that they happen to me does not mean that I have incurred God's wrath. Jesus is quoted as saying in John 16:33: "In this world you will have trouble. But take heart! I (Jesus) have overcome the world." Christ Himself confirms that I will have trouble, suffering, pain, but he also assures me that he has overcome the world and is the means by which I, too, can overcome the tragedies that befall me.

In spite of Christ's assurance, at the point of deepest pain, in the midst of tragedy, God seems absent and even the scriptures may not help much. Dr. William Sloan Coffin, pastor of Riverside Church, New York City, lost his son in an automobile accident. Shortly after that, on January 23, 1983, he said in a sermon:

> I know all the right biblical passages, including "blessed are those who mourn," and my faith is no house of cards. These passages are true, I know. But the point is this: while the words of the Bible are true, grief renders them unreal. The reality of grief is the absence of God—"My God, my God, why hast thou forsaken me?" The reality of grief is the solitude of pain, the feeling that your heart's in pieces, your mind's a blank, that "there is no joy the world can give, like that it takes away." [Lord Byron]. That's why immediately after such a tragedy people must come to your rescue, people who only want to hold your hand, not to quote anybody or even say anything, people who simply bring food and flowers—the basics of beauty and life—people who sign letters simply, "Your brokenhearted sister." As the pain that once seemed unbearable begins to turn to bearable sorrow, the truths in "right" biblical passages are beginning, once again, to take hold.

The meaning of tragedy is God's secret. Job's friends went wrong when they ceased being comforters and tried to be interpreters. The meanings will never be explained by another person, and they will never be discovered by ourselves. God can reveal the meaning when He chooses to, but most often He does not. I have to trust God, look to him for support, and leave the meanings to Him.

God is the great salvage worker. God does not cause the wreck, but steps into the wreck and salvages good, even when the situation is unsalvageable from man's point of view. Much of God's business is salvage, turning hopeless situations into something good, glorious, of eternal value. There is a lot we, too, can do as individuals to work in cooperation with God to salvage good out of tragedy.

We will always have mixed emotions in the face of tragedy, no matter how much faith we have. There will be doubt and confidence, despair and hope, resentment and thanksgiving. But God lets us feel and express our emotions without putting us down for it.

One of the things we will have mixed emotions about, in the midst of tragedy, is the biblical truth expressed in Romans 8:28, which says that "in all things God works for the good of those who love him, who have been called according to his purpose." How do we respond to this in the midst of our tragedy? I find that I begin to doubt that it is really true.

As I ponder this scripture in the midst of a tragedy, I will try to remember the following:

- This scripture does not say that the actual tragedy is *good* nor that it is *for* our good, but rather that even in the midst of a tragedy, God is working "for the good" of those who love him.

- My idea of what is good is much more limited than God's. I think in terms of its direct impact on me. My perspective is limited, but God sees the big picture and knows what I really need. Furthermore, God's ways are superior to my ways, His plans are superior to my plans, His understanding of the correct timing is perfect, and His provisions are accurately appropriate to my real need. All of these may well differ significantly from my own perception.

"For my thoughts are not your thoughts, neither are your ways my ways," declares the Lord. "As the heavens are higher than the earth, so are my ways higher than your ways and my thoughts than your thoughts." (Isa. 55:8–9)

Do not forget this one thing, dear friends: With the Lord a day is like a thousand years, and a thousand years are like a day. (2 Pet. 3:8)

Many of the saints didn't see as "good" what happened to them and their suffering, but look at the good it has meant for succeeding generations! I want to remind myself that God is at work and will use me in His way and in His time.

- What happens *in* us is more important than what happens *to* us. The good that will emerge on the far side of the tragedy may depend on how we react to the tragedy and learn from it.
- God is at work "in *all* things"—even the things we could least imagine. He has promised to be with us and to work with us "in all things." We, in turn, have to be with Him and work with Him "in all things"—paying attention and being prepared to let go of some things, even things we cling to, including such things as doubts, old habits, etc.
- "Of those who love Him"—John 14:21, 23 says that those who love Him obey His commands. Am I one of those? If I can turn more toward Him and do a better job of following His will, then can I believe that He can produce good, even out of this tragedy?
- "Who have been called according to his purpose"—His purpose is to conform us to the likeness of His Son in our attitudes and our actions (v. 29). We may have to *want* to be conformed to the likeness of Jesus in order for God to accomplish His good in us. It is hard for us to surrender self-will until we are in pain. As long as things are going our way, we tend to give lip service to God. It is when things don't go our way, and we hurt, that we reach out for God. If that is the only way He can get our attention and our obedience, it's a wonder more good, steady people don't hurt more often.
- Since pain and suffering may lead me closer to God and are sometimes necessary for that, I should try to get every bit of good I can from those situations which cause me pain and suffering. We know that some blessings flow from

working our way through pain and suffering. That raises an intriguing question. How far should we go in trying to obliterate all pain and suffering? Since so much good can come from it, should we refrain from suppressing pain? If I see someone suffering or in pain, I want to do whatever I can to mitigate that suffering. I believe that God wants me to do that. On the other hand, it is not good for me to strain to avoid all situations that might bring pain or suffering (we might then not even marry or have children) or to anesthetize ourselves so much that we can't gain the blessings that might flow from the suffering that does befall us.

As we think of the trauma that surrounds us as we engage our dislocations, we realize that we need to think also about the resources that are available to us, which will help us to survive in the midst of the dislocations and help us to recover and to move on after we have emerged on the other side of the dislocation.

Building Relationships and Spiritual Strength That Will Sustain Us

When I think of the things I can do to equip me to deal with dislocations, I am drawn to my favorite Bible verse, Isaiah 12:2–3. We will discuss this more in the next chapter, but let me share a few thoughts with you here, because they are so important in the context of our dislocations.

Isaiah 12:2–3 says, "Surely God is my salvation; I will trust and not be afraid. The Lord, the Lord, is my strength and my song; he has become my salvation. With joy you will draw water from the wells of salvation."

"I will trust and not be afraid." How that contrasts with the doubt and fear we experience in the midst of our dislocations. We fear the future and also the present. We fear being thrust into a wholly new situation, we don't know how to handle. We doubt our abilities to cope, and our conviction that God can and will sustain us is shaken. Isaiah found a way to trust and not be afraid.

In this verse I observe the following things:

- In all situations, including my dislocations, it is because I am in God's hands that I can trust and not be afraid. He has promised to care for me and I have entrusted my ultimate salvation to Him.
- I appropriate God's salvation by joyously drawing living water from the wells of salvation.
- There are many wells and of different kinds. (The verse uses the plural, wells.)
- I have to draw the water. It doesn't just overflow me. I have to recognize my need for the water, seek the well, draw the water, and drink it with faith.
- I draw it with joy because from it I receive salvation, trust, confidence, strength, and continual refreshment. I am rescued from doubt and fear, uncertainty and anxiety.

So I see that doubt and fear and discouragement are defeated and replaced by confidence, conviction, and joy, through God's Spirit, which comes as I draw water from the wells of salvation. We will discuss these wells and the process of drawing water from them, as well as other sources of strength, in the next chapter. If you are in the midst of coping with a dislocation, I encourage you to read that chapter next.

The most important thing we can do in advance to deal with all dislocations. is to "dig wells" and "maintain wells." Digging wells involves hard work, and there are often distractions from it. However, it is important and necessary work that we must do in the valleys and also on the mountain-tops in anticipation of the valleys. In the midst of our dislocations, we are too occupied by our problems, which absorb all our energy and time. It is then almost too late to accumulate the spiritual strength and friends who can support us.

During and after the event we also want to draw on the support of friends. Obviously it is important to have deep friendships. We may find it difficult to find the time and energy to cultivate friendships when we are absorbed with our families and our work, but that must not be neglected. Our deep friendships are one set of "wells" from which we will draw the water that will save us.

Drawing on the Experience of Others

After a dislocation we want to benefit from the experience of other people. One of the advantages of being in a church is that there are loving people who have been through almost any kind of dislocation we can think of. We can either consult them in person or join one of the support groups composed of such people who are ready to assist us. In addition, some people who have had to deal with particular dislocations have written books, which can be very helpful.

I would like to make some brief comments about one dislocation that seems to be increasingly prevalent—the loss of one's mate. That dislocation can be devastating, but it is amenable to modest preparation.

Loss of Our Mate

Loss of our mate can happen either through abandonment or untimely death. If we are happily married, and in relatively good health, the probability of such dislocations may seem very remote. However, we all know people, both men and women, who have lost their spouses very unexpectedly. It is especially not that uncommon for a woman to lose a husband. In our society, all too often women are left bewildered, with too little understanding of the family finances, especially some of the financial obligations that may have been undertaken by their husbands. Ruth is just one example.

Ruth had been happily married with two wonderful children. Then her husband, Jeff, suddenly died. Jeff's death was a tremendous shock, naturally, to Ruth, the two children, and to everyone who had known and loved Jeff. People rallied round, and gradually the shock and grief subsided enough that Ruth could take stock of her situation. Jeff had a very good job and Ruth had a modest career of her own. Between the two of them they had made a comfortable living, and Ruth did not anticipate financial problems even with Jeff now gone. However, she had let Jeff take care of the financial planning, so she wasn't sure just how well off she was. For instance, the children were teenagers now, and she wasn't sure how much Jeff had been putting aside for their education.

Fortunately, Jeff was reasonably organized and had files in his den, that contained the basic records Ruth needed. These records listed the insurance policies and investments as well as the expected cash flow. Ruth was able to deduce that the cash flow would be sufficient to sustain the family's normal lifestyle, especially with the temporary continuation of Jeff's salary, which was a company benefit. However, Ruth was horrified to discover that Jeff had made several investments and had signed papers pledging to make substantial payments into those investments over the next few years. Jeff had been mindful of the need to accumulate capital for the kids' education and for retirement, and had selected investments that seemed to have the potential for significant growth. Jeff knew they could handle the promised subsequent payments with their combined income.

With Jeff's untimely death, however, Ruth couldn't make those payments. She was inclined to just let the payments go and sacrifice the current value of the investment. But there was a signed promise to pay, and the company would pursue the required payments. Ruth was in danger of having to use her insurance proceeds to make the payments, or of losing her house and other assets. What a nightmare!

Of course, Jeff's death was a very remote possibility, but should Jeff and Ruth have taken that remote possibility into account in their planning? And was it a mistake for Ruth to be so uninvolved in the financial planning and the commitments that were made on behalf of the family? Prudent financial planning is a major aspect of living intentionally.

We all need to know enough about how to do each other's household jobs, so that we can carry on when our mate is not there. I have prepared a notebook that is in the right-hand upper drawer of my desk. It is intended to be available to Jean to help her cope in the event of my untimely demise. A woman obviously should make sure she knows how to manage the household finances. In addition, she might also make sure that she has some means of earning a living, perhaps part-time for mothers with dependent children. Jean and I each take responsibility for handling a portion of our family finances, using the same procedures, so we would have no difficulty taking over each other's accounts.

We probably need to simplify some things (such as financial affairs) and document others. When my father died, I helped my step-mother put all their investments in one brokerage account. That made things much simpler for her. Then she died eighteen months later, and I had inadvertently made things much easier for myself as executor. Having had to clean out their house, I also realize we should all try to get rid of some of our junk and not leave that job to our heirs. Jean and I are in the process of getting rid of some of ours.

Helping a Friend with a Dislocation

When a friend is suffering or in pain, we usually want to do something to help, but often feel awkward, not sure what would be appropriate. At those times I have found these suggestions helpful:

1. It is very important to be our unique person; formulas are not the answer; no one can give us a recipe for what to do. Almost anything we do, if it is from the heart and genuine, will be blessed and used by God for the benefit of the person we want to help.
2. Quiet support is needed in the midst of suffering and pain: presence, food, prayers, cards, etc.

When three of Job's friends heard of all the tragedy that had befallen him, they got in touch with each other and traveled from their homes to comfort and console him. . . . Then they sat upon the ground with him silently for seven days and nights, no one speaking a word; for they saw that his suffering was too great for words. (Job 2:11–13)

3. While a card or phone call is helpful, nothing replaces the face-to-face visit. Especially be sure to visit when the water is very deep and others haven't the stomach for it. However, never intrude when not really wanted.

4. Preparing for the visit:

   a) Go in quiet confidence that you go in the enabling power of the Spirit (Ex. 33:14–15: Moses said to God, "If your presence does not go with us, do not send us up from here." God said to Moses, "My presence will go with you and I will give you rest").

   b) Pray for God's peace, compassion, and sensitivity to ways of being helpful.

5. During the visit:

   a) Do not force intimacy, but be open, available, attentive.

   b) State the purpose of being there: "I came because I care about you" (not "about what happened to you").

   c) Be an active, sensitive listener.

   • Be active in asking appropriate questions, such as "What would you like to talk about today? What are your greatest needs? What are you worried about? How does it hurt? Where are you finding the strength you need? Have you tried sharing what's going on in you with God?"

   • Be sensitive in listening to the person and not just to the words he or she is saying. Some want to talk about it, and some do not. There is a time for silence as well as for listening. In some cases it is necessary to turn around the old adage: "Don't just stand there, do something" to "Don't do something, just stand there."

   d) Be sensitive to the dynamics of the situation (including who else is present) and let them influence how long you stay, what you say, etc.

e) The use of scripture and prayer: It may be appropriate to pray and read scripture and it may not. In any event, don't read or pray too long. Sometimes give one verse of the Bible on a three by five inch card, e.g.:

Fear not, for I am with you. Be not dismayed, for I am your God. I will strengthen you and help you; I will uphold you with my righteous right hand. (Isa. 41:10)

Surely, God is my salvation. I will trust and not be afraid. The Lord, the Lord is my strength and my song. He has become my salvation. With joy you will draw water from the wells of salvation. (Isa. 12:2–3)

Perhaps take their Bible, open it, and put a marker at an appropriate passage.

f) Offer to do things for your friend:

- Can I read to you?
- Can I answer some cards or letters?
- Can I run an errand or do some chore? (e.g., mow the lawn, drive your family somewhere, house sit, etc.)

g) Seek to comfort, not to interpret!

h) Be realistic. Don't say, "Don't worry. Everything is going to be all right."

i) Be aware of the grief process (which is our reaction to many dislocations) and give permission for its expression: denial and isolation (it can't be happening to me; why to me? no one else can understand what I am going through), then anger, bargaining (if only . . . then I promise . . .), depression, acceptance, and finally hope.

j) Leave with a word of assurance

- of your availability for help
- that you will be praying for them

6. Following the visit: send a simple card, or phone—it is often what you do after the visit that solidifies what you did during the visit, especially after a death.

Our Zigzag Path

As we cope with our forks and dislocations, we recognize that we are growing, during the process, into someone who is much more mature. We would not want to remain in our naive infancy. So our path must be upwards, and climbing involves some stress. Sometimes we wish that our path could ascend very gradually. However, our paths are not gradual; they go up and down and zigzag back and forth, dipping into deep valleys, then rising back into high country. Would we forgo some of the delightful highs of our lives if we could also be spared the deep lows? Not likely! Can we find some benefit in this convoluted path?

An unknown author has written:

> We climbed the height by the zigzag path
> and wondered why–until
> We understood it was made zigzag
> to break the force of the hill.
>
> A road straight up would prove too steep
> For the traveler's feet to tread;
> The thought was kind in its wise design
> Of a zigzag path instead.
>
> It is often so in our daily life;
> We fail to understand
> That the twisting way our feet must tread
> By love alone was planned.

In the midst of my forks and dislocations, it has been hard to remember that there is purpose behind the existence of those disruptions in my life. But I have discovered that in those disruptions I have learned the greatest lessons of life; my character has been strengthened as in the refiner's fire; and I have been drawn closer to God.

In Conclusion

Intentional living is partly dealing with dislocations or forks when they suddenly come upon us. But it is also a process of keeping an intelligent, running inventory of things that we will want to consider as dislocations or forks do come upon us, and wisely preparing ourselves for those that might befall us. For those dislocations we know we will ultimately have to face (retirement, death), we clearly should make some preparation. For others, which might or might not occur (e.g., loss of employment, earthquake, loss of spouse), we want to do those things which are prudent.

I encourage you to ask yourself:

- What are some of the dislocations that you can anticipate in your life?
- In particular, for what dislocations should you make some modest preparation even now?
- In what ways could you prepare?

As we face these issues we can feel quite inadequate. We need to remember that God will direct us in our dislocations and that he will empower us, knowing full well that we have little strength.

- "I am the Lord your God, who teaches you what is best for you, who directs you in the way you should go" (Isa. 48:17). He will direct us at our dislocations.
- "Whether you turn to the right or to the left, your ears will hear a voice behind you, saying, 'This is the way; walk in it'" (Isa. 30:21). We need to pray, be quiet before him, and listen for that voice saying, "This is the way; walk in it."
- "See, I have placed before you an open door that no one can shut. I know that you have little strength" (Rev. 3:8).

That verse reminds us that God will open doors of challenge and opportunity for us, but we have to choose to walk through them. He knows that the doors are scary and that we have little strength for this, but He will provide for us. He will not open new doors until we walk through the present doors.

He also gives us the necessary reassurance and power when we seek it from him. Paul says in 2 Timothy 1:7:

> For God did not give us a spirit of timidity or fear, but a spirit of power, love, and self-discipline.

Let us go forward with a spirit of power, love, and self-discipline as we attempt to live intentionally.

In our thinking about forks and dislocations, we have glimpsed some of the resources that are available to us in coping with such events. In the next chapter we want to look a little more closely at those resources and what we can do to appropriate them.

Synopsis

- Preparing for dislocations implies the following:

  a) Identifying the ones that are amenable to modest preparation, and doing what is prudent to prepare for them.
  b) Recognizing the nature of traumatic dislocations, so we are not stunned by the experience of dislocation when it does come.
  c) Building the relationships and spiritual strength that will sustain us during and after dislocations.
  d) Drawing on the experience of others who have experienced the same dislocation.

- It is clear that we should prepare for our changes in season or predictable dislocations, e.g., marriage; having children, or learning that you can't have children; disruption of employment; loss of mate; midlife crisis; children leaving the nest; retirement; dependent parents.

- We should also prepare somewhat for those sporadic traumatic dislocations which are highly likely to occur, or which have severe consequences if they do occur, even if the probability of their occurring is not that large. Possibilities include loss of possessions by an uncontrollable event (such as an earthquake, fire, or failed investment); catastrophic loss of physical, mental, or spiritual health (cancer, heart attack, nervous breakdown, severe depression); abandonment by a spouse; abuse in the marriage relationship; rebellion and rejection by a child; death of a child; a child succumbing to substance abuse.

- Suffering and pain are realities of this life, falling on the good and the bad. We will always have mixed emotions in the face of tragedy, no matter how much faith we have. There will be doubt and confidence, despair and hope, resentment and thanksgiving, etc. But God lets us feel and express our emotions without putting us down for it. The most important thing we can do in advance to deal with all dislocations is to "dig wells" and "maintain wells"—the wells from which we draw strength during dislocations.

- It really helps to know what to expect in dislocations. It especially helps to understand about the emotional phases we go through and about the scars, the allergies, the possible need to deal with guilt, the promise of new life afterwards.

- Intentional living is not just dealing with dislocations or forks when they suddenly come upon us, but rather a process of keeping an intelligent, running inventory of things that we will want to consider as dislocations or forks do come upon us, and wisely preparing ourselves for those which might befall us.

Personal Reflection

- What has been the greatest dislocation of your life so far?
- Which of the features of dislocations, listed in the chapter, characterized that dislocation?
- Which were particularly hard for you to handle?
- What helped you?
- What scar and/or allergy remains due to this dislocation, and how does it affect your behavior or attitudes today?
- Can you identify any compensating strengths that emerged from this dislocation?
- What have been other consequences of that dislocation?
- What do you want to remember about anticipating and dealing with dislocations?
- What are some of the dislocations that you can anticipate in your life?
- In particular, for what dislocations should you make some modest preparation even now?
- In what ways could you prepare?
- What was your reaction to the section in the text, *Suffering and Pain in Tragedy*?
- What do you think are the best ways to prepare/condition oneself for the dislocations that will come unexpectedly?

Points I Want to Come Back To

Later, when I have more time, I want to think more about the following sections, questions, or ideas associated with this chapter:

_____

_____

_____

_____

_____

_____

_____

_____

CHAPTER 8

Realizing Our Resources

Where Do I Find the Help I Need?

I have a friend who lost her husband very unexpectedly when he collapsed from a heart attack. Suddenly she needed help. First of all, she had to deal with her own emotions. She also had two teenage daughters to be concerned about. She was co-owner of a small business, which her husband had managed. She wasn't sure where she stood financially.

Fortunately, she was a well-connected member of a loving church community. There were many people in that church who were eager to help her. Some of them were well acquainted with grief and the process of restoration. Others were accountants, business consultants, lawyers, etc., and they immediately helped with her personal and business finances. They helped her evaluate the business and find a competent person to run it and eventually buy it. They also helped her sort out the legal complications that resulted from some of their previous investments. She was obliged to make further payments into these investments, payments that would have been covered by her husband's future earnings. Thankfully, that woman is a very intelligent, competent, levelheaded person, and, with all the support she received, everything worked out pretty well, after a long period of transition.

That example helps to illustrate the resources we all need to develop and cultivate, because we will need them when we face our dislocations. In addition, we saw in the chapter on coping with our forks that we also need similar resources to help us sort through the many factors involved in our major decisions.

Our first tendency is to try to do everything ourselves. Indeed, we do need to recognize that we have a unique contribution to make to the accomplishment of our goals and the solution of our problems. No one else has the knowledge that we have of ourselves. No one else knows the details of our history and what has made us what we are. No one else has our unique insight into what goes on inside of us: our aspirations, anxieties, frustrations, fears, etc. No one else is as highly motivated to realize our goals. Therefore, no one else is going to commit the time and energy that it will take. So we do need to look first to ourselves.

Having said that, we also need to let our relatives and close friends help us. We need to have someone to provide a check on what we perceive and think. We also need people who will provide new ideas and a different point of view. We obviously need people who are motivated to help us and who know us well. Our relatives and close friends have a vested interest in our well-being and are in a wonderful position to help. In addition, many of them have previous experience or professional talent that will be very helpful to us. Even if they can't help us in particular areas themselves, their experience often makes it possible for them to suggest other people.

With the advice and support of friends and relatives, we can reach out to other professionals. This category includes teachers, pastors, counselors, and professional organizations. There are specialists in many of the areas in which we will have goals and/or problems: financial planning (budgeting, investments, real estate, insurance, wills, etc.); career planning and placement; relationships (counselors in marriage, child rearing, family planning);

physical fitness (coaches, trainers, gyms, YMCAs), and many others.

In addition to the people we personally know, we can profit from the experience of other people through the books they have written. There are books on almost every subject we can imagine. Some of those books recite the experience of other people, which can be helpful to us. Some of these give how-to advice, based on the successful accomplishment of similar goals and the resolution of similar problems by other people. We can read good books even before we have some of the problems they anticipate, and then file away our notes on the good advice they contain. Even if it turns out that we never need those notes for a problem of our own, they might show us how to help a friend at some future time.

We can also meet people who may be trying to accomplish similar goals or solve similar problems in classes. Many churches have groups or classes that deal with a variety of human problems: grief, single parenting, coping with cancer, etc. In addition, classes are available in community colleges, recreation departments, and various specialized institutes. These classes not only offer valuable facts, techniques, and training, but provide an opportunity for us to connect with other kindred souls who, because of their involvement with the same issues, will help to give us compassion, comfort, and encouragement.

The most important resource of all is God, the spiritual resource of the universe. God wants us to prosper and to grow. He has the power to help us cope with our dislocations and our forks, to help us to accomplish our goals. He has provided the connection to himself through Jesus, the Holy Spirit, the Bible, prayer, meditation, etc. While we can utilize all the other resources we have cited above, we quickly realize that the most important and effective resource comes directly from God. Of course we cannot just go to a bank of spiritual resource in our time of need. Such a bank has to be personalized, and it has to be built up by our personal investments over a substantial period of time. Living intentionally is not very successful unless we fully realize our dependence on God and continually invest in our relationship with Him.

Realizing Our Resources

It is no good if we just list our resources; we really have to make use of them. I intentionally labeled this chapter "Realizing Our Resources," rather than something else like "Identifying Our Resources," because the word *realizing* has such a rich implication.

The word *realize* has four connotations:

1. To recognize or discern. For instance, "At that instant I *realized* that what you named was, in fact, a valuable resource."
2. To understand and to comprehend fully. "Do you *realize* the depth of the resources that are available to you?"
3. To fulfill, complete, achieve, attain. "If I want to *realize* my full potential I need to utilize all of my resources."
4. To profit from, to make capital of, to obtain a return. "What did you *realize* from all that time and effort?"

We need to *realize* the resources that are available to us in all four of these ways: to discern what they are; to fully comprehend them; to appropriate and absorb them; and to obtain the benefit from them.

What are some of the things we have to do to realize these resources? Let me mention just a few things that come immediately to mind.

Certainly we have to understand ourselves and we have to apply ourselves. This book is intended to provide help in more fully comprehending ourselves. This is accomplished through the many Personal Application questions and also the chapters of section 3. It should also stimulate our incentive to apply ourselves to living more intentionally, as well as understanding what we have to do in order to live more intentionally.

In the personal realm, our mind is the most powerful resource we have. Here I am not talking about intellectual power, but just the ability to direct our thoughts to the right things. My teacher, Ken Olson, taught me that I can change my mood rapidly by redirecting my thoughts. He has identified a series of images that bring him happy memories and kindle pleasant feelings. When he is feeling blue, he intentionally reviews that series of images in his mind. And he finds that his mood improves. If we doubt that power, we have only to think of what happens to us at the movies. Our emotions swing from fear to delight, from sadness to joy as the celluloid images change on the screen. His teaching persuaded me to intentionally make a list of images that can produce pleasure or gratitude when I play the series through my mind. Some of those images include a picture of my little granddaughter when she was in a mischievous mood, showing off for her Grandpa; the view from the porch of our cabin at Lake Winnepesaukee as the morning sun obliquely lights the lake and surrounding hills; hundreds of people, in an open-air auditorium on a hillside in the Adirondack mountains, enthusiastically singing "How Great Thou Art." Of course, my memories can fade. But I also have photographs or audiotapes of those things with which I can periodically refresh my memory.

Similarly, there are scriptures and other truths that can do wonders for me if I play them through my mind. Here, too, I have to identify them and periodically refresh my memory, so they are vivid when I need them.

In almost every round of golf I have some wonderful holes and some dreadful ones. After the game I have a tendency to be depressed about the bad shots. But I am learning to shift my thoughts to the holes where I did particularly well, or to the magnificent scenery I enjoyed, or to evidences of friendship from those with whom I played.

Our pastor, Greg Ogden, pointed out that God told Adam and Eve that they could eat of every tree in the Garden of Eden, except for one. They promptly focused on the one tree they couldn't have and ignored God's expansive generosity with all the other trees. I find that I, too, tend to become preoccupied with that one thing I can't have, inclined toward frustration and, in some cases, even to bitterness. I can change my attitude dramatically if I direct my thoughts to the many wonderful things that I do have and the marvelous mercy God has shown me.

Yes, we can change our moods by redirecting the focus of our thoughts. In order to live intentionally we must focus our minds on the right things.

One way to realize the help of friends or a spouse is to study this book with them and, in particular, to intimately discuss the issues that are covered in it. As we talk with others who are involved with forks, facing dislocations, trying to find ways of passing on their legacy, etc., we substantially increase both our own insights and also our incentive. Those who have participated in our eight-person groups have discovered that in abundance.

Individuals in our study groups have said they have been gratefully surprised at how much help they have received from professional counselors. Sometimes we think we should go to such persons only when we have problems that are so tough we can't solve them ourselves. One couple told me they thought every married couple should go together to a marriage/family counselor, because when they did, their insight into their relationship was so greatly illuminated and they received so many good ideas as to how they could enrich their relationship. We probably should also avail ourselves more of professional financial counselors. We already know that a good doctor or trainer can help us achieve and maintain good health; we don't go to them only after we become sick. The same can be true of other professionals. Pastors are a particularly good source of references to other professionals.

As we try to build and maintain our physical, mental, and spiritual health before we face a critical situation, we need to use selected classes and books. The classes give us needed information. They also enlarge the circle of our relationships with people who might be interested in interacting with us in the areas where we want to make progress. Many of our ideas about which books can be really helpful can also come from the people we meet in classes; they will have found some particularly helpful and they save us from casting around. But to realize the benefits that can be obtained from the books, we have to apply ourselves to reading them. We need to set aside particular time to read and reflect. A group study of a book can provide both incentive to our discipline of reading, and also greater depth in what we absorb from the book. Sometimes we just don't really study a book unless we have to get ready for a meeting in which we are scheduled to discuss the contents.

We have already said that the spiritual resources are the most important of all. In this chapter I would like to discuss some of the ways that we can realize the spiritual resources that are available to us. Before we do that, though, we should perhaps discuss the other side of the coin. We can make progress only when our spirits are uplifted, enlightened, and strengthened. Yet we realize that there are spiritual or emotional things that can demoralize us, confuse us, and inhibit our progress.

Hindrances: Those Things That Deter Us, Distract Us, and Defeat Us

What are some of the things that can greatly hinder us, distract us, and defeat us as we attempt to live intentionally? I think particularly of three things: failure to think straight and logically, doubt, and fear. Let us think a little more about each of these.

Failure to Think Straight and Logically

All of the aspects of living intentionally require us to think straight and logically. We have to think things through sufficiently to generate an intention that we are convinced is important and worthy. Then we have to think through the ways of accomplishing our intention.

In dealing with forks, we have to be able to think through the various factors that are involved and to realistically appraise their relative importance. We have to think about what dislocations we should prepare for and then how we should go about preparing. We need to accurately appraise the characteristics of our own person: what we prefer, what we can realistically do, etc.

We may fail to think straight and logically for a number of reasons:

- *Limited ability.* We may be limited in our own mental ability to think analytically. If we are strongly *intuitive* or *affective* (as we will discuss in chapter 12), we need to consult with a friend who is a logical thinker to help us think it through.
- *Being distracted.* We may be preoccupied by worldly necessities and cultural pressures. We may be so absorbed in the activities of making our living or raising our family, or fatigued by the stress of those activities (preoccupied with fending off the rocks) that we can't bring ourselves to devote the time and energy to anticipatory thinking.
- *Distorted perception or understanding.* We may have a distorted perception of reality or distorted understanding of truth. Our thinking is based on certain truths we believe, assumptions we accept, and what we believe are facts. Any of these may be in error. We may have a distorted perception of some of our abilities or of what is really most important to us. We may have a distorted view of some other people's intentions or their reliability. We may have a distorted assessment of the probability of occurrence of a particular event. We may have unrealistic expectations. There are so many ways in which we can err in our perception of the factors that enter into the calculation of our intent, or of the best way to accomplish that intent. That is where relatives and close friends can be of great help—as a check on our perceptions of reality and understanding of truth.
- *Seductive temptation to rationalize.* Even when we are perfectly capable of thinking clearly and logically, and we are not distracted, and the facts and perceptions at hand are clear and undistorted, we have a strong temptation to rationalize inappropriate conclusions or actions. For instance, we are tempted to take the easier path, or the one with least conflict, or the one that appeals to our sense of pleasure. In our clear thinking, we do need to give some

favor to the easier path, the one with least conflict, and the one that appeals to our sense of pleasure, but what we want to avoid is distorting our thinking by unconsciously succumbing to these factors. We realize that even though we may know it is wrong to go along with the group we're with, it is so easy to rationalize going their way based on any number of subtle factors.

So there are a number of reasons why we may succumb to faulty thinking. Our best protection from this is to have a discerning and logical confidant with whom we can candidly review our thinking.

Now let us consider two other things that can deter us, distract us, and defeat us: doubt and fear.

Doubt and Fear

We could list doubt and fear as separate problems, but they are both stimulated by many of the same things, and they are also overcome by the same approach.

Uncertainties in any aspects of our situation can produce doubt and fear. Those uncertainties can play havoc with our emotions and our wills. The resulting doubt can be tremendously upsetting and the fear can paralyze us.

Also, changes occur in the factors that influence our decisions and our actions. Things may change while we are in the process of deciding, or they may change after we have become committed to the new direction. If we had known that they were to going to change, would we have chosen the alternate path? Let a couple of things change, and all of a sudden we are assailed with doubt and fear.

We need to keep in mind the following:

- There are many uncertainties involved in any fork decision. We can't precisely know what the final conditions will be. We have to be prepared for the anxiety the uncertainties produce.

- We also need to recognize that the assumptions we are using in our fork decisions may indeed change. We need to imagine some of the ways things can change and do a little thinking about what our response would be if they did change.

Let me give you an example from the story I told you about, when I was confronted with the decision whether to move back to New York.

Remember that one of our reasons for wanting to stay in California was that our daughter and her young family lived there. If we stayed there we would have a chance to be with the grandchildren often and watch them grow and develop. We also wanted to be near our daughter and our son-in-law for the same reason. Now suppose we stayed and our son-in-law got a job offer he couldn't refuse, and our daughter and her family moved away from there. Now one of our important family reasons for staying there would have disappeared.

On the other side, one of our reasons for wanting to go back east was that my elderly father lived near where we would be, and if we went back we would have been near him while he was still alive. Now suppose my father suddenly died of a heart attack while he was watching TV right after New Year's (That is what happened). Now one of our important family reasons for going back there would have disappeared.

Yes, we need to imagine some of the ways things can change, and do a little thinking about what our response would be if they did change.

- It is natural and commonplace, during a transition and even afterwards, to be assailed by doubts. Am I making a huge mistake? Did I pressure my family too much in trying to satisfy my own interests? Should I reverse my course even though that might be very costly? In addition to doubt, I can be assailed by fear of the consequences of the move I am making. As soon as something changes, I can say, How many other things are going to go wrong? What will happen if some of my assumptions don't work out?

We might be assailed by doubt and fears during the transition and then find that everything works out fine. So many blessings materialize out of the decision we made that it was all clearly worth it. The decision was the right one even though we had a lot of grief in the process. On the other hand, we might be sort of euphoric during the process of change, and only later find that the end result wasn't what we had hoped, and wish that we had made the decision differently. In any case, we have to be prepared for periods of conviction and periods of doubt; periods when we are swamped with fear and periods when we are basking in confidence.

I have friends who had taken my course before making a major decision. They were well aware of the likelihood of uncertainties and doubts, but they felt that they would be able to handle them. However, they found that handling them emotionally, while in the midst of the process, was much more traumatic than they expected. They really fretted and agonized.

If we have a spirit of conviction and confidence, we have courage and move forward. If we develop a spirit of doubt and fear, we become discouraged and give up. We can begin to doubt the importance of our goals, our ability to achieve them, or even God and his eagerness or ability to help us. We can fear any element of the unknown, anything that we can't control. We can fear exposing ourselves to "failure." We know how difficult it is to change, and we don't even try because we know we will feel bad if we don't succeed. Our greatest *struggle* in our attempt to grow and to live intentionally is spiritual. Our greatest *resource* for growth and living intentionally is spiritual.

It is pretty clear that we need something very firm to hang onto while we go through our forks and our dislocations. It may be a conviction that God's leading is very clear to us, and we know that, whatever happens, He will sustain us and bring us to a right conclusion, because he powerfully supports what he clearly purposes. Or it might be that we rest in the confidence that God honors even our mistakes and will open doors of recovery for us even if we make a mistake while trying our best to live intentionally.

I would like to share with you some things that I have found to be a real help to me.

The Whole Armor of God

The apostle Paul clearly recognized that our attempts to live intentionally constitute a spiritual battle involving our minds and our spirits. He knew the importance of spiritual strength and our need for armament as we enter such battles. In Ephesians 6:13, Paul tells us that we need to daily put on the whole armor of God. He urges us: "Therefore, take up the whole armor of God that you may be able to resist in the evil day, and having done everything, to stand firm." God has provided this *armor* for us in order that we might be firm in our resolve and in our progress. Let us review the ingredients of that armor.

Paul described this *whole armor of God* in verses 13–18 of Ephesians 6:

> Therefore, take up the whole armor of God, that you may be able to resist in the evil day, and having done everything, to stand firm. Stand firm therefore, having girded your loins with truth, and having put on the breastplate of righteousness, and having shod your feet with the preparation of the gospel of peace; in addition to all, taking up the shield of faith, with which you will be able to extinguish all the flaming missiles of the evil one. And take the helmet of salvation and the sword of the Spirit, which is the Word of God. With all prayer and petition pray at all times in the Spirit, and with this in view, be on the alert with all perseverance and petition for the saints.

When I first read that, I didn't really know what it meant, and didn't see it as advice that relates very well to my struggles. But the more I studied it, the more help I received (so true of all scripture!)

Paul sees that our integrity, our well-being, our progress, and our success are threatened, as by various weapons and blows of an enemy who is trying to thwart us. He cites items of battle clothing (armor) we can put on and weapons we can use to repel the threats and the consequences those threats produce. Notice that we put on the armor in the normal order: girding the loins (putting on the basic undergarments); then putting on the breastplate and the boots; then accepting the shield, helmet, and sword from our armor bearer.

I have made Fig 8.1 to list the items of the "armor" Paul describes, the composition of each item, what it is that the item protects us from, and the consequences to us if we are not adequately protected from these threats.

Let us consider each element in sequence:

a) Paul says, first of all, "Wrap yourself in truth." The primary threat to our ability to live the way we should and to grow is our tendency to rationalize God's truth. Society urges us to accept half-truths and distorted truth. We persuade ourselves that these alternative interpretations of the truth are reasonable. That leads us into all kinds of incorrect principles, beliefs, and attitudes. Our most basic protection is the whole truth as revealed by God and Christ. We need to immerse ourselves in it. Remember how Jesus said, "If you abide in My word, then you are truly disciples of Mine; and *you shall know the truth and the truth shall make you free*" (John 8:31–32). So the first element of equipping ourselves for the battle is to "wrap ourselves in truth—the whole and undistorted truth—which gives us a new freedom to live intentionally. That is the basic undergarment.

b) Next we put on the breastplate of righteousness. The second greatest threat to our well-being is the seductive temptation to rationalize God's intention for us and to find acceptable all kinds of behaviors that harm others as well as ourselves. Soon we not only make excuses for those behaviors, but actually condone and accept them. We can all think of many things we have accepted and, indeed, may do ourselves because the general culture has accepted them.

Fig. 8.1

Items of Armor	Composition of Armor	Protects Against This Threat	Consequences of Threat
Clothes	"truth"	Primary Threat: The seductive temptation to rationalize God's truth	Incorrect principles, beliefs, attitudes
Breastplate	"of righteousness" (right living)	Secondary Threat: Seductive temptation to rationalize God's will for us	Accepting actions that harm others and ourselves
Boots	"preparation of the gospel of peace" (peace with God = security)	Anxiety, loss of security, alienation from God	Loss of footing, stability, maneuverability
Shield	"of faith"	"Extinguishing flaming missles" hurts coming from beyond our control	Becoming penetrated and burned
Helmet	"of salvation" God is able to save us; is determined to do it	Fatal blow to the head, loss of our center, our balance	Confusion, lack of coordination
Sword	"Word of God" (Scripture)	Though protected, we are ineffective with no offensive power to destroy what threatens	Enemies run rampant, threats abound
Communication w/leader	"pray at all times" ("prayer and petition") ("in the Spirit")	Loss of contact with His will, insight, strategy, direction, response	Out of sync with leader and others; confusion
Intelligence (awareness)	"be on the alert" ("with all perseverance")	Insidious invasion that cripples because we are not prepared	Don't realize what threatens; defeated before we can react

However, if we go back to basics we know they aren't what God would bless. Our protection from this is our persistent determination to live righteously, according to what is right with *God*, not our culture.

c) Thick leather boots with nail heads in the soles are necessary for the warrior both to maintain his footing and to be able to sustain long marches. What gives us our firm stance and endurance is the preparation of ourselves beforehand with the reestablishment of our peace with God: "Shod your feet with the preparation of the gospel of peace." Having made peace with God preserves us from the threat of anxiety, loss of security, and alienation from God. If, on the other hand, we are not sure about our standing with God, our footing is very tenuous, we are unstable, and we lack maneuverability. Thus these boots are an important part of our uniform.

d) Next Paul calls on us to take up the shield of faith so that we will be able to extinguish all the flaming missiles. What are those flaming missiles? The fact that they are missiles indicates that they are hurts that come from a distance, beyond our control, not in up-close, hand-to-hand combat. It may be that someone tells untruths about us and assails our reputation. It may be that misfortunes descend upon us. Those things which come our way with no warning nor rationale can cause us to even doubt God and his protection of us. Even if we can counteract distortions of the truth and temptation, we will also be assailed by more brutal weapons, which not only penetrate deeply, but can burn out our courage and our determination. We need an impervious, flexible shield to blunt, deflect, and extinguish those: a sturdy, unshakable *faith* in God's love and his faithfulness. We need to remember, as Paul says in Romans 8, that God is for us, and if *God* is for us, no one nor no thing can defeat us nor separate us from his love. Faith not only keeps us steady, but renders the assaulting missiles impotent.

e) Finally, after we have dressed ourselves for battle, the armor bearer hands us our helmet and sword—the helmet of *salvation* and the sword of the *Spirit*. A warrior's head is his most vulnerable part. A blow to the head can cause us to lose our center, our balance. We suffer confusion and a lack of the coordination that our head is supposed to give us. Our ultimate protection from this confusion and lack of coordination is our "helmet of salvation," the knowledge that God has promised to save us, is able to save us, and is determined to save us, as we go faithfully out in the fulfillment of His purposes, armed with all the protection He has provided.

f) It is not sufficient that we be purely defensive, able to ward off the attack upon us. We must also have an offensive weapon to destroy what threatens us, our families, and society. It doesn't do us any good to be personally protected if our enemies are allowed to run rampant to threaten our families and all we hold dear. We need to be alert to what threatens, and we need to appropriate God's power to defeat those enemies. Jesus used the Scripture to defeat those who attacked Him, including the Tempter (Matt. 4:4). That too, must be the weapon we rely on. Our best offense is found in the *Word* of God, which is the *sword* of the Spirit. God's Word has answers and has power. That is where we should look for our ammunition.

g) Even if we are armed to the teeth, we are in trouble if we are not in good communication with our leader. We need communication with our leader at all times, but even more so in the times when we are under attack or are fighting the battles, on behalf of God, for His people and purposes. Paul says, "pray at all times in the Spirit." Thus we need to be in prayer daily, finding time to sit apart, to communicate, and especially to listen.

h) The other thing a warrior needs is defense intelligence—an awareness of what the threats are. Paul admonishes us to be "on the alert with all perseverance." If we aren't sensitive to what threatens us, no matter how fine our armor, we can be invaded and crushed before we have a chance to put it on.

As we come to understand this scripture, we see what we must do. Each day we need to put on the *armor of God*. So, let us each day

a) immerse ourselves in the whole truth as revealed by God and Christ;

b) maintain a persistent determination to live righteously;

c) reconfirm our peace with God, repenting of our mistakes of the day before and reappropriating His forgiveness;

d) preserve a sturdy, unshakable faith in God's love and faithfulness;

e) remember that God is fully able to save us and is determined to do so;

f) spend time in the scriptures and search them out for the ammunition with which we can defeat whatever threatens us and our families;

g) stay in constant communication with God to know His will and discern his direction;

h) be continuously alert for what it is that threatens us and the identity of those who would destroy what is precious in God's sight. The threats are subtle and they sneak up on us. We need to spot them when they first arise; if they become too entrenched, our battle becomes very difficult. This is especially true of the subtle threats to our children and grandchildren. Before we know it they can be seduced almost beyond our reach.

God provides the armor for us in this spiritual battle. We just have to appropriate it, stay in close communication with Him, and be alert to the things that threaten us, our families, and our society. These include failure to think straight and logically, due to either our limited *ability* to think straight and logically; or our being *distracted* by worldly necessities and cultural pressures; or our *distorted perception* of reality or our understanding of truth; or the seductive *temptation to rationalize*; as well as rampant *doubt* and *fear*.

Drawing Water from the Wells of Salvation

When we talk about combating our two greatest enemies, doubt and fear, I am once again taken back to my favorite verse of Scripture, Isaiah 12:2–3. The prophet Isaiah experienced his own doubt and fear, but found there was a basis on which he could replace the doubt with trust and the fear with peace. Isaiah tells us we need to daily draw water from the wells of salvation. Furthermore, we need to dig such wells before we are in the midst of doubt and fear, in anticipation that we are going to need them.

We mentioned some of the highlights of these verses in the previous chapter. Because this is so crucial to realizing our resources, I would like to share my further thoughts about that great scripture with you.

> Surely God is my salvation; I will trust and not be afraid. The Lord, the Lord, is my strength and my song; he has become my salvation. With joy you will draw water from the wells of salvation.

In this scripture I observe the following things:

- God can save me from the two most insidious and discouraging things in life: *doubt and fear.* Instead of doubt, I can have trust. Instead of fear, I can be unafraid. I can trust and not be afraid *only if* God is my salvation. I will trust and not be afraid *because* God is my salvation.
- It is *God* who is my salvation. I have a tendency to look to other people or things to be my salvation: money? my in-

tellect? institutions? Help me to avoid seeking salvation in other people or other things.

- *My* salvation. It is not that He is *our* salvation (although that is also true), but He has to be my own personal salvation.
- *Surely.* There is no uncertainty; it has been confirmed and continues to be confirmed in my experience as I rely on Him.

"The Lord, the Lord, is my strength and my song; he has become my salvation."

- The Lord is my *strength.* I have to look to the Lord for strength, not try to be self-sufficient, and I also have to recognize my own weakness in order to appropriate His strength.
- The Lord is also my *song.* At first I was a little surprised to find this word here. I expected "strength and shield" or "strength and hope." But it says "strength and song"! Because I have been so blessed by God I have a song in my heart that I am compelled to sing. But the song is also a stimulus: singing it stimulates my joy. Over fifty years ago I learned a song at a summer camp that has rung in my heart ever since. It is the song, " "In My Heart There Rings a Melody," by Elton Roth, which begins: "I have a song that Jesus gave me." The Lord is also my song.
- The *Lord*, yes, it is the Lord, who is my strength and my song. The doubled word is always used in the scripture for emphasis. There is no question as to who is my strength and my song. I have to keep remembering that it is the Lord who is my strength and my song.
- *Has become.* Salvation is a continuing process, not just one event: God continues to provide it; I need to continue to appropriate his provision.

How *do* I appropriate God's salvation? I appropriate God's salvation by joyously drawing living water from the wells of salvation. "With joy you will draw water from the wells of salvation":

- The verse uses the plural form: wells. There are many wells and of different kinds. Wells are beneath the surface. They have great capacity; they never run dry. They are often closer to the surface in the valleys of hardship than they are on the peaks of delight, but they are accessible whatever the circumstances.
- I have to draw the water. It says, "With joy you will draw water." It doesn't just overflow me. I have to recognize my need for the water, seek the well, draw the water, and drink it with faith.
- The water that I draw is the *living water*, which is God's very own Spirit. It is in Jesus (John 4:10) and in God's Holy Word (the "law" of his universe). As Psalm 1:2–3 says, "His delight is in the law of the Lord, and on His law he meditates day and night. He is like a tree planted by streams of water, which yields its fruit in season and whose leaf does not wither. Whatever he does prospers." We evidently need to meditate on God's word continuously.
- Why do I draw it with joy? Because I receive salvation, trust and confidence, strength, continual refreshment. I am rescued from doubt and fear, uncertainty and anxiety.
- These wells are wells of salvation. They are not just wells of *convenience*, but of *necessity*; not just for *comfort*, but for *survival*. I am not only *revived*, but *sustained!*

So I see that doubt, fear, and discouragement are defeated and replaced by confidence, conviction, and joy through God's Spirit, which comes as I draw water from the wells of salvation.

Now for the million-dollar question: What are these wells? When I was looking to learn more about these wells I found a sermon that Stan Johnson preached on July 12, 1987. Stan talked about the experience of Isaac in Genesis 26:12–15. As Isaac moved from one valley to another in response to the events of his life, he reopened wells which had been dug earlier, and he also dug new wells. In these wells he found water that sustained him in the valleys. After the water sustained him he went up onto the mountain, worshipped the Lord, and dug another well. The wells of salvation, both old wells to be redug and new wells to be dug include the following:

a) The Scriptures that we have previously discovered to have deep meaning for us and to bring us God's own strength. We can not only revisit familiar ones, but also uncover new ones.

b) Prayer; seeking communion with the Holy Spirit, the "Comforter" whom God has provided for us (John 14:26–27). We can use the familiar prayers we have used before, and also create new ones for our new circumstances.

c) Particular human relationships that sustain us; we all know people from whom we can draw strength and wisdom. We have old friends who have helped us before, and we also want to develop new friends who will be a source of strength for us as we go on.

d) Remembering significant truths, we have recorded for this purpose, such as these:

  • In the "valleys" of life we are often closer to the water of cleansing and renewal than we are when we're on the mountaintop.
  • Being in the valley occasionally is important, in that it persuades us to open old wells and to dig new ones.
  • What happens to us when we are in the valleys depends to a large extent on what we do there.
  • It takes more than one mountain to make a valley—at least one on both sides. There is another mountaintop experience coming on the other side.

- When on the mountaintop again, it is important to remember to continue our worship of the Lord and the digging of wells there also.

Bible verses that especially give me courage include these:

Fear not, for I am with you; be not dismayed, for I am your God. I will strengthen you and help you; I will uphold you with my righteous right hand. (Isa. 41:10)

Yet this I call to mind and therefore have hope: Because of the Lord's great love we are not consumed, for His compassions never fail. They are new every morning; great is His faithfulness. I say to myself, "The Lord is my portion; therefore I will wait for Him." The Lord is good to those whose hope is in Him, to the one who seeks Him; it is good to wait patiently for the salvation of the Lord. (Lam. 3:21–26)

What, then, shall we say in response to this? If God is for us, who can be against us? . . . Who shall separate us from the love of Christ? Shall trouble or hardship or persecution or famine or nakedness or danger or sword? . . . No, in all these things we are more than conquerors through him who loved us. For I am convinced that nothing in all creation will be able to separate us from the love of God that is in Christ Jesus our Lord. (Rom. 8:31, 35, 37–38)

I am confident of this, that he who began a good work in you will carry it on to completion until the day of Christ Jesus. (Phil. 1:6)

I have learned to be content whatever the circumstances. I know what it is to be in need, and I know what it is to have plenty. I have learned the secret of being content in any and every situation, whether well fed or hungry, whether living in plenty or in want. I can do everything through him who gives me strength. (Phil. 4:11–13)

For God did not give us a spirit of timidity or fear, but a spirit of power, love and self-discipline. (2 Tim. 1:7)

It is as we meditate on the words of scripture, and see them confirmed in our own experience, that we receive the spiritual strength to go forward with our resolve to live more intentionally and become the persons God designed us to become.

Remaining in Christ

Meditating on such words of scripture is just one of the ways in which we can "remain in Christ." Jesus told His disciples (and us) that the key to living (intentionally, successfully, joyfully, etc.) is to "remain in Him."

For instance, from John 15:1–11

[1] I am the true vine and my Father is the gardener (vine dresser). . . . [4] Remain in me, and I will remain in you. No branch can bear fruit by itself; it must remain in the vine. Neither can you bear fruit unless you remain in me. [5] I am the vine; you are the branches. If a man remains in me and I in him, he will bear much fruit; apart from me you can do nothing. [6] If a man does not remain in me, he is cast forth as a branch and withers. . . . [7] If you remain in me and my words remain in you, ask whatever you wish, and it will be given you. . . . [9] As the Father has loved me, so have I loved you. Now remain in my love. [10] If you obey my commands, you will remain in my love, just as I have obeyed my Father's commands and remain in His love. [11] I have told you this so that my joy may be in you and that your joy may be complete.

Look at the insights we gain from this passage:

1. We can't succeed by ourselves, totally out of our own strength, wisdom, etc. We must "remain" in Jesus and, through Him, the Father (v. 4). Apart from Him we will ultimately fail (v. 5).
2. We relate to Jesus as the branches relate to a vine (v. 5). As the vine sustains the branches, so Jesus sustains us (as we "remain" in Him). As a branch withers if its connection to

the vine is weakened, so we too wither if we do not remain intimately connected to Him. (v. 6)

3. I need to pay attention to his words, as part of "remaining in Him" (v. 7) so that my thoughts are purified and potentially destructive aberrations are "trimmed" out. It is as his words remain in us that our well-being is realized.

4. Remaining in His love involves obeying His commands (v. 10). Do I sometimes try to remain in His love while neglecting to obey His commands?

5. Jesus found His greatest enjoyment as He remained in tune with His Father and did what His Father wanted Him to do, and He says we will find our greatest enjoyment as we remain in tune with Him and do what He tells us to do. His desire is that we will experience the same joy that He enjoyed, and that is why He gives us this teaching (v. 10–11).

Evidently, the most important thing for me to concentrate on is *remaining* in Jesus.

I need to further understand how to *remain* in Christ. *Remain* means to "stay, continue, endure restfully in a given place, condition, or relation." That is difficult for me. I am inclined to try to figure out what to do and how to do it, and go get it done. I tend to be compulsive about fruitfulness and am eager to see the harvest. I keep telling myself that I should enjoy the process of accomplishing things; that the result is merely the culmination and not as important as the process. However, I find myself rushing to get one thing done so that I can get on to the next thing. Stan Johnson told me, "Working for Christ should be a natural result of walking with Christ." This teaching says that even more important than the process of bearing fruit is the time spent in *remaining* in Christ. My real significance is as a child of God and a disciple of Christ, whereas I act as if my real significance is found in my busyness; as if inactivity is laziness and waiting is wasting time. I even take reading matter with me if I have to wait for an appointment, and am very impatient at traffic lights. I know that *remaining* in the Lord includes trying to be faithful to the things he has taught me, but another essential part of it is to cultivate a spirit of patience and waiting upon God:

Be still and know that I am God. (Ps. 46:10)

Wait for the Lord; be strong and take heart and *wait* for the Lord. (Ps. 27:14)

Make me know thy ways, O Lord, teach me thy path. Lead me in thy truth and teach me, for thou art the God of my salvation. For thee I *wait* all the day. (Ps. 25:4–5)

Rest in the Lord and *wait* patiently for Him. . . . those who *wait* for the Lord, they will inherit the land. (Ps. 37:7–9)

I wait for the Lord, my soul does *wait* and in His word do I hope. (Ps. 130:5–6)

Yet those who *wait* for the Lord will gain new strength. . . . (Isa. 40:31)

I need to cultivate a time of being quiet with the Lord and *waiting* for Him to speak to me and strengthen me. It seems that this is a vital part of *remaining* in Christ. We do this through prayer and meditation.

Prayer and Meditation

Prayer seems to be an instinctive drive, yet most people have some difficulty with it. A recent Gallup poll reported that 90 percent of all Americans say that they pray, and 75 percent pray every day. Some don't have the slightest idea of who is on the other end of their prayer, but they do it anyway, expressing their gratitude, their concerns, appealing for help.

Even though people feel driven to pray, there are problems with prayer that may discourage us from doing it. What are the chief problems with prayer? I think there are two main problems. The first can be called the apparent *silence* of God and the other is the *difficulty* of prayer.

The silence of God. Henri Nouwen says in *The Way of the Heart* that if we think of prayer as *speaking with* God, it more often seems like *talking to* God because it feels so one-sided. This is the problem of the apparent silence of God. When I speak to God, I expect an answer, and when it doesn't come I can feel like I am engaged in a silly monologue, that I may be talking to myself. We don't want a one-sided conversation, and we get little benefit from a one-sided conversation. In the extreme it is like the space program where scientists are constantly busy beaming messages into outer space in the hope that, one day, they will be acknowledged and answered. So we don't have that sense of an active two-way conversation. Furthermore, even if we are satisfied with a one-way conversation, too often it seems that our prayers are not answered, even long after we have finished our prayer. If there is no result from our prayers, what is the point of praying? In the face of God's apparent silence, many people are discouraged from prayer.

Then there is the *difficulty of prayer*. First of all, we are not sure what kind of prayer is acceptable to God. We do not want to babble in the face of our Creator. So we have the problem of trying to construct our prayers so they are efficient, concise, and to the point. In addition, Nouwen says, "If we consider meditation as *thinking* about God, that sounds like serious mental effort that will add to our fatigue. How can we possibly expect anyone to find real nurture, comfort, and consolation from a prayer life that taxes the mind and adds one more exhausting activity to the many already scheduled ones?"

So prayer and meditation can be difficult for us, because of both the apparent silence of God and the difficulty inherent in prayer and meditation. Fortunately, there are people who have grown tremendously in that dimension of their lives, and I look to them for guidance. Books I have found particularly helpful include these:

a) *The Way of the Heart*, Henri J. M. Nouwen (New York: The Seabury Press, Inc., 1981).

b) *Space for God,* by Don Postema (Grand Rapids, Michigan: CRC Publications, 1983).
c) *Nurturing Silence in a Noisy Heart,* by Wayne E. Oates (Garden City, New York: Doubleday & Co., 1979).
d) *Breaking through God's Silence,* by David Yount (New York: Simon & Schuster, 1997).

These authors offer help in dealing with the problems we experience with prayer and meditation.

In Isaiah 30:15–16 God is quoted as saying, "In returning and rest you shall be saved; in quietness and in trust shall be your strength; but you would have none of it. You said, 'No, we will speed upon horses.' Therefore you shall speed away." If I insist on speeding He will allow that, but that is not the way—"in returning and rest you shall be saved." Nouwen says that our prayer life should be "an experience of rest where we open ourselves to God's active presence."

Nouwen suggests that our prayer should have five components (op. cit., p. 50):

1. Be quiet and let God's love soak in! Ponder the realization that I am loved by God as I am. His love is not based on my performance, but on His character and the fact that I am His creation, His child. Simply let myself be loved by God. This realization stimulates adoration.
2. Spend time just adoring God for who He is and what He does. Dwell upon His characteristics:

"The Lord is my light and my salvation." (Ps. 27:1)
"The Lord is my strength and my shield." (Ps. 28:7)
"The Lord is good." (Ps. 34:8; 100:5; 135:3; 145:9)
"The Lord is merciful and gracious." (Ps. 103:8; 111:4; 145:8)
"The Lord is faithful." (2 Thess. 3:3)
"The Lord is my helper." (Heb. 13:6)
"The Lord is righteous." (Exod. 9:27; 2 Chron. 12:6)

"The Lord is my rock." (2 Sam. 22:2; Ps. 18:2)
"The Lord is my refuge." (Ps. 14:6)

3. Pick out a gospel event, from the Bible, and contemplate it, not as an onlooker but as a participant. That is, identify either with Christ and what He was seeing, feeling, etc., or with a person with whom Christ was dealing. Try to let the Christ who is in you communicate the essence of Himself.
4. Then comes the prayer of petition. Once we are in real communion with the Lord, it is appropriate to speak the needs of our hearts or those needs we want to bring before Christ on behalf of someone else.
5. Finally, there is meditation, where we listen, think, analyze, imagine, and seek to hear the leading of the Lord, and to understand it's meaning and significance for our lives.

I am the Lord your God, who teaches you what is best for you, who directs you in the way you should go. (Is. 48:17)

Whether you turn to the right or to the left, your ears will hear a voice behind you, saying, "This is the way; walk in it." (Is. 30:21)

In his book *Breaking through God's Silence,* Yount points out that prayer requires practice, application, and attention. We should realize that no one (least of all God) is judging or scoring us. Effective prayer requires the humility to attempt it, knowing we will be clumsy. We should combat the temptation to be prodigies of prayer, and begin by learning the language of prayer through familiarizing ourselves with its classics. When the apostles asked Jesus to teach them to pray, he did not counsel them to be creative; rather, he gave them the Lord's Prayer, which has proved serviceable for two thousand years. We can use the prayers that have been written by those who are more experienced than we are. They usually include the same basic ingredients: praise, sorrow, gratitude, petition. But, after all, Nouwen quotes Dom Chapman: "Pray as you can and don't try to pray as you can't."

Conclusion

We have many resources available to us as we try to live intentionally. Of particular importance is the digging and maintaining of our wells before we need them, so that they are available when we do need to draw strength and wisdom.

Synopsis

- We can't live intentionally without drawing deeply, fully *realizing* all of the resources available to us.
- With all the other resources there are, we need to look first to ourselves and recognize that we have a unique contribution to make to the accomplishment of our goals. We also need to have someone to provide a check on what we perceive and think, and to provide new ideas and a different point of view. Our relatives and close friends have a vested interest in our well-being and are in a wonderful position to help. We also want to utilize qualified professionals (there are specialists in many of the areas in which we will have goals), books (there are books written on almost every subject we can imagine), and classes (which not only offer valuable facts, techniques, and training, but provide an opportunity to meet other people who are interested in the same areas we are). We need to be sure that we are grafted in to the power of the universe. God has the desire and power to help us grow and to accomplish our goals.
- The things that can greatly hinder us, distract us, and defeat us as we attempt to live intentionally include failure to think straight and logically; doubt; and fear.
- We may fail to think straight and logically for a number of reasons, including a) limited ability to think straight and logically; b) being distracted by worldly necessities and cultural pressures; c) distorted perception of reality

or understanding of truth; or d) the seductive temptation to rationalize.

- Even though we can think clearly and logically, we know that there are great uncertainties, and these uncertainties can lead to doubt and fear, which can play havoc with our emotions and our wills.

- In our fork decisions, we need to recognize the questionable reliability of our assumptions, imagine some of the ways things can change, and do a little thinking about what our response would be if they did change.

- If we have a spirit of conviction and confidence, we have courage and move forward. If we develop a spirit of doubt and fear, we become discouraged and give up.

- Paul urges us each day to equip ourselves by immersing ourselves in the whole truth as revealed by God and Christ; maintaining a persistent determination to live righteously; reconfirming our peace with God, repenting of our mistakes of the day before and reappropriating His forgiveness; preserving a sturdy, unshakable faith in God's love and faithfulness; remembering that God is fully able to save us and is determined to do so; spending time in the Scriptures and searching them out for the ammunition with which we can defeat whatever threatens us and our families; staying in constant communication with God to know His will and discern His direction; and being continuously alert for what it is that threatens us and the identity of those who would destroy what is precious in God's sight. The threats are subtle and they sneak up on us. We need to spot them when they first arise; if they become too entrenched, our battle becomes very difficult. This is especially true of the subtle threats to our children and grandchildren. Before we know it they can be seduced almost beyond our reach.

- The prophet Isaiah experienced his own doubt and fear, but found there was a basis on which he could replace the doubt with trust and the fear with peace. We can understand this by really examining the implications of two verses of Isaiah 12: "Surely God is my salvation; I will trust and not be afraid. The Lord, the Lord, is my strength and my song; he has become my salvation. With joy you will draw water from the wells of salvation." Doubt and fear and discouragement are defeated and replaced by confidence, conviction, and joy through God's Spirit, which comes as we draw water from the wells of salvation. There are many wells: Bible verses; prayers; hymns; other people; books of insight. They are to satisfy many needs: for peace, confidence, patience, endurance.

- Digging wells involves hard work and there are often distractions from it. Nevertheless, it is the important and necessary work we must do in the valleys and also on the mountain tops, in anticipation of the valleys.

- Jesus tells us that the key to living intentionally is to "remain" in Him. Remaining means to "stay, continue, endure restfully in a given place, condition, or relation." Remaining in Christ includes prayer and meditation.

- Prayer and meditation should be an active but restful process, not an exhausting chore or tedious discipline. Nouwen suggests five sequential steps: First, be quiet and remember all of the ways that God loves me. Then, spend time just adoring God for who He is and what He does—dwell upon his characteristics. Next, contemplate a Gospel event, trying to let the Christ who is in you communicate the essence of Himself. Then comes the prayer of petition for ourselves and on behalf of others. Finally, there is meditation, where we listen, think, analyze, imagine, and seek to hear the leading of the Lord and to understand it's meaning and significance for our lives. But, after all, Nouwen quotes Dom Chapman: "Pray as you can and don't try to pray as you can't."

Personal Reflection

- If you have had to go through a traumatic experience (death of a loved one, failure of some endeavor, betrayal by a friend, a very difficult decision, etc.), what have been some of the things that helped you most to carry on through it all? to recover afterwards?
- If some persons have been really helpful, what were their relationships to you, and how did they help?
- Do you think you are digging and maintaining your wells, and, if so, how do you do that?
- What wells do you think you are underutilizing? What could you do to probe that well further?

What is your reaction to the following sections of the text:

- The paragraph at the bottom of page 144 of the text on playing mental tapes in our minds?

- Failure to Think Straight and Logically, p. 147.

- Doubt and Fear, p. 149.

- The Whole Armor of God, p. 152.

Points I Want to Come Back To

Later, when I have more time, I want to think more about the following sections, questions, or ideas associated with this chapter:

_____

_____

_____

_____

_____

_____

_____

CHAPTER 9

Exploiting Our Occasions

I Don't Want to Miss My Chance!

My granddaughter, Stephanie, is eleven and this year graduated from her elementary school into junior high school.
Stephanie is a sweet, intelligent, energetic young lady. But I have
seen too many such lovely girls corrupted by the cultural pressure of junior high schools. I have been worried about my
Stephanie and wondering what I could do to help her stand up
against these negative influences. Two weeks ago I had occasion
to be in the local bookstore and noticed a book entitled *Reviving
Ophelia.** It's subtitle is *Saving the Selves of Adolescent Girls.* That
book is full of case histories that illustrate both the problems and
the pressures that confront junior high girls. It also discloses
things parents and grandparents can do to counteract those evil
forces. Discovering that book was an occasion for me to rejoice
at the happy coincidence that connected my concern to that
resource. (Was the "coincidence" accidental or part of God's response to my justified concern?) I read some of the book and
then bought another copy for Stephanie's parents. Now that will

---

* *Ballantine Books,* Mary Pipher (Random House: New York) 1995.

help us discuss together both the problems and possible solutions. I hope to find the right occasion for a casual talk with Stephanie about what she encounters at the school and the problems that presents to her. I already know that she has been confronted by a gang of girls who are antagonistic to anyone who doesn't buy into their values. And Stephanie has recently lost a girl friend who was her constant companion, because the girl decided it was better to join the gang than to buck it. We are all going to Disneyland together in two weeks to celebrate the occasion of her brother's eighth birthday. We will be together in an apartment at the local Residence Inn. Perhaps that will present an appropriate occasion for the kind of conversation I want to have with Stephanie.

Did you notice how many times I used the word *occasion* in the previous paragraph? Perhaps it's a little contrived, but it illustrates the several connotations of the word *occasion* and the types of occasions that happen in our everyday life. If we are alert to these occasions, we can accomplish a good result, in keeping with our intentional goals.

One of my goals is to be a positive influence on my grandchildren and to try to help them acquire the strengths and characteristics that will enable them to live happy and productive lives. A particular subgoal is to support Steph in this dangerous but opportune time in her life. As a part of living intentionally, I want to take advantage of every "coincidence," opportune moment, or propitious occasion that allows me to accomplish these goals.

Remember the dictionary definition of "occasion":

1. A time when everything is just right to accomplish an important objective if only we seize the opportunity. A favorable time, a fit time, an opportune time, a suitable time, a convenient time. I am looking for an appropriate occasion for my talk with Stephanie about what she confronts at the junior high school.
2. A particular time or happening. It was on the occasion of my happening into the local bookstore that I discovered the book *Reviving Ophelia*.

3. A fact, event, or state of affairs that makes something else possible. This could be thought of as a priming occasion. It prepares for and facilitates an additional occasion. I am hoping that our trip to Disneyland will turn out to be an occasion that provides the right setting for my conversation with Stephanie. It therefore is an occasion facilitating another occasion. Discovering the book *Reviving Ophelia* was also this type of occasion, in that it has provided me with needed background for my future conversation with Stephanie.
4. A special time or event suitable for celebration. Andrew's birthday is an occasion for celebration, and we are going to celebrate that occasion by all going together to Disneyland.

Our trip to Disneyland is a compound occasion: a special time to celebrate Andrew's birthday, an occasion for us to build great memories that we all will enjoy in the future and, I hope, also an occasion for my initial talk with Stephanie in a relaxed and congenial atmosphere.

These occasions resemble forks and dislocations in that they involve conscious choices and, we hope, make a significant difference in our lives. However, they are not major branch points where we have to make tough decisions—we single those out as forks. And afterwards we do not find ourselves in a drastically different situation where we have to struggle to adjust—we single those out as dislocations. But they are significant times when we have an opportunity to really make a difference, if we are alert and prepared. They may be less dramatic than forks or dislocations, but there are many more of them and, taken together, they also have a profound impact on the course of our lives.

Importance of Occasions

Why is it important for us to be alert to such occasions and to try to make the most of them? Well, first of all, we want to accomplish our objectives, and these occasions can be the significant steps in doing that. We don't accomplish our objectives, usually, through one magnificent happening, but by a succession of small steps, each involving the exploitation of an occasion that looks like a step in the right direction.

We also want to enjoy life. There can be a lot of occasions for joy and celebration, if we are alert. Of course, we have anniversaries, birthdays, perhaps times when someone gets a promotion or a raise in salary. But we can also celebrate together other occasions, such as when one of the children is in a recital or has participated in an athletic event or gets a good report card. It is amazing how many occasions we can find for celebration if we think about it, and such mini-celebrations increase the joy in our lives.

We also want to create and enrich the legacy we leave behind us. We can find many occasions to demonstrate important life principles for our children and grandchildren, to pass on important lessons we have learned, the wisdom we have accumulated. Part of the reason for our going to Disneyland is to create fond memories for our children and grandchildren. Fortunately, there have already been enough of those that the children and grandchildren want to include us, and our lives are blessed in the process. When we go on trips together, things always happen that give us a chance to communicate our values and wisdom in indirect, delicate, and natural ways.

So, taking advantage of the many occasions that either naturally present themselves, or we concoct on purpose, we can more readily accomplish our objectives, increase the joy in our lives, and contribute to the legacy we leave behind us. We can make good things happen if we are alert to these opportunities, and we can create a result or a memory that will have continuing benefits. If we live intentionally, we want to anticipate such times and events and make the most of them.

Observations about Occasions

What we have discussed already about occasions leads us to a number of observations.

- We need to be alert to the potential of particular occasions for accomplishing our objectives, increasing our joy, or enhancing our legacy. We can easily pass right by occasions, which could be very valuable, if we aren't alert to their potential. We need to ask ourselves: *"Here are some of the things that could happen this week. Do they have potential to advance my purposes if I handle them in the right way?*

- We need to have explicit goals, and also know what we want to model, if we are going to recognize particular occasions as presenting opportunities to advance those goals, or model what we want for the children. Having such goals and knowing what we want to model and to pass on is part of living intentionally.

- We need to sacrifice something in order to take advantage of these occasions. When my grandson is playing a baseball game, or my granddaughter is doing a recital, or my son is conducting a concert by his high school music classes, I have an opportunity to demonstrate my interest in them and their activities, as well as to enjoy myself as I observe their talent and their enjoyment in performing. It is usually also an opportunity to be with other members of the family who attend. But if I didn't go I would be doing something else. I may have an "important" meeting or a scheduled game of golf. I am going to have to make a choice and give up some other activity in order to take advantage of those occasions. It usually costs us something to take advantage of our occasions; the benefits are not free. That means we need to know our priorities.

- We need to prepare for our occasions. I am looking forward to my conversation with Stephanie, but I know that I need to anticipate and prepare for that occasion. It is not enough that I purchased the book. I have had to read it, to highlight the items that seemed particularly relevant, then create a summary of those key points. I also had to make a list of questions that I would like to ask Stephanie, which will help her to think about those issues and easily communicate her thoughts and feelings about them to me. I also know I need to pray about our time together—and more than one time! I feel I need some preparation for all of my special occasions.

- Time flies and those opportunities are quickly lost. Let me come back to that issue when I have completed this list of observations.

- Occasions build on other occasions. Here I am writing this book, and I hope that is an occasion to pass on to others some of the observations that I have found very valuable. How did I get to this point? First, I always took the occasion to write down and preserve the important lessons I learned, whether from experience, books, sermons, or other observations. Then there was an occasion when I was invited to discuss some of my observations at a men's breakfast. That went so well, and the men were sufficiently interested, that they asked me to come back for a second session. There followed an occasion where I was asked to lead a weekend men's retreat on Living Intentionally. It was built around the theme "Faithfulness, Fruitfulness, and Fellowship." Many men encouraged me to write down some of the things we talked about. In order to further firm up these ideas and to explore their applicability to real lives, a pastor invited me to lead a twelve-week discussion group of men. We had two men from each decade of life: twenties, thirties, etc., up to seventies. It was a fascinating experience. One of the men invited me to speak to his Kiwanis group, and I learned a lot from that experience with men outside of the church. That was followed by other men's groups, until some women asked why I was limiting the discussion groups to men. An eleven-week study with eight wonderful women followed. What other man has had such an opportunity to hear eight women candidly discuss the most meaningful issues of their lives? That occasion helped me to understand how this material relates to women. In the small group studies, the participants read the material outside of our sessions, and we spent the whole session discussing a particular topic for which I had given them provocative questions. I then tried a large class of fifty where I mostly lectured. Most recently I was invited to conduct discussions at a series of weekly meetings of a club for young married couples. Now I was able to see the issues that those young people have to face and how my material could be particularly helpful to them. Those occasions appeared to build one on top of another, and were presented to me in an amazing sequence that just seemed miraculously designed to make progress toward this book. What will happen next? I don't know, but I do know I want to be alert to whatever occasions there are to move forward. One occasion leads to another.

- Sometimes we need to take the occasion to back off, to not use the occasion in the way that first appeals to us. It might be an opportunity to lecture a child, and we should really refrain. It might be an opportunity to give a group the benefit of my experience and to tell them what they ought to do, while I really should refrain, let them make their own mistakes and learn for themselves. We need wisdom as to which occasions to exploit and in what way to use the occasions that are presented to us. I need to consider not only *my* long-range objectives, but those of other people and of God. On any occasion, the preferred action might well be different, depending on whose long range-goals we consider paramount.

- We need to be realistic. It is my hope that during our trip to Disneyland, I can communicate to my grandchildren important characteristics such as patience, tolerance of other's opinions and idiosyncrasies, pervasive joy and contentment, etc. But I know that things will happen during which my worst attributes will be revealed. I will undoubtedly show impatience with the traffic and long lines, annoyance at things that happen or at other people's behavior. Perhaps I will lose my temper and say things I will regret and be embarrassed about. So those are also occasions when we can demonstrate our humanity, our ability to acknowledge mistakes and eagerness to make amends, to say we're sorry, to admit that others were right when we thought they were wrong, to express affection and respect even in the midst of turmoil, to show how love can rise above and heal disagreements. While we run the risk of revealing attitudes that are contrary to the ones we want to teach, even that can be an occasion to convey important, positive lessons.

Time Flies

Let me come back to the reality that "time flies" (*tempus fugit*) and opportunities are quickly lost. In my discussion groups, each participant makes a compound time line, as illustrated in Fig. 9.1. In this figure I have drawn the most basic elements of my own time line. The bottom scale shows actual calendar years. The upper scale shows my actual ages corresponding to those years and my thirteen-year eras. The middle line represents the time sequence of my own life, and on it I can enter some key events. It begins at the time of a person's birth and ends at the time the person dies. The M and C stand for the times when I married and when I finally finished college after my Ph.D. The R is the date when I retired from IBM. This line also shows the births of my two children (Thomas and Susan) during my young adult years. I did not put a line on for my wife, Jean, because it complicates the display, but it really should be there. The $ symbol indicates a major traumatic event. In my case the earliest one was the accidental drowning of my brother; the second, the death of my mother; the third, my father's grave heart attack; the fourth my father's death. Obviously the markings on the line can be as few or as numerous as desired, depending on the detail we want to represent.

I added the time lines of my parents and grandparents on the bottom half of the figure. My parents were Grace H. and Andrew F. Josephine is the woman my father married after my mother died.

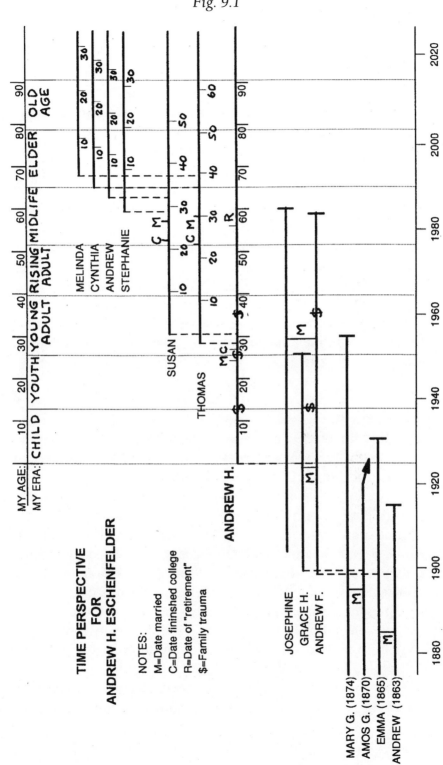

Fig. 9.1

My father's parents were Andrew and Emma Eschenfelder, who were born at the time of the Civil War. My mother's parents were Amos and Mary Griffith, and they were born about ten years later. The M stands for the date of their respective marriages. Amos Griffith departed for places unknown before I was born. You can see that by the time of my Youth I had only one grandparent still living. She is the only grandparent I can actually remember. You can observe the $ on my parent's lines, where their traumatic event was the same as mine. The second M on my father's line indicates the date of his marriage to Josephine.

The upper lines show the lives of my children and those of their children, my grandchildren. Looking at this chart I see how quickly the children will change and how quickly I will age at the same time. I observe, with some trepidation, that I will have to survive to 80 if I want to see my granddaughter Stephanie reach 21; and at that time Andrew would be 18; Cindy, 15; and Melinda, 12. I guess I'd better take better care of myself.

I also observe how quickly I moved through my earlier eras. I have recently finished my Midlife period (age 52–65). It was an exciting era during which I entered semi-retirement, my children entered their careers and married, my grandchildren were born, and both my father and stepmother died. During my Rising Adult period I did not anticipate all the fascinating things that would happen in my following Midlife period. This Rising Adult period appears fairly empty on the chart. However, it was the most stressful time of my career, and I was undoubtedly more absent than I should have been from my children, who were finding their way through their teens. But we did have some good family vacations that are a source of fond remembrance for all of us. And we did try to be present to each other, especially when one of us had a major event or celebration. It was near the beginning of my Rising Adult era that we relocated from New York to California, and this had a major influence on our lives.

Now I am into my Elder years, which may well be the richest years of my life, with the opportunity to watch my children evolve, help my grandchildren to grow, and to have the time to do things I want to do (including the reflection on my life and the preparation of this material). But if I want this picture of my future to be a reality, I will have to make the most of all of the occasions that come along to accomplish my objectives and to enjoy my life.

This chart is useful because it shows the rapid change in family structure and reminds us that we have a brief time to take advantage of opportunities to interact with our children and grandchildren when they are of particular ages and in particular circumstances. There is also a brief time to interact with our parents and grandparents when they are of particular ages and in particular circumstances. We need to be conscious that time flies, and we need to take advantage of all of our occasions while we can.

I encourage you to make a similar chart. I have included a basic chart in the appendix upon which you can construct your own timelines.

Synopsis

- Occasions are opportune times when we can move our lives forward in the way that we want, if only we seize the opportunity. We might take a step forward in accomplishing an important objective. We might be able to make one more contribution to the overall joy of our lives. We might be able to have a beneficial impact on those around us. These occasions may be less dramatic than forks or dislocations, but there are many more of them and, taken together, they also have a profound impact on the course of our lives.
- Some occasions naturally present themselves; others we concoct on purpose.
- Some occasions prepare for or facilitate other occasions. Taking advantage of the first occasion makes the second occasion possible or increases the chances that the second occasion will have a good result.

- Occasions build on other occasions. By hindsight we see that our objectives are accomplished, our life is enjoyed and, our legacy is enhanced, not in a single occasion, but by a continuous succession of occasions. Taking advantage of one occasion opens the door to the next important occasion.
- Occasions abound in our lives. Each day presents a variety of occasions. But we can so easily pass them by without actually realizing the benefit that we might from them. We have to be very alert to the opportunity they present and prepare ourselves to use them well.
- Occasions do not usually repeat themselves. If we overlook one and fail to use it well before it has passed, we have missed a golden opportunity!

Personal Reflection

- Make a short list of some of the recent "occasions" in your life:

  a) A time or event that was suitable for celebration, whether or not you did celebrate
  b) A time when everything was just right to accomplish an important objective, whether or not you seized the opportunity
  c) An occasion that made possible or facilitated another occasion

- Can you see how some occasions facilitated or led to others?
- Can you name some that substantially increased your joy in life?
- Can you think of some occasions when you probably should have backed off and not used that occasion in the way that first appealed to you?

- Can you think of some opportunities you may have missed?

  a) Times when you might well have celebrated, but didn't?
  b) Times when you might have strengthened personal relationships, which you didn't take sufficient advantage of?
  c) A chance to minister to someone's need or to expand your Christian knowledge and experience?
  d) Opportunities that might have advanced a particular objective of yours, which you missed, or almost missed?

- What are some of the things that have caused you to miss what might have been a significant "occasion"?
- Make a timeline for your family, using the form in appendix B.
- What impressions do you get from the process of making this timeline, or from reflecting on what it displays?
- Can you think of some occasions that either naturally lie in your future already, or that you could construct, that could be used to advance your objectives?

  a) Times when you and/or your family might well celebrate?
  b) Times when you might strengthen a personal relationship?
  c) A chance to minister to someone's need or to expand your Christian knowledge and experience?
  d) Opportunities to advance a particular objective of yours?

- What do you have to do to take maximum advantage of these opportunities?

Points I Want to Come Back To

Later, when I have more time, I want to think more about the following sections, questions, or ideas associated with this chapter:

_____

_____

_____

_____

_____

_____

_____

_____

_____

_____

CHAPTER 10

Recognizing Our Givens

Taking My Uniqueness into Account

Would you have made a different decision than I did when offered a promotion that required a move from California to New York (chapter 6)? You might well have. At that time improvement in our family's financial well-being and a career promotion were outweighed by other important family and personal factors. We decided to stay in California. At a different time of our lives, when our circumstances were different, the balance might tip the other way. Other people might well decide the fork differently, depending on their particular values, preferences, overall objectives, history, circumstances, and particular stage in life.

It is essential, in deciding my forks, that I decide which direction suits *me* best. To do that I have to clearly understand what's important to me. How relatively important are position and prestige, time to do things with my family, the power to buy them things they would enjoy, opportunities to travel, a larger home, living in a benevolent climate, a job in which I can really make a mark, even if it does consume my time and energy? I also need to know these things in order to shape my daily life for maximum enjoyment. We all spend money to improve our enjoyment of life. On what do we spend it? If we are wise, we carefully ascertain what things mean the most to us, and that clarifies our priorities for spending. So I need to understand such truths about myself and my situation whenever I am thinking about how to respond to my *forks*, to my *dislocations*, and to the many other singular *occasions* when my decisions and actions have a significant impact on the course of my life.

We all have to deal with the same kinds of events. And we can use some of the same wisdom and techniques in dealing with those events. But the actual decisions we make may indeed be different. In order to make plans that really suit me and are realistic in terms of what I can accomplish, I need to *assess my givens*.

The dictionary defines *givens* as "that which is assumed to be true or is accepted as fact; premises." My givens are the things that are true about my particular situation, which I should take into account in making my decisions. We call them givens because they are the premises for our personal deliberations. We assume they are going to continue to be true. Of course, we may be able to change some of these givens, but, for the most part, they are the conditions of our lives that we have to live with. In this chapter we want to think about assessing our own givens.

What is it about each of us that makes our situation unique, and could be listed as our *givens*? We can list the following categories:

- Personal goals and aspirations. The things that you hope will happen for you may be different from what I long for.
- Values, preferences, and inclinations. The things that are most important to you may not be the most important for me. The things that you enjoy may be quite different from what I enjoy. The things that you abhor may be quite tolerable to me.
- Personal skills and limitations. The things that you are good at, I may not be able to do at all, and vice versa.

- Constraints. You have commitments that are quite different from those that bind me.

Let us think a little more about some of those categories.

Our Personal Goals and Aspirations

Our aspirations are what we hope we might become, or what we hope will happen. Some of you might aspire to own your own home, to win a particular promotion, to live in a given area, to acquire a certain skill, to have a child, to become more patient. Our aspirations may be for very specific things we want to acquire or achieve or become. Some of our aspirations may be more general and pervasive. For instance, I recognize that I want to be a good grandfather, to help my grandchildren in significant ways to develop into the marvelous individuals they were destined to become. I want to work on things that intrigue me, that use my abilities well, where my efforts make an important difference. I want to shape my environment rather than have my environment shape me. I want to be imaginative, rational, and creative.

We see that we all have aspirations in a number of different areas:

- Our personal nature: what we want to be; attributes in which we want to grow and improve; our physical fitness (exercise, dieting, etc.); our emotional harmony (being more content, etc.); our patterns of thought and behavior (e.g., living more intentionally); our spiritual maturity.
- Our relationships: perhaps with our spouse; with our children or grandchildren; with our parents or grandparents; with our business associates, our good friends and confidants, our neighbors, our siblings or other family members.
- Our family prosperity: financial security (perhaps involving budgeting, insurance, wills, investments, etc.); our physical home (obtaining one; repairing or protecting the one we have, etc.); our family happiness and serenity.

- Our personal accomplishments: what we want to do; perhaps things we want to make, to write, to complete; perhaps places we want to visit or experiences we want to have.
- Our lifestyle and environment: the way we spend our time/energy; the environment in which we dwell, work, play.

Some aspirations are subtle and perhaps even subconscious. How can we identify our aspirations? We can perhaps pin down our general aspirations by thinking about what seems to drive us forward, or what changes in our situation we would hope could occur, or what we would personally hope to become, what we would hope that other people could say about us, or what we long for, to what we feel ourselves drawn, what we sense to be our "growing edges" (aspects of our person where we feel we are growing).

One aspiration can collide with another. Then we have to think about our relative priorities. For instance, if one of my aspirations is to have the most beneficial influence on my family that I can and to really enjoy them, that involves spending more time with them. But if I am also trying to be as productive as possible with the time, energy, and talents I have been given, and to provide for my family to the best of my ability, then I would be tempted to spend more time at my work, resulting in less time with my family. Which has the higher priority?

Some of our aspirations may not be realistic in terms of our givens. For instance, an aspiration you might have in the arena of lifestyle could be to have one of the partners in the marriage stay at home with the children. You may feel this is impossible because you need two incomes to maintain your lifestyle. If we have an aspiration and there are things that impede its fulfillment, we need to think about other compromises we could make that would make our aspiration more possible.

In this particular case, your discussion of compromises could include the following:

- Would it be possible to get along on one salary and lower your expectations in other areas? Some spouses do stay home and their families live on lower salaries. This is not true just for high-salaried doctors, but for families of firefighters, police, schoolteachers, etc.

- Even though you think you could get along on one income, you may feel that you need to have two incomes to protect against sudden loss of income because job security is so low.
- Are there ways to have two incomes and still have one spouse home when the children are out of school?

Aspirations that have been clearly defined and firmly committed become my specific goals for the future. Some people have *explicit* goals in these arenas; some have *subconscious* goals; everyone has at least *implicit* goals. By *explicit* I mean a defined list. By *subconscious* I mean that while they do not have a list, they do have specific goals and would not have any difficulty writing out such a list. Some people have thought very little about goals, might even think they had none, and would have a very difficult time writing out a list. However, they do have *implicit* goals. By this I mean that we all shape our decisions and actions by an internal drive that moves us toward certain ends. Those ends can be said to be our implicit goals.

In each of the several categories of our aspirations, we may well have one or more goals. Those goals are usually rather broadly defined. Then for each of those goals we would have subgoals, which need to be quite specific and must be accomplished for the major goals to be realized. Let me give you an example of one of my major goals and some subgoals that might help me to achieve the major goal.

I presently have a goal to build a life that is satisfying in the present for Jean and myself. We often postponed pleasures in our younger years in order to build a better future. Now, it doesn't pay for us to put pleasures off, for we are growing older and we may not be here that much longer. That goal implies some subgoals: for time spent on our relationship; for fixing up our house and yard so we can enjoy them to the fullest; for sustaining our health; for planning some fun trips; for designing more activities together, although still maintaining some of our favorite separate activities also.

Some of our goals and aspirations persist throughout our lives. For instance, no matter what age we are, we may want to do well at whatever we attempt. Some aspirations change as we grow older. I read somewhere that when we are ten our aspiration is to wake up with a day off from school, at twenty we want to wake up romantic, at thirty to wake up married, at forty to wake up successful, at fifty to wake up rich, at sixty to wake up contented, at seventy to wake up healthy, and at eighty we want to just wake up. Incidentally, if we are living intentionally, we have to anticipate some of our future aspirations. For instance, if at seventy we think we will want to wake up healthy, we have to take care of our bodies when we are younger. Some young people think they can abuse their bodies in all sorts of ways and they won't notice the difference when they are older. If at forty we want to wake up successful, we are going to have to take the appropriate steps when we are much younger.

Certainly we want the decisions we make at our forks, the adjustments we make at our dislocations, and our planning for our "occasions" to move us in the direction of our aspirations and goals. It is therefore obviously essential that we have our aspirations and our goals explicitly in mind. If we haven't thought them out, we need to do that. If we have previously thought them out, we probably need to update them.

Our Values, Preferences, and Inclinations

Our values, preferences, and inclinations are closely related, but they are not the same thing. Into the category of preferences we put those things that represent what we like the most and also, in contrast, those things that annoy us and that we want to avoid. Perhaps inclinations overlap preferences. However, I think of preferences as reflecting our desires, whereas inclinations reflect more our habits, tendencies, the patterns of behavior we have developed. Our values represent things we esteem very highly and want to see sustained. If we are going to make wise choices at our forks, dislocations, occasions, etc.—choices that are most suitable for us as individuals—we have to be fully aware of our values, preferences, and inclinations and give them precedence in our choices. Let us consider a few examples.

First of all, consider preferences. I recognize that I have preferences in all kinds of realms: preferences in what kind of activities I want to undertake, preferences in the kinds of surroundings in which I want to work and live, preferences in the kinds of people with whom I want to be involved, etc.

For instance, I might prefer short-term projects that show immediate and visible accomplishment rather than long, tedious projects requiring persistence. I might prefer to have only one project at a time, without the complication of having to juggle several balls at once. I might prefer to have a project I can work on alone at my own pace, rather than having to integrate my skills and schedule with those of other team members. I might prefer to live and work in a rural setting with clean air and little traffic, or I may prefer a more urban environment with lots of cultural activities and convenient access to all kinds of resources. I may abhor noise or cold winters. I may want to avoid dealing with political persons who delight in manipulating situations and people, and who may pressure me to compromise my ideals. I would have to take all such preferences into account at forks where I am trying to decide which employment to accept.

In the category of inclinations, I might be much more inclined to talk than to listen. That might *not* be my preference. I might prefer to restrain my talking and spend more time listening to what others have to say, believing that is a good and important thing to do. But I might nevertheless be strongly inclined to do too much of the talking because it is a habit. I might also be inclined to put off things that might be enjoyed today in order to concentrate on building a better future. I might not so much desire to do that, but might have developed an attitude and a pattern of deferred gratification and find it difficult to do otherwise. Clearly I ought also to understand and take into account my inclinations in dealing with my forks, etc.

Now what are my values? Well, I certainly value the things I prefer. And I would usually be inclined towards those things I value. But we think of our values as stronger than preferences or inclinations. I very much value certain people, such as my wife and my best friend. I very much value certain personal characteristics, such as commitment and faithfulness—that a person will commit himself to something specific and then fulfill that commitment, whether it is to a person, to a task, or to a principle. We want to uphold and honor what we value. So we want to be very explicitly conscious of our values when making decisions, lest we choose an alternative that does not honor our values. We may sacrifice our preferences in a decision, but we do not want to sacrifice our values.

Our Personal Skills and Limitations

My skills are the tools I have available to me in doing the things I do. These may be mechanical skills or intellectual tools. I seem to have an ability to sort out complex matters, understand the parts and the way they fit together, and then explain the substance of the matter, clearly and succinctly. This is an important skill, which enables me to play a special role that not everyone else can play. I need to be aware of my special skills. What is it that you can do better than most other people?

I also need to be aware of my limitations. There are skills I just don't have, and I should be sure to rely on other people who are more competent than I in those areas. There are areas in which I have a great deal of knowledge, and there are areas where my knowledge is very limited. I have habits that limit me. I have physical and economic limitations. Can you think of the areas in which you have real limitations? It might even be that you have limitations on the time available to you because of your responsibilities. Clearly there are certain things we should not try to do because of our limitations.

Constraints

I am bound to certain people and bound by particular conditions. We can look at that positively and ask: Who are the people

that God has given to me, with whom I possess a very special relationship, who are in a position to strongly influence my life and to
whom I also can be a real blessing? Those are positive givens in my
life, and I don't want to weaken those connections. We can also
look at that from the negative side and ask: Who are the people
with whom I have to contend whether I like it or not (perhaps an
employer or a difficult relative)? My constraints also include the
situations with which I am involved and certainly the restrictions
on my financial flexibility. We ask: What are the financial constraints which now limit what I am able to do, and what are my
prospects for the future; obligations I have that claim resources;
financial dependencies that exist, and how long they will persist?

The Essentials of My Life

We see that our list of *givens* can be pretty long. One way of
isolating the most crucial ones is to ask, "What do I feel are the
essentials of my life?" By the *essentials* I mean two things: the greatest
necessities of my life and the greatest *keys* to the way I live. Suppose I say to you, "The companionship of my wife is essential to
my life; I don't think I could get along without her." There are
some things that are so necessary to my life as I know it and want
to live it that I can't imagine getting along without them. That is
one meaning of the word *essential*. A somewhat different connotation is related to the word *essence*. We consider the essence to be
what something really is, in its concentrated or pure form. Boil it
all down and what have you got? You've got the essence. As with
an onion, peel away all the layers and what is at the core? Both
essential and essence come from the Latin verb, *esse*, which means
"to be." We are talking about the core of our being. Suppose I say
to you, "An essential aspect of my nature is a compulsion to use
wisely every minute available to me." That is a key to the way I
live. So think of those things that largely determine the way that
you think and behave. Also think of the greatest necessities of your
life. What is it that you can't do without? These are the *essentials*
of your life.

Section 3 contains three chapters strongly related to our givens: chapter 12, Our Uniqueness—Personal Characteristics; chapter 13, Our Uniqueness—Beliefs and Attitudes; chapter 14, Our Uniqueness—Personal and Family History. We have already recognized that we have to take into account our personal characteristics, as well as our beliefs and attitudes. I also realize that my personal and family history is an important part of my givens. They have shaped what I believe and value and have also helped to shape the way that I think and react. These chapters are intended to help the readers who want to explore further these dimensions of themselves and to be more precise in identifying the details of their givens.

Our Self-Worth

As I think about my characteristics, my skills, and my limitations, I begin to compare myself to other people. I am certainly different from other people. Am I better or worse than they are? As I list my attributes, I might feel good about myself or I might feel chagrined. I can easily begin to feel inferior or inadequate. I think it is important, first of all, to make the distinction between being better and being different.

If we consider an attribute in conjunction with its opposite, we realize that some attributes are commonly acknowledged to be *better* than their opposites, while others are only *different* from their opposites. An example of a better attribute would be "honest." Clearly honesty is better than dishonesty. We value the honest person and disdain the dishonest one. An example of a *different* attribute would be "logical." Being logical is different from being intuitive, but it is not better. We value the logical person and the intuitive person, and both can make equally important contributions to a project or the enrichment of our lives. In fact, we would like to be a composite of both, and if we are predominantly one or the other, it is good to have a partner with the opposite strength. I group the *better* attributes into a category called *character*, and they might well be called *virtues*. I group the *different* attributes into a category called *personality*. Those attributes just describe the particulars of our personalities. We need to keep the distinction clearly in mind and not confuse virtues with personality particulars.

Even as we recognize the difference between being better and just being different, we can still feel chagrined. How do you feel? Can you write down a substantial list of virtues you have (even though you are aware of those that don't measure up to your ideals), or are you more conscious of what you consider your inferiorities to other people you know? Do you feel that you have some outstanding talents, or do you feel you have been shortchanged in that area? Do you, perhaps, have more behavior patterns that you are ashamed of than that you are proud of? It is somewhat dangerous to reflect on these aspects of our character and personality because it can lead to dismay, to a feeling that we do not amount to much, after all.

How valuable am I, anyway? The Bible declares that God knows us full well, including our inadequacies. At the beginning of Psalm 139 it says, "O Lord, you have searched me and you know me." At the same time, God had a large hand in making us what we are, including our inadequacies. Later verses in Psalm 139 (13–16) say, "for you created my inmost being . . ." So, to some degree He is responsible for what we are. The essential thing we must remember is that God considers each one of us as infinitely precious, even with all of our inadequacies and our warts. He knows we don't have all the talents or personality we would like to have, but He just wants us to use well whatever opportunities we have, with whatever talents we have been given. This is demonstrated in the Parable of the Talents (Matt. 25:14–30).

In the Parable of the Talents, Jesus clearly declares that even if two men have very different resources, they are rewarded equally if they show the same diligence in using what they have. That is true even though they accomplish quite different levels of results. On the other hand, the man who fails to use his resource, whether it is small or large, is dealt with severely. Quite clearly, our lives are valued not in terms of the resources we *have* (personality, skills, opportunities, etc.—most of which we didn't earn anyway), but in terms of *what we do with what we've got*. In a sense, the game of life is similar to the game of golf. I like golf because it is a handicapped sport. That is, everyone can compete, no matter what his ability. In tennis, you can enjoy the game only if you play with someone of comparable ability. But in golf, everyone has a handicap, which is determined by his skill level. Taking the handicap into account, each player is measured in terms of how he plays, not against an absolute standard, but against his own skill level. I can have an enjoyable match with someone else whose golfing ability is much better or much lower than mine. Clearly, our job is to use well what we have and not think about whether what we have is more or less than someone else. We may be a mighty tree or a small bush, but in either case we can yield some delicious and beautiful fruit that is commensurate with the nature of our plant.

I had a few other thoughts about the differences between us that I want to keep in mind and that I would like to share with you. It seems to me that we tend to expect others to think in our patterns. That is, to act as we do and to react as we do; to respond as we would respond; to want personal support in the same form that we want it. It is true that some people might be much like us, but more often they are not.

Almost everyone is familiar with the Golden Rule, "Do unto others as you would have them do unto you." As I have thought about our differences I have concluded that the Golden Rule can lead us to a wrong conclusion. I think the rule that governs our behavior should really be stated: "Do unto others the way that they want to be done unto." When we treat others in the way we would like to be treated, instead of the way they want to be treated, we are asking for trouble. For instance, suppose I like to be quiet and left alone and my wife wants companionship and conversation. The Golden Rule would have me leave her quiet and alone, because that is the way I want to be treated. If I did, she would complain, "Why isn't he interested in me?" However, when we take into account human variations and act accordingly, we breed harmony instead of conflict. My wife wants to talk? . . . I'll talk!

I have realized new things about myself and have come to appreciate differences in other people as I have thought about my givens and talked to other men and women about theirs, as I have thought about the variations between people and the expectations we tend to have for each other. I want to really appreciate that "variety is the spice of life." Wouldn't it be terrible if we were all carbon copies of each other! Our variations give joy and interest to our relationships and our activities. We have to remember: "It takes all kinds to make a world." It takes all kinds to make most anything go: a project, a church, a community. Vive la differènce! We can all make a real difference and find a happy life, if we use well our *givens*.

Synopsis

- The dictionary defines *givens* as "that which is assumed to be true or is accepted as fact; premises." My givens are the things that are true about my particular situation, which I should take into account in making my decisions. We call them givens because they are the premises for our personal deliberations.
- Because we have different *givens,* different ones of us can be expected to make different decisions, even when many aspects of a particular situation are similar. Therefore, to make decisions that are right for ourselves, we have to be explicitly conscious of our givens.
- Things that are unique about ourselves, which we need to take into account, include our personal goals and aspirations; our values, preferences, and inclinations; our personal skills; and our constraints, which include the people and situations with which we have to contend and restrictions on our financial flexibility.
- We should make sure we know our aspirations for our personal nature; our relationships; our family prosperity; our personal accomplishments; and our lifestyle and environment.
- Aspirations, which have been clearly defined and firmly committed, become my specific goals for the future. In

each of the several categories of aspirations, our goals must exist in at least two levels: a) major goals for each category, which are necessarily rather broadly defined, and b) subgoals for each major goal, which need to be quite specific and must be accomplished for the major goals to be realized.

- We also need to take into account our preferences: those things we like and enjoy, as well as those things that annoy us, and which we want to avoid. Those arise in a number of arenas: preferences in the kind of activities I want to undertake, preferences in the kind of surroundings in which I want to work and live, preferences in the kinds of people with whom I want to be involved, etc.

- As we list our givens, we may feel good about ourselves or chagrined because we feel we aren't as good as someone else. We need to clearly differentiate between being better or worse and merely being different.

- Quite clearly, our lives are valued not in terms of the resources we *have* (personality, skills, opportunities, etc.—most of which we didn't earn anyway), but in terms of *what we do with what we've got*. That is a biblical principle and should also be a cultural principle.

- Variety is the spice of life. Our personal variations give joy and interest to our relationships and our activities. It takes all kinds of people to make most anything go. Thank goodness we are so different, one from the other.

- The Golden Rule should really be "Do unto others as they want to be done unto." That may well be different from the way we would have them do unto us.

- We can all make a real difference and find a happy life, if we use well our *givens*.

Personal Reflection

- What are some aspirations you have? How realistic do you think they are?

- What are some compromises you could consider or have considered that could help them to become reality?
- Can you think of some things that really bring you a sense of peace or enjoyment, which you would like to emphasize? Can you think of some things that really annoy you, which you would like to avoid?
- What are some of the things that are so necessary to your life as you presently know it, and want to live it, that you can't imagine getting along without them?
- What are some of the convictions or attitudes that are central to the way you think and behave?
- If you are facing a specific fork now, or know of one in your near future, which of your *givens* seem most relevant to that fork?
- What are some of your primary constraints that limit what you could do (responsibilities you must carry out, other people you depend on, skills you lack, financial obligations, etc.)?
- Are you basically content to play the game of life with the givens that you have, and do you accept the fact that your life is valued in terms of what you do with what you've got? Or are you burdened with feelings of personal inferiority and inadequacy . . . or feelings of superiority?

Points I Want to Come Back To

Later, when I have more time, I want to think more about the following sections, questions, or ideas associated with this chapter:

_____
_____
_____
_____
_____
_____
_____
_____

CHAPTER 11

What Next?

My First Steps on a New Road

In this chapter I would like to help you answer the following questions:

- How satisfied are you with your life today and with how it will likely be in five years if you continue on your present path?
- What changes should you try to make at this time in yourself and in your situation so that you will be more satisfied in five years than you would be if you continued on your present path?
- What specific steps are you going to take next?

In this book we have considered many aspects of living intentionally. Recognizing that our life is precious, the only one we're ever going to have, we are determined to make the most of it. Obviously, the crucial question is, *"What are you going to do next in order to enrich your life?"*

Whatever you do next, it will be a step in a given direction from the point where you are now. We are all at a given point in our life's journey and we are heading in a particular direction. You may be at a high or low point in your life. I hope you are headed upwards, but you could be on a downward slide. It is important for you to assess where you are and where you are headed. I want to help you to do that.

But are you headed in the direction you want? We are who we are, but not yet what we are becoming. We can't change who we are today, but we are becoming someone else and we can influence that. We may not be able to change the situation in which we find ourselves today, but we can strongly influence the situation in which we will find ourselves in five years. Are you satisfied with where you are headed? I also want to help you assess that. Most of us see room for improvement and want to make some course corrections.

What course corrections should you attempt? What changes do you want to make? What are you going to try to do differently? Alcoholics Anonymous has a definition of insanity that goes as follows: "Insanity is continuing to do what we've always done and expecting different results." If we want things to go differently in our lives, we are going to have to do some things differently! I want to help you decide what you want to do differently. But first, let's consider your current situation.

Analyzing Your Current Situation

In order to analyze your current situation I suggest you ask yourself a sequence of questions that help to answer the principal question, *How do you feel about the way things are right now?* How do you feel about

- Your economic state? You might feel that you are too much in debt; or that you are not saving enough; or that you are spending your money on the wrong things; or you might feel that everything will be fine as long as you can keep your financial posture as it is today, while keeping up with inflation.

- Your employment? Is there a good match between the requirements of your job and your talents and interests? Do you look forward to going to work? Do you think you are being treated fairly? Can you see room for growth?
- Your family situation? Is there some deficiency in your relations with your spouse? or with your children? Is there a family problem you are allowing to fester that needs to be resolved?
- The expenditure of your time and energy? Do you seem to work too much and play too little? Are there things to which you feel you should devote more of your time and energy?
- Your health? Should you lose weight? Have you been putting off your physical? Do you feel you are in satisfactory physical condition? Are you taking care of yourself?
- Your state of happiness/unhappiness? Do you always seem tense? Are you a grump? Do you experience the joy that the Lord wants for you?

Those are, of course, very private questions. I suggest you take a piece of paper and write down how you feel right now about each of those areas. Then, if you are married, you may want to ask your spouse to do the same thing and compare notes.

You can clarify how you feel now by asking yourself these additional questions:

- Which of the factors of your life/situation are most satisfying to you?
- Which of the factors of your life/situation are most disappointing to you?
- What is it that currently troubles your spirit about your present situation; about your future prospects; about your past?

Then, after assessing your feelings about the present, it is appropriate to turn toward the future and ask: *Where do you seem to be heading?*

As you look at the various dimensions of your situation (your economic state; your employment; your family situation; your activities; your health; your state of happiness) try to project into the future:

- Are there significant changes to be expected at a particular time? (e.g., children leaving home, parents becoming infirm, inadequacy of your present house, your employment situation, retirement, etc.)
- What significant events and/or forks can you anticipate in the reasonably near future?
- How is your situation likely to look five or ten years from now if you don't make any changes?
- Are you likely to be satisfied in the future as you look back, if you continue on your present course and don't make some changes or begin to prepare now for some of the forks? In what areas do you anticipate dissatisfaction?

If you conclude that you are not thoroughly satisfied with your present trajectory, you need to think about what changes you would like to see.

What changes would you like to see

- In the person you are?
- In what you are likely to accomplish in the coming years?
- In the relationships of your life?
- In your lifestyle?

Those questions help to identify potential next steps.

Another way to get a handle on the next steps you might like to take is to assess each of the roles you currently fill. We each serve simultaneously in quite a number of roles. Some of these roles are continuing and some are temporary. I see my own continuing roles as husband; father; grandfather; brother; uncle; close friend; Christian agent/witness. I also have the following temporary roles in this particular year: President of the Seniors at my golfing club; Elder at my church; author/teacher in the subject of living intentionally. You probably have additional roles as an employee and/or employer, as a son or daughter, etc.

For each of my roles, I ask myself the same questions: Whom do I serve in that role? What do they need from me in that role? What could I do to meet that need? What could I do to better equip myself to serve in that role?

The last question is as important as the others. We expect to do some good in each of our roles, to have a positive impact. At the same time we know that a plant becomes exhausted and unproductive as it bears fruit, unless it is continually nourished, watered, and fed. So, I need to consider what would nurture me in my role as well as how I could better perform that role. For instance, as a husband, I can ask: What do I perceive as the greatest needs my wife currently has, and what specific thing could I do to help satisfy those needs? I should also ask: What are my greatest inadequacies as a husband, and what could I do to improve on those inadequacies and become a better husband?

I have answered those questions for myself and discovered that thinking along those lines immediately brings to mind a variety of potential "next steps." Some are so obvious and imperative that I leap to the task. But the importance of my taking such steps was not at all obvious before I asked myself those questions.

The same thing happens in my discussion groups. As we have had those discussions, one man immediately decided he should take steps to rebuild his relationship with a brother from whom he had become estranged. A woman quickly concluded she should go back to school. Another resolved to set limits on her time commitments so she could have some opportunity for solitude and rejuvenation. A man decided that the future prospects for his job were bleak enough that he intended to start preparing for a change of employment. A mother decided that it was time she and her husband agreed on a plan of "tough love" to deal with a wayward child. One father realized that he had become curt and aggressive in response to the needs of his career and resolved to find ways to soften his personality at home. A couple decided it was time to get some counseling for their marriage. I hope that pondering those questions will also reveal "next steps" for you that might enrich your life.

Considering Your Next Steps

After you have analyzed your current situation, it is time to ask yourself the important question: In view of all that, *what do you need/want to confront at this particular time?*

Once again, take pencil and paper and answer the following questions:

- What decisions should you resolve right now (career, family, personal issues, etc.)?
- What changes seem called for in the allocation of your time and energy?
- What people should you really pay more attention to?
- What other relational situations are there that need mending or more attention?
- What modifications in your house, yard, autos, etc., would enhance the quality of your life?
- What future events can you anticipate, and which should you begin to prepare for?
- What changes would you really like to see in your personality?
- Are there any threats to the well-being of yourself or your family that you perceive, and that you ought to do something about?
- Which of those items are most urgent and should have the highest priority?

I know how I answer those questions. As I think about the ways *you* might respond to those questions, I can visualize a variety of possibilities:

1. There may be decisions pending in your life that you need to make, to get resolved. If so, I hope that our discussion in

chapter 6 on forks will be helpful, including the worksheet for analyzing previous forks as well as the observations and guidelines for dealing with forks.

2. You may have a desire to make changes in your allocation of time and energy. That might have been stimulated by a desire to be more fruitful, or by constructing the timeline in chapter 9 and realizing that time is flying past and your children and grandchildren are growing rapidly.

3. You may have realized that there are particular people you want to pay more attention to. In some cases those are parents who are aging and may not be around much longer. In other cases it may be a friend (do I spend a "friendly" amount of time with that person?), a mentor (I'd better learn from him/her while I can), or someone you are mentoring (I can be an unusual blessing to that person if I seize the opportunity before it has passed).

4. There may be other relational problems you realize you need to deal with. It might be someone with whom you have become estranged and you know there is something you can do to heal or strengthen that relationship.

5. You may have been stimulated to make some changes in your environment to better suit you. It was such a stimulation that caused me to retire from IBM in 1981 at only fifty-six, to leave the church staff three years ago, to remodel our backyard two years ago, and to install the little waterfall, where I can enjoy the peaceful sound of water trickling. And it also caused us to remodel my den last year. I spend so much time in there working on these things, we concluded I ought to have it the way I can really enjoy it and work more efficiently.

6. You may have become aware of some events that are likely to lie in your path in the near future for which you ought to prepare (at least somewhat), or some events you could cause to occur that would enhance your life.

7. You may perceive some threats to the well-being of your family that you had better tackle. It could be a relationship

at work that is currently innocent, but could easily mushroom into a threat to your marriage. It could be a shaky financial investment that you realize you ought to get out of. It could be the need for some safety feature or repair in your car or house. As I discussed in a previous chapter, I became aware of the threats of junior high culture to my granddaughter and felt that I could help fortify her against them. We need to be alert to the threats to our well-being and diligent in combating those threats.

8. Finally, you have probably identified some characteristic of your personality that you would like to change. None of us are satisfied with what we are. That task of trying to change ourselves is a very difficult one, and we should probably talk more about it in this chapter.

I would like to tell you what I have discovered about the difficult process of changing oneself.

Because it is difficult to change our personal characteristics, I expected that the men and women in my discussion groups would say that they had not changed much. I was surprised to hear so many of them say they felt they had changed considerably. However, they confessed that they changed because it was essentially forced upon them. Each of us has some characteristic that is counterproductive. In their cases, their undesirable characteristics had produced such damaging consequences, in either their marriages or their employment, that it was a matter of changing or losing those marriages or employment. They felt it was important to go through the kind of introspection we were having in the class so we could recognize the need for change at an earlier, non-crisis stage. Otherwise the "grapes of wrath" continue to mature, as they put it, and the situation is pretty far gone when we finally discover the negative impact we are having on our spouse, our children, or fellow workers.

Sometimes we are prompted to change when we reflect on the characteristics of our parents. What was it we admired in our parents? What was it that we abhorred in our parents? A number of women said that they were inclined to be critical because their mothers had been so critical. Having experienced the destructive impact of their mothers' personality, they wanted to change their own behavior. Several men had a similar reaction to their fathers' controlling nature. A surprising number wanted to reverse a pattern of destructive behavior or attitude that had theretofore been passed down from one generation to another. Have you inherited any characteristic that you can see is really unhealthy and you would like to change? Have you drifted away from some of the wonderful qualities of your parents or grandparents, and do you want to reinforce those qualities in your own self?

In addition to trying to check myself on the desirable qualities that I want to have, I also try to check whether I have begun to slip into some undesirable qualities. I ask myself, Do I show signs of becoming

- Self-centered? How important to me are the needs and welfare of others compared to my own?
- Hardhearted? Do I have sympathy and compassion, or do I steel my heart and shut my eyes when I become aware of oppression or affliction?
- Lustful? Am I reasonably content with what I have, or am I always hungry for more (enough is never really enough)?
- Envious? Do I have a grudging resentment of what others have, or get, or are?
- Haughty? Do I delight in seeing myself above or before others? Do I consider others inferior? or inconsequential? Am I too eager to have my virtues exalted?
- Arrogant? Do I insist on having my own way? Do I use the power I have to get my way, even if that manipulates others or ignores their rights?
- Bitter? Am I bitter toward any other person or about some situation?
- Infected with a persecution complex? How often do I feel that my rights are being violated or that I am a victim?

- Contentious? Do I have a spirit of contention and try to provoke arguments?
- Devious? Am I honest and straightforward, or do I find myself using devious methods to avoid confrontation or difficulty or to get my own way?
- Unfaithful? Do I fulfill my commitments and responsibilities, or find convenient excuses when it becomes difficult or inconvenient?
- Slanderous? How often do I repeat untruths or unexamined accusations about someone?

If I see any signs of those, I want to make a special effort to reverse that trend.

It may be we want to rebalance a pair of our complimentary attributes. Contentment and dissatisfaction are complementary attributes. To live successfully, we need a certain amount of contentment and a certain amount of dissatisfaction (in order to be motivated to change). We have problems if we lean too much toward one extreme of a complementary pair of attributes. Appendix C lists pairs of such complementary attributes that we might want to rebalance.

Once we know what qualities we want to change, we embark on the difficult process of changing ourselves.

The Process of Changing Ourselves

Some people feel that we can change ourselves by our own power if we will just work at it hard enough and apply the right set of disciplines. Other people believe that it is impossible to change ourselves and that we make a big mistake to try. They say we should concentrate on opening ourselves to the Holy Spirit and that then the Spirit will transform our personalities so that we exhibit the *fruits of the Spirit*, which include the attributes we desire.

I don't think either of these extremes is right, but that the right course is a combination. I think we all agree that we cannot change ourselves solely through our own power. But does that mean that we don't need to *work* to improve in specific attributes? I believe that we cannot change without the help of the Holy Spirit, but that there are certain disciplines we have to exercise, in cooperation with the Holy Spirit, if we want to improve in a given attribute.

I decided that I should try to become more *patient*. One thing I did was to use a concordance to discover scriptures that relate to patience and then see what those scriptures teach. My study of the scriptures revealed that God expects me to *strive* to be patient. I have to work at it! Paul's writings say that many times. Consider the following examples:

- In Romans 12:1, Paul writes, "I appeal to you, brethren, by the mercies of God, to present your bodies as a living sacrifice, holy and acceptable to God, which is your reasonable worship . . . be patient. . . ." He doesn't say, "seek patience" or even "pray for patience," although those are undoubtedly good things to do. He says, "*Be* patient."
- Then, in Ephesians 4, he says, "I, therefore, a prisoner for the Lord, beg you to *lead a life* worthy of the calling to which you have been called, with all lowliness and meekness, with patience. . . ." He says, "lead a life . . . with patience." That implies intentionality and effort.
- In Colossians 3:12 he says, " *put on then*, as God's chosen ones, holy and beloved, compassion, kindness, lowliness, meekness, patience . . ." He tells us to put on patience. It is something we have to put on; nobody puts it on us.
- Again, in 1 Thessalonians 5:14, "And we exhort you, brethren, admonish the elders, encourage the fainthearted, help the weak, be patient with them all." There's that "be" again.

Well, I'm sorry. I just can't "be patient." I've tried. But one thing I know, I can't expect the Spirit to do all the work, or that patience will come automatically if I pray enough for it. I have to work at it.

I have become convinced that if we want to improve in one of these Christlike characteristics, we have to have a combination of knowledge and discipline. We have to, first of all, have knowledge about that particular characteristic, and then we have to have a process which will train us up in that particular characteristic.

If we want to accomplish change, a few things are required:

1. First of all, we need a strong desire for that particular kind of change. Stan Johnson once said in one of his sermons, "Usually we won't change until we get to the point where we are so exasperated we explode: 'I'm just not going to live like this anymore'!" Maybe that's what it takes. But we would like to think that if we live intentionally, we could make some changes before the present becomes intolerable and change is forced upon us.

2. We also need a strong belief that the changes are possible. We might feel that the changes are too difficult and that to try to change will only lead to frustration. We might think it would be better to not try! We need to be convinced that "I can change those things, at least somewhat!"

3. Then, during the process of change, we need a few things to keep from becoming discouraged:

    a) We need a recognition that personal growth and other changes involve a long, continuing process—they usually aren't accomplished quickly.

    b) We need to be satisfied with gradual, stepwise progress—no progress for a while and then a change, perhaps noticeable only by hindsight.

    c) We need to avoid becoming discouraged by an occasional setback—they will occur. That is like the problem I had with my knee after I fell and tore some ligaments. Some days I felt that my knee was really getting better. At other times it gave me such pain that I didn't know whether I had gone back to square one. And occasionally I did something that hurt it again, and I had a major setback. However, when I took the longer view, by hindsight, I could see that it slowly got better, but with real ups and downs.

4. We need to break up our effort into manageable pieces. That means that a) we have incremental objectives (we don't look to become totally patient, but only somewhat more patient); b) each presents a stimulating challenge (not a trivial improvement); c) we are able to measure progress; d) we have a realistic time scale. We shouldn't try to do the whole thing at once. We just need to break off a piece and work with that.

5. An important assist in accomplishing change is to have someone who knows what we are trying to do, and who will both support us and also hold our feet to the fire. This can be our spouse, our children, a close friend, or a small group of intimates. It can also be a professional counselor who has substantial experience helping people who want to change. Those persons will affirm us when they see us take a step in the right direction, and they will stimulate us when they see us backsliding. We have to approach each day as an opportunity to reinforce the new pattern, and we can use help in that reinforcement.

6. Finally, we need to use the manual that God has given us, the Bible. I have found very practical helps by using my Bible, concordance, and Bible dictionary. I will show you how in appendix D.

In appendix D, I have included some notes on my own attempt to grow more patient as an example. I hope this appendix will be of help to you if you want to improve in a given personal attribute.

Having thought about the things you might like to change in your life, it is time to plan specific actions.

Things You Are Going to Do Next

Now it is time to ask yourself the crucial questions about specific things you are going to undertake next:

- What particular personal relationships in your life are you going to immediately try to improve, and what specifically are you going to do now to begin that process?
- What are some of the things you are going to do next to improve the well-being of your family?
- What are some of the patterns of thought or behavior you are going to try to modify soon, and what particular steps are you going to take to do that?
- What are some of the things you are going to do next to improve your health and fitness (physical, mental, spiritual)?
- What are some of the things you are going to do next to improve your lifestyle and environment (house, yard, allocation of time, etc.)?
- Are there other things, not included in the above categories, that you want to achieve or accomplish soon? What first steps are you going to take?

There usually isn't a problem of thinking of some things that we want to do. The danger is that we think of too many and become overwhelmed by the task of accomplishing all those things. Which are the most important? Let's take them one or two at a time.

Conclusion

I can almost guarantee you that your efforts to think through the questions in this chapter and act upon your conclusions will produce gratifying results. I continually encounter people who have been through my discussion groups, and they're always eager to tell me how their life was changed by the process. The most common lament is that they didn't go through this exercise when they were younger. They are convinced that their lives would have been different and more satisfying.

You are probably familiar with some of the published interviews with people who have had *near-death experiences* (NDE). These are people who appeared to have died as the result of heart attack, car accident, surgery, or other trauma, but were successfully resuscitated. Dr. Raymond Moody, Jr., in his book, *The Light Beyond*, reports on his interviews of over a thousand such people, as well as some similar studies by others.* He describes the NDEs as related to him by these people, as well as the ways in which their lives were changed by the NDE. Three aspects seem particularly relevant to our study. The first is that "after the NDE, people tend to declare that life is precious, that it's the 'little things' that count, and that life is to be lived to the fullest." (p. 39). The second is that "all NDEers feel more responsible for the course of their lives." (p. 36). They are more careful in choosing their actions, especially if they have experienced the instantaneous "life review" where they witness all the actions they have done and also feel the reactions of other people to those actions. The third is that NDEers "have newfound respect for knowledge." They seem convinced that acquired knowledge is carried over into the afterlife and that we continue to learn in the afterlife. "The short time they were exposed to the possibility of total learning made them thirst for knowledge when they returned to their bodies"— knowledge that helped them to become whole persons. (p. 35). We may or may not have confidence in the reality and implications of these NDEs. But even the possibility of their truth, strongly reinforces our desire to live intentionally.

Let us remember what we said at the end of chapter 5. We have to recognize the following truths:

- *Living intentionally* is easier for some persons than for others. Some people will be naturally inclined to live in this way. It will be quite foreign and difficult for others.

---

* *The Light Beyond*, Raymond A. Moody, Jr., M.D., (Bantam Books: N.Y.) 1988.

- The same principles, described in this book, apply for everyone, no matter what their proficiency in living intentionally; no matter that each person has a very different situation in detail; or that their particular forks and dislocations may be quite different.
- We need to first put our toes in the water, then try to wade, and finally learn to swim. The important thing is to try to live a little *more* intentionally, not necessarily to become a master at it.
- Whatever effort we apply to this, even if only a little or at an elementary level, will enhance our lives.
- Every person is capable of doing enough of this type of introspection, with the help of suggestions contained in this book, to substantially benefit his or her life.

It helps to remember that the Lord is on our side and will help us to improve our lives.

We remember what God promised, "Fear not, for I am with you; be not dismayed, for I am your God. I will strengthen you and help you; I will uphold you with my righteous right hand" (Isa. 41:10).

Then there is Paul's encouragement: "I am confident of this, that He who began a good work in you will carry it on to completion until the day of Christ Jesus" (Phil. 1:6), and "For God did not give us a spirit of timidity or fear, but a spirit of power, love and self-discipline" (2 Tim. 1:7).

Then there is my favorite scripture: "Surely God is my salvation; I will trust and not be afraid. The Lord, the Lord, is my strength and my song; he has become my salvation. With joy you will draw water from the wells of salvation" (Isa. 12:2–3).

May the Lord be your strength and your song as you try to do the things you have decided upon. Don't forget to

- Draw water from the wells that are already available to you, (remember the resources we talked about in chapter 8).

- Have as one of your goals the digging of new wells, which will be a source of strength for you in the future as you try to live intentionally, including dealing with the forks in your path and coping with some of the dislocations we have talked about.

Synopsis

- In deciding what to do next, I need to think about various arenas of my life: my economic state; my employment; my family situation; the expenditure of my time and energy; my health; my state of happiness/unhappiness.
- In each of these areas I need to evaluate how I feel about them now and also how they will look in the future if I don't make some changes.
- Considering my present trajectory (both where I am and where I seem to be heading), what specific changes would I like to see in the person I am? in what I am likely to accomplish in the coming years? in the relationships of my life? in my lifestyle?
- What do I need/want to confront at this time: decisions to be made; changes in the allocation of my time and energy; modifications of house, yard, autos, etc; people I want to pay more attention to; other relational situations; preparations for future events; changes in my personality?
- If we want to change some aspect of our personality (the hardest change of all), we have to recognize that we cannot change without the help of the Holy Spirit, but that there are certain disciplines we have to exercise to cooperate with the Holy Spirit. The Bible makes clear that we have to *work* at accomplishing change.
- We have to recognize the following truths:

  a) *Living intentionally* is easier for some persons than for others.

b) The same principles apply for everyone, no matter what their proficiency in living intentionally; no matter that each person has a very different situation in detail; that their particular forks and dislocations may be quite different.

c) We need to first put our toes in the water, then try to wade, finally learn to swim. The important thing is to try to live a little *more* intentionally, not necessarily to become a master at it.

d) Whatever effort we apply to this, even if only a little or at an elementary level, will enhance our lives.

e) Every person is capable of doing enough of this type of introspection to substantially benefit his or her life.

- Remember, the Lord is on your side and will help you to live intentionally.

Personal Reflection

This chapter is filled with many specific questions for personal reflection. But by way of summary, you might ask yourself:

- Have you been specific in identifying those changes you want to see in your life? What are the few most important changes?

- Do you see some specific things you can do next to initiate some of those important changes?

- Do you think your spouse and family would be enthusiastic about those changes and would collaborate in accomplishing them?

- Do you have someone who will help you (holding you responsible for the commitment you have made to yourself, stimulating you to make progress and encouraging you as you take steps in the right direction)?

Points I Want to Come Back To

Later, when I have more time, I want to think more about the following sections, questions, or ideas associated with this chapter:

_____

_____

_____

_____

_____

_____

_____

_____

_____

Our Uniqueness

CHAPTER 12

Personal Characteristics

Can you describe your SHAPE?
By your SHAPE I do not mean whether you are tall and thin, or whether you are wide around the middle. SHAPE is an acronym that is used by some to remember the different aspects of a person's individuality. Your SHAPE is what you are as a person, what you bring to any relationship and to any situation, and what you should keep in mind when making vital decisions. Let us use this acronym to designate the following dimensions we need to consider in describing any person:

S: *strengths* and *skills* (and, by contrast, weaknesses and limitations). All of us have some things we can do especially well, as well as other things for which we might better rely on someone else.

H: *heart* (our passions, our values, the things that deeply concern us). All of us have something to which we want to apply our strengths and skills because our hearts are in it.

A: *attitudes* (including our preferences and our inclinations). Our behavior is shaped by our attitudes.

P: *personality type* (extrovert vs. introvert, energetic vs. lethargic, etc.). We go about things in different ways because our personalities are of various types.

E: *experience* (what we have learned from our history). Our past experience and personal history have shaped our strengths and skills, our hearts, our attitudes, and even our personalities.

How complex a person is! Have you ever tried to enumerate the many things that describe your uniqueness? or that of a friend?

Let me try to describe my friend Bill. Bill is forty, an accountant, is married to Sally and has two children, a boy twelve and a girl nine. He is five feet eleven inches with a large frame, and happens to be a good golfer with a handicap of ten.

Those are the first things we might say about Bill when someone asked us about him. I would call those things some of the *facts* of Bill's life. Such facts are definite and measurable. They are relevant to Bill's personhood, but they don't help you to really know or understand him. They don't define how he behaves, or what goes on inside of him, or what motivates him.

Now let me add that Bill is a very careful worker. He does things thoroughly, persistently, logically, faithfully, honestly, and joyfully. Now we are beginning to discover some of Bill's *traits*. Traits describe the way that a person does things, rather than what he does, and also the roles that he acts out—whether he is a leader, a bully, a victim, childish, dependent, or something else.

All of those things can be ascertained by observing Bill's actions. If you observe him long enough, you will also discover some of Bill's *virtues* and his *skills*. Bill is honest, faithful, fruitful (produces abundant and good output), and is a very genuine person (without guile or deception). Those are some of his virtues. You might guess from his profession that he is very good with numbers, but you might not also realize that he is a master woodworker and also an accomplished pianist. He has a number of other skills. On the other hand, Bill has his limitations: he is not very empathetic (has little ability to walk in someone else's shoes) and consequently is not very compassionate (willing to share another's burden or inclined to try to relieve another's pain). He also doesn't like to work in a mode where he has to dovetail his work with that of other people or be a working part of a team—he's a lone ranger.

By now you are beginning to get a pretty good picture of Bill. But, if you really want to know and understand him, you will have to learn some of the things that lie behind his outward traits and his behavior. He would have to relate to you some of his key *beliefs, values,* and *fears.* Those are the things that fundamentally underlie why Bill does things the way he does. Most of us could identify some of the strong beliefs and values we have, but it may not be easy to identify our fears. They are often disguised and obscure to us. However, it pays to try to identify our fears so that we can recognize how influential they are in our attitudes, behaviors, and goals.

Often values, skills, and traits will complement each other. That would occur because someone who has a particular value will probably develop skills along that line, and then is also inclined to act accordingly, which shows up as a trait.

We know that we want to take into account our own particular idiosyncrasies when deciding our forks, responding to our dislocations, and in taking advantage of our "occasions." From our picture of Bill, we see it takes a multitude of parameters to define one's self. First, there is the host of personal characteristics, that describe our personality, including personal skills and dependencies, preferences and aversions, limitations, etc. Then there are the beliefs, values, and attitudes that underlie so much of our behavior, and also play such a big factor in our decisions. We also realize that our decisions are shaped by what has already happened in our lives so far, and by the families to which we belong. All of those are important in understanding ourselves well enough to make wise decisions, and to really live intentionally. In this chapter we will say a little more about personal characteristics, move to the beliefs and attitudes in the next chapter, and then discuss our family history in the final chapter.

Personal Variations

We want to try to be explicit about our own personal characteristics. We need to know our own desires, attributes, etc., in order to live intentionally. We also need to be cognizant of the characteristics of others with whom we interact: spouse, children, others. It is essential that we recognize how we are similar and how we may differ. So, let us talk about how we are different.

When we think about personal variations, we realize that we are different in a variety of dimensions. I have labeled some of these variations: *temperament*; *social* (some of us are introverts and some extroverts); *sensory* (some of us are more attuned to sounds, some to sights, some to movements and actions); *perceptive* (some are more logical, some intuitive, and some affective); and then there is the *planetary* dimension (whether we are more Martian or Venusian.)

The following chart illustrates what I mean by variations in *temperament*.

Temperament:	Theoretic	Economic	Aesthetic	Idealistic
Attribute:	logical	practical	sensual	personal
Occupied with:	what I can understand	what I can do	what feels good	what is sound
Values:	intelligence reason	efficiency responsibility	beauty freedom enjoyment	truth authenticity health
Currency:	ideas	abilities	feelings	ideals
Vocation:	science	business	arts	religion, medicine

Those four temperaments are theoretic, economic, aesthetic, idealistic.*

1. The *theoretic* person is very logical and occupies himself with what he can understand. He values intelligence and reason and deals primarily with ideas. He may well excel in a field of science.
2. The *economic* person is very practical and occupies himself with what he can do. He values efficiency and responsibility and deals primarily with abilities. He may do well in business.
3. The *aesthetic* is sensual and occupies himself with what feels good. He loves beauty, freedom, and enjoyment, and deals primarily with feelings. Many of the people in the arts are aesthetics.
4. The *idealistic* is very personal and occupies himself with what is sound or right. He values truth, authenticity, and health, and deals primarily with ideals. We find such people in religion and medicine.

Probably none of us is purely one of these temperament types. We are each admixtures of all of them, but one or more usually predominates. Before thinking about it much, I felt like I was a real theoretic type—perhaps 85 percent theoretic; 5 percent economic; 5 percent aesthetic; 5 percent idealistic. Now that I have thought more about it, I feel that I am much closer to an even distribution,

---

* There is a long history of describing individuals in terms of four temperaments. Twenty four hundred years ago, Hippocrates used four, which he called choleric, phlegmatic, melancholic, and sanguine. In succeeding years other writers used somewhat different divisions and names. In 1920 Spranger used theoretic, economic, artistic, and religious. I have found a book by David Keirsey and Marilyn Bates most helpful (*Please Understand Me*, D. Keirsey & M. Bates, Prometheus Nemesis Book Co., Del Mar, CA 92014, 1978). It was from their descriptions that I formulated this chart. Another shorter booklet, which can be very helpful to the reader who wants to learn more about this, is by Isabel Myers Briggs (*Introduction to Type*, Consulting Psychologists Press, Inc., 577 College Ave., Palo Alto, CA 94306, 1980)

perhaps 40 percent theoretic; 30 percent economic; 20 percent aesthetic; 10 percent idealistic. Would someone who is primarily aesthetic have as much interest in this book as a theoretic person would? Perhaps if I were not theoretic I would not have written it. I think it would be interesting to see in what order a given person would list his goals, values, skills, and traits. We might expect the theoretic to list his goals first, the economic to first put down his skills, the aesthetic his traits first, and the idealistic his values. I wonder if it would be better to be an even mixture of the types (25/25/25/25) or almost a pure type (e.g., 5/5/85/5)? Perhaps to enjoy all aspects of life it would be better to be an even mixture, but for real excellence we might need to be almost a pure type. For instance, an excellent musician or painter might need to be highly aesthetic (5/5/85/5).

The difference between men and women is also very important. A man or a woman could be the same blend of theoretic, economic, aesthetic and idealistic. But are there fundamental differences between men and women? Do women think the way men do? Do they tend to react similarly or differently?

Male/Female; Martians/Venusians

John Gray wrote a book called *Men Are from Mars, Women Are from Venus.*[*] His overall thesis is that men and women by nature have very different instincts and inclinations. Those differences are so contradictory that it is as if men and women came from different planets. The differences exist particularly in the ways that each sex reacts to stress and the way they are inclined to support each other. Men tend to react to women and to support them in the way that men would want to be supported, but that is not the way women want to be supported (and vice versa). Each sex will also misinterpret the actions of the other if they are not aware of those differences. Therefore conflict easily arises. We need to understand the differences and take them into account in the way we react to others. When we act in accordance with this understanding, we create harmony instead of conflict.

---

[*] *Men Are From Mars, Women Are From Venus,* John Gray (Harper Collins: NY) 1992.

Let us consider briefly the two different personality types, Martians and Venusians. It does seem that many men recognize themselves in the description of Martians and many women see their tendencies in the description of Venusians, but we don't want to get hung up on whether all men are Martians and all women Venusians. Think of these differences, which were cited by Gray, and see where you can recognize yourself.

Some of the major contrasts between Martians and Venusians, as well as the problems that can arise because of their differences, are as follows:

- Martians especially value power, competency, efficiency, and achievement. Venusians would put communication and relationships higher on their list of values.
- Martians experience fulfillment primarily through success and accomplishment. Venusians experience fulfillment through the quality of relationships and the sharing of feelings.
- Martians need to win, even if a friend loses in the process. Venusians are accustomed to giving (losing) so that others may prosper (win). Martians may get tired of always having to win. Venusians may get tired of always giving. Venusians need to learn how to receive, while Martians have to learn how to give up.
- A Martian's greatest fear is that he is not good enough or that he is incompetent. A Venusian is afraid of needing too much and then not being supported; she hesitates to express her need.
- When a Martian has a problem, he expects to solve it himself, and retreats into his cave to deal with it alone. When a Venusian has a problem, she seeks someone who will share her feelings and her distress about the problem.
- A Martian feels good about himself when he quietly solves his problems on his own. A Venusian feels good about herself when she has loving friends with whom she can share her feelings and problems.

- Because Martians understand that Martians want to solve their own problems, they try not to offer advice unless it is asked for; to offer a Martian unsolicited advice is to presume that he doesn't know what to do, or that he can't do it on his own. However, Venusians believe giving advice and suggestions is a sign of caring, and they are eager to do that.

- Since a Martian is fulfilled by working out the intricate details of his problem in solitude, it is natural for him to try to find relief from the stress of a major problem by withdrawing and dealing with little problems that he *can* solve. He doesn't want to talk! He may want to go into the garage and tinker, or even want to watch a football game on TV, observing others deal with problems. But since a Venusian is fulfilled through talking about the details of her problems and sharing her feelings about it, talking is the natural and healthy way for a Venusian to find relief from such stress. She doesn't want the Martian to withdraw! Withdrawing and not talking are the natural course for a Martian, but totally unnatural for a Venusian and misunderstood by them.

- Martians talk about problems primarily for one of two reasons: They are seeking advice, or they are blaming someone. A Martian assumes a Venusian is talking to him about one of her problems either because she wants help or because she is holding him responsible for her problem. He reacts accordingly. However, a Venusian doesn't want solutions or to blame anyone; she just wants to find relief by expressing herself and being understood. Venusians talk about problems to get close, not to get solutions. When the Martian offers a quick fix or rebels against being "blamed," she gets upset. For those same reasons, a Martian becomes frustrated when a Venusian talks about problems where he can't help.

- Martians and Venusians use the same words, but they mean different things. A Venusian sees that something is troubling a Martian, and she asks him about it. He responds, "It's nothing." What he means is, "Nothing is bothering me that I can't handle alone. Please don't ask any more questions about it." However, she interprets him to mean, "I don't know what is bothering me. I need you to ask me questions to assist me in discovering what is happening or how to handle it." So she tries to help him by asking unwanted questions. Furthermore, Martians tend to interpret words literally because they use words to convey specific facts and information; Venusians express their feelings with poetic license, using superlatives, metaphors, and generalizations. One of the big challenges for Martians is to correctly interpret and support a Venusian when she is expressing her feelings; the biggest challenge for Venusians is to correctly interpret and support a Martian when he isn't talking. Silence is most easily misinterpreted by Venusians. The only time a Venusian would be silent is when what she had to say was hurtful or when she didn't want to talk to a person because she didn't trust him. No wonder Venusians become insecure when a Martian suddenly becomes quiet!

- A Venusian is very sensitive about being heard and feeling understood; a Martian is very sensitive about feeling trusted and accepted, just the way he is.

- Martians want space. Even when a Martian loves a Venusian he needs to periodically pull away before he can get closer. A Martian can get moody and irritable when he gets too close and isn't allowed to pull back. If he is allowed to withdraw for a while, he will rebound with renewed vigor and enthusiasm. However, Venusians don't like to let him withdraw because they interpret that as rejection. Just as Martians have their oscillations between wanting to be close and pulling away, so Venusians also have their oscillations. They rise and fall in their ability to love themselves and others. Venusians are capable of intense feelings of love, happiness, trust, and gratitude. We marvel at that ability. But they can't keep it up indefinitely. Periodically they also will feel anger, sadness, fear, and sorrow. They go into a depression. Martians need to be patient. If they wait a while, the Venusians will rise again. When a Venusian goes down into her well, she deals with her negative emotions and finds emotional rejuvenation. But Martians are not good at waiting. They will try to talk the Venusian out of her depression. Telling a Venusian she shouldn't feel hurt is about the worst thing a Martian can say. Just sympathize with her. Venusians want understanding. Martians argue for the right to be free; Venusians argue for the right to be upset.

Gray suggests the following guidance for Martians and Venusians in learning to accomodate to each other:

- A Martian should learn that a Venusian is looking for understanding and a chance to express herself, not for quick fixes. If you are a Martian, listen whenever a Venusian speaks, and try to show her you understand what she is going through. Bite your tongue whenever you get the urge to offer a solution or change how she is feeling.
- A Venusian should learn that when a Martian withdraws to deal with his problem, he is not rejecting her. Refrain from pursuing him. Also remember that he does not welcome helpful suggestions for improvement, because that suggests he isn't competent to handle it adequately. If you are a Venusian, refrain from giving any unsolicited advice or criticism.
- When a Venusian brings up a subject or problem, a Martian will typically go silent. The Venusian can easily think he is not responding because he's not interested or he feels what she has said is not important. However, he is more likely saying, "I don't yet know what to say, but I am thinking about it." Martians should always try to respond to whatever a Venusian says, even if it is only some sign that he is still connected, like, "oh," "uh-huh," or "hmmm."

- Venusians need to have intimate friends because of their need for relationship and expressing their feelings, and because of the Martian's need to withdraw and be silent. When a Venusian goes into the doldrums and her partner is working things out alone in his den, it is essential that she have other friends to provide support. Otherwise she will feel powerless and resent her partner's absence.

It seems to me that Gray has accumulated some marvelous insights about contrasting personality types. Here, too, each person may be a blend of the two types, but one type predominates. When I read Gray's book, I recognized a lot of my Martian characteristics, and I realized that I tend to expect others to react the way I would react. I welcome each reminder that we are as likely to be different as we are to be similar, and that I need to take the differences into account in order to have congenial relationships. So I need to know myself, and I need to be sensitive to the ways in which others are different.

Other Types

There are a variety of other types into which we might sort our differences. Among these are the *sensory* types, the *social* types, and the *perception* types.

SENSORY TYPES

The sensory types are *auditory*, *visual,* and *kinesthetic*. It is surprising how much one of those senses predominates in our personalities. Our dominant sense is reflected in how we seek tranquility, remember, spend our time, learn, react to other people, sense what other people are really saying and feeling, and communicate to others; as well as the qualities about which we are most self-conscious and the way in which we are most effectively convinced.

At first I thought I was kinesthetic because I find that I learn best through the act of writing notes. I did that in school; I do it during the sermon in church. I also find that I know how to do something only after I have done it once. But after reflection I have concluded that I am a strong mixture of all three, but primarily auditory. For instance, if I want to be peaceful, I do want to be comfortable (kinesthetic) and be in a spot where the view is pleasant (visual), but the thing that most contributes to a feeling of serenity is to hear water lapping on the rocks at the edge of a lake or stream and to hear an occasional bird chirping in a predominantly quiet ambience (auditory). Also, I am most disturbed by noise or disharmony. I have found that the following examples are helpful in discerning whether our emphasis is auditory, visual, or kinesthetic:

- The things that are most conducive to tranquility for me are "soft, pleasant sounds against a quiet background"; "a beautiful setting or having my eyes closed"; "relaxation and physical comfort." I am particularly bothered by "noise or disharmony"; "clutter or clashing colors"; "discomfort or sadness."
- I remember best by recreating "what was said or how it sounded"; "a picture of how it looked"; "a sense of how I felt or reacted."
- I love to "talk and discuss"; "read or watch"; "go out and do things."
- I learn best by "being told"; "by watching or by reading"; "by actually doing it myself one or more times."
- When things seem right I tend to say: "that sounds right to me"; "that looks right to me"; "that feels right to me."
- In my imagination I can best visualize how something "sounds"; "looks"; "feels."
- When talking to another person, I am most profoundly influenced by "her tone of voice"; "the look on her face"; "what I am feeling or sense that she is feeling."
- I admire someone with "a clear, strong voice"; "a sparkle in his eyes and a square jaw"; "a firm handshake and a warm embrace."
- For the impression I make, I am most concerned with "what I say and how I say it"; "my appearance and how I look"; "the mood I convey or how I affect other's feelings."

- I most often communicate in words that are related to "sound" (such as "noisy"); "sight" (such as "hazy"); "feel" (such as "confusing or clumsy").
- In order to believe it, I need to "hear it with my own ears"; "see it with my own eyes"; " touch it with my own hands."

Note that Christ can be equally real to each type, as described in 1 John 1:1–2, "That which was from the beginning, which we have heard, which we have seen with our own eyes, which we have looked upon and touched with our hands, concerning the word of life . . . was made manifest to us."

SOCIAL TYPES

The social types are *extrovert* and *introvert*. I used to think I was an extrovert, since I have always been in leadership positions and quite public. But, I have concluded that I am fundamentally an introvert. This is for a variety of reasons, including these:

- I tend to be "introspective, private, internal" rather than "gregarious, open, external."
- I tend to "become exhausted when involved with too many people, and prefer to work quietly and alone," whereas extroverts tend to be "bored when they are alone, but stimulated when they are with people."
- When in doubt "I want to think and sleep on it" rather than wanting to "brainstorm with people about it."
- When under stress "I want to be alone" rather than feeling that "I need contact with other people."
- I have very few "close friends," whereas I think extroverts tend to have "many friends and acquaintances."
- I prefer "solitary spiritual disciplines" and get less "pleasure out of shared devotions."

Considering these factors, would you view yourself as an extrovert or an introvert?

PERCEPTION TYPES

The perception types are *logical, intuitive,* and *affective.* The primary difference here is whether we tend to think things through very logically and can trace the series of steps by which we reach a conclusion (logical), or our minds instinctively reach conclusions without our being able to trace the sequence of steps (intuitive), or we reach conclusions based more on perceptions of our hearts rather than perceptions of our brains (affective). I am very logical, but my wife is intuitive. She just reaches conclusions by some undecipherable mental process, and she is usually right without being able to trace out the logic for you. I also have some friends who disdain logic and are happy to be totally affective. Here are some clues to these types:

- How do you reach conclusions? The logical person might say, "I need to have facts, which I can organize into a series of logical steps." The intuitive person: "My brain seems to integrate impressions into a conclusion and I don't know where it comes from, but I have learned to trust it." The affective person: "I go with what I feel is right."
- You want me to make a decision? "You need to tell me the pros and cons in order for me to form a judgment" (logical); or "Don't bother me with details, just paint for me the big picture" (intuitive); or "tell me why you're for it" (affective).
- What do I like to deal with? "What can be seen, felt, heard" (logical); or "what I can visualize, imagine, conceive" (intuitive); or "those things for which I have a strong instinct" (affective).
- What kind of people do I most value? "I particularly value people with common sense who face reality" (logical); or "I particularly value people who visualize with imagination" (intuitive); or "I particularly value people who have an instinct for the right or best path" (affective).

We realize that these variations in type of personality are the spice of life—how dull life would be if we were all the same! But why is it important for us to understand our own type as well as to discern the types of the other people with whom we interact? We need to understand our own so that we will make the right decisions for ourselves. It can make a big difference in what employment I select, in how I spend my time and energy, in the things I will emphasize in my living and working environment. We spent good money in the design and decoration of our backyard to accommodate our aesthetic tastes. This included a small waterfall after I realized the role that the sound of water plays in my tranquility. Now we don't need to seek peace away from home, but can revel in it in our own backyard.

When we understand such things about other people with whom we interact (our spouse, our friend, our employer, our customer, etc.) and take them into account in our relationships, harmony is created instead of conflict. Our human interactions are enriched and misunderstandings are minimized.

Synopsis

- In a sense we are like an onion: a number of layers that can be peeled away to reveal an even more basic underlayer, which provides shape and substance to the outer layers. The most superficial and obvious layer comprises the *facts* of our lives. Facts are definite and measurable, and include things like age, sex, marital status, profession, etc. More important to what the person is really like or how he/she behaves are his/her *traits, virtues, skills,* and *limitations.* Even these don't define what goes on inside of that person or what motivates him or her. If you really want to know and understand a person, you will have to learn some of the things that lie behind his outward traits and his behavior. He would have to relate to you some of his key *beliefs, values* and *fears.* These are the things that fundamentally underlie why we behave the way we do.
- Most of us could identify some of the strong beliefs and values we have, but it may not be easy to identify our fears.

239

They are often disguised and obscure to us. However, it pays to try to identify our fears so we can recognize how influential they are in our attitudes, behaviors, and goals.

- Our personal differences come in a variety of dimensions: *temperament* (theoretic, economic, aesthetic, idealistic); *social* (some of us are introverts and some extroverts); *sensory* (some of us are more attuned to sounds, some to sights, some to movements and actions); *perceptive* (some are more logical, some intuitive, and some affective); and then there is the *planetary* dimension (whether we are more Martian or Venusian.)

- We are never of a pure type, but a blend. We might be almost a pure type (5 percent theoretic, 85 percent economic, 5 percent aesthetic, and 5 percent idealistic) or an even mixture (25/25/25/25). Perhaps to enjoy all aspects of life, it would be better to be an even mixture, but if we want real excellence we might need to be almost a pure type. For instance, an excellent musician or painter might need to be highly aesthetic (5/5/85/5).

- Martians and Venusians are two different personality types where the differences are so drastic that it is as if the two types came from different planets. These types naturally have quite different instincts and inclinations. Their differences exist particularly in the ways that each type reacts to stress and the way they support each other. Martians tend to react to Venusians and to support them in the way that the Martians would want to be supported, but that is not the way Venusians want to be supported (and vice versa). Each will also misinterpret the actions of the other if they are not aware of the differences. Therefore conflict easily arises.

- We need to be explicit about our own personal characteristics, and we also need to understand such things about the other people with whom we interact: our spouse, our friend, our employer, our customer, etc. When we understand our own we will make better decisions for ourselves. When we understand our differences and take them into account in our relationships, harmony is created instead of conflict.

Personal Reflection

- Make a list of some of your preferences, inclinations, values, skills, and aspirations.
- Are you quite similar to or quite different from your spouse? How do you handle that? Have you changed over the years in order to accommodate your spouse? Has your spouse changed in order to accommodate you?
- What incompatibilities are there currently between your temperament, skills, preferences, style, etc., and the requirements of your work? What is the result of this?
- To what extent do you think we have to learn to be content with the personality we have, and to what extent do you think we ought to work at changing that characteristic which most disturbs us or gets us into the most trouble?
- What characteristic of yourself most disturbs you or gets you into the most trouble?

Points I Want to Come Back To

Later, when I have more time, I want to think more about the following sections, questions, or ideas associated with this chapter:

_____

_____

_____

_____

_____

_____

_____

_____

_____

CHAPTER 13

Beliefs and Attitudes

Archie is a very different person from Sam. Sam is a person who continually manipulates every situation and every person so as to maximize his own power, position, and personal reward. With Sam you want to beware! Archie behaves in a very different way. He spends a great deal of his time trying to help people who are less fortunate than he is, so that they can obtain some joy and satisfaction from their lives and surroundings. It is a joy to interact with Archie. What a contrast!

How can we explain this difference in behavior? I believe the explanation lies in the difference in *prevailing attitudes* and in *core beliefs*. Our traits and behaviors, which we considered in the previous chapter, are really an outward expression of our beliefs and attitudes. Our traits and behaviors are evident to other people; they can only guess at our beliefs and attitudes based on how we act. We can understand ourselves and others better when we begin to comprehend attitudes and beliefs.

The dictionary defines an attitude as "one's disposition, opinion, mental set." The adjective *prevailing* has three connotations, related to strength, frequency, and scope. A prevailing attitude is the attitude that seems to have the most influence on our behavior. A prevailing attitude is the one that is most noticeable and that we observe most frequently. A prevailing attitude is the mental set that seems to permeate so many of our actions, feelings, and thoughts. Sam's prevailing attitude is one of arrogance, selfishness, and competitiveness. Archie's is one of compassion and generosity.

We recognize that our prevailing attitudes stem from our core beliefs. *Core* beliefs are those which are most fundamental to the way we live. Sam's behavior and his prevailing attitude really stem from a basic belief that there is no purpose in life other than to obtain the most personal satisfaction from it and to survive as one of the "fittest." Sam believes that if you don't overwhelm the other person, you will be overwhelmed by him. His is a win-lose philosophy. Archie's behavior and his prevailing attitude stem from a belief that we were all created to be God's children, that everyone is supposed to share in the goodness of life, and that we have a responsibility toward each other. His is a win-win philosophy.

As you think about the way that you behave, can you identify an attitude that seems to lie behind many of your actions, feelings, and thoughts? Then, can you identify a core belief that seems to account for that attitude? Our attitudes and beliefs may not be immediately obvious, even to us, but it is important that we try to identify them, because they are at the root of the way we behave. What is it that seems to drive you?

As an illustration, I would like to discuss what I find to be my current prevailing attitude. Then, I want to discuss with you the issue of our beliefs, including the act of believing and the process by which we develop our convictions and establish our beliefs.

My Current Prevailing Attitude

When I try to decide what attitude seems to have the most influence on my behavior, I think of a combination of two closely related things: a) a compulsion to be productive, to make a difference, to use well the time and energy that I have; and b) a compulsion to pass on to others, especially my grandchildren, whatever wisdom I think I have accumulated in my 70+ years. Attitude a) is one I have had for years. The most recent embodiment of this attitude is manifested in attitude b). These are the attitudes that seem to permeate many of my actions, feelings, and thoughts. I seem to spend almost all of my time trying to be productive in general and to find ways to pass on my accumulated wisdom to my grandchildren and to others, through this book and the courses I conduct.

I have always found it hard to just relax and take it easy, because I feel that somehow I am wasting time. I have always felt that if I am not part of the solution, I am part of the problem. I am a problem-solver and leap at the opportunity to do something constructive. That inclination, which is more like a compulsion, is not altogether good. As usual, any good trait can be taken to an extreme, can be our undoing. We need to have balance.

Now, why am I so driven? Undoubtedly, some of that attitude was bred into me by my parents. Both of them were earnest workers. Both of them were eager for me to accomplish. So by their example and by their approval or disapproval, they inclined me toward productivity. My sister is very different from me in some respects, but in this respect we are the same.

Even though some of that attitude can be traced to my upbringing, it also reflects my earnest beliefs. I think it stems from my belief that we are on this earth for a purpose and, as I stated in chapter 4, my belief is that our purpose is to be good stewards of the time, energy, and opportunities we have been given. A good steward ensures that the vineyard is productive, that it yields good and abundant fruit. My attitude also stems from a belief that someday we will be invited to account for the stewardship of our lives. This is, of course, a consequence of believing in the existence of God and that He is not only loving, but also expects much from us. "From everyone who has been given much, much is expected" (Luke 12:48). How much differently another person thinks and acts if he believes that nothing exists beyond the physical world; that death is the end of existence and there is no God.

There is no doubt that my Christian faith shapes my attitudes. There is also no doubt that I often have attitudes that are not consistent with my Christian faith. These include, too often, an attitude of selfishness—looking to my own best interests without sufficient regard for the interests of others; or an attitude of criticism—finding fault with others and dwelling too much on their inadequacies; and I could go on. I could well say that the biggest attitude problem in my life is being too self-centered.

Sometimes I think that my *prevailing attitude* may be shaped more by my culture than by my Christian faith. The attitude that prevails is sometimes one of reaction, formed as a backlash to our current culture. On December 30, 1993, there was an article in the *San Jose Mercury News* about the phenomenon of backlash: its origins, symptoms, and consequences. The overall thesis of the writer was that our society is in a state of universal backlash, which is an unusually high state of rebellion against all movements and institutions.

This *backlash* is a product of unsettled feelings due to change, disillusionment, and fear. Many things are so up in the air in our culture. We realize we are on the verge of big change. At the time of the article the pending changes involved health care reform (which might have negative impact on the health care that many enjoy, so that all could have some health care), NAFTA, public education (should parents be given vouchers to send their children to any school, private as well as public?), etc. Those are all things that could quite profoundly change the life we were used to. At the same time, we are disillusioned about our government, about corporations we previously trusted (e.g., IBM abandoning their tradition of loyalty to the employee, GM faking a fiery crash of a pickup truck); about religious leaders (ministers who bilk congregations, pedophilic priests, etc.); about the media (slanting of information to advance their own leanings, liberal or conservative). In addition, we fear changes in the economy, assaults on children, proliferation of guns and violence, and many other things.

The symptoms of this backlash include rebellion against politics as usual (e.g., the popularity of Ross Perot and the Reform Party);

rebellion against the proliferation of movements ("save the ———";
"stop the ———"); rebellion against legitimate, but exaggerated
causes (gay rights, feminism, other "minorities"); distrust of religious institutions; distrust of corporations; distrust of media.

As a result of that backlash, we seek out other people who feel
as we do, commiserate with each other, and augment the backlash. People separate into narrow, like-minded cliques of victims
and reinforce each other via specialized newsletters and computer
bulletin boards. We become inclined to negative reactions to everything; we become numb to legitimate claims on our compassion and our drive for social justice wanes.

I confess to having some of those symptoms and wonder how
much of my attitude is one of *backlash*. I realize that I have to be
careful that my prevailing attitude is one that is worthy and purposeful, and not one of reaction.

When I think about what I *want* to have as my prevailing attitude, I think of my desire to have an attitude of gratitude permeate
my living, gratitude to God and to other people for what they mean
to me. However, after careful thought I would say that my *prevailing* attitude is a compulsion to establish my legacy. Perhaps all
older people want to ensure their legacy—to feel that they are going to leave an important part of themselves behind in their descendants and others. It does seem to me, though, that I have this
in an unusual degree. I would like to tell you how that attitude
manifests itself, as an example of the outworking of an attitude.

I realize that we all bear important fruit in a number of different categories.

- For those of us who have children, we think first of them,
  as the precious fruit of our marriages and of our lives. And
  we hope that fruit bears additional fruit, spreading our influence to succeeding generations.
- Other important fruit is the influence we have on other
  people, through our friendship, encouragement, teaching,
  leading them to faith, etc. People pay attention to what we
  say and do, and we can have a very positive effect on them.

We want to bear the "fruits of the Spirit" (Gal. 5:22) and are dismayed when we don't.

- Then we think of the work product that we produce in our vocation. We are paid to bear that fruit and, after our children, we probably put more energy into this fruit than any other. First of all there is the *direct* work product, which is the primary output of our employment. There is also our *indirect* work product, which is not the immediate purpose of our employment, but is more of a by-product, such as books we may author along the way, procedures we may generate and that we hope will survive us, plus contributions we make to the organizations with which we are associated by virtue of our profession.

- There are also things which we produce in our avocations. For example, some of us produce lovely things as a hobby. These may be objects (perhaps beautiful furniture) or perhaps wonderful performances that other people can enjoy (music, theater, etc.)

- We include the ways we help to shape institutions with which we are involved, such as the companies we have worked for, the church, community organizations and projects, the government, or universities.

- Finally, there are other forms of service, such as serving effectively on a church or community board.

What Fruit Really Counts?

I have thought about the things I have accomplished in these categories of fruit-bearing so far. And I have thought about what, of those things, I will leave behind me. How permanent are they? What is my legacy? To make a long story shorter, just let me say that I concluded that very little of the fruit we produce lasts more than one generation. It has been over fifteen years since I left IBM, and most of the people who knew who I was and what I had done are themselves leaving, and as time goes on more and more have died. Even the book I wrote on technology, which was so unique, became out-of-date and languishes on library shelves. Institutions that I worked so hard to shape and improve have gone through other phases under the influence of succeeding leaders. So none of these things last. I conclude that there are only two important things of eternal significance:

1. One is the influence on our children and our grandchildren, as well as other people in our lives. As I look back, I can see the influences of my forebears on me and my children, and know that the Bible is true when it says that our influences persist strongly through succeeding generations.
2. The second important thing is the quality of the story we write with our lives and our ability to say at the end along with Paul, "I have fought the good fight; I have finished the race; I have kept the faith" (2 Tim. 4:7).

What is the most important fruit of our lives? What should be our first priority? Dr. James C. Dobson is convinced that a man's top priority is to lead his children into the faith. He writes in his book *Straight Talk*, "According to the Christian values which govern my life, my most important reason for living is to get the gospel safely in the hands of my children."* He quotes from a letter from his father, which woke him up. The letter includes the following: "Danae is growing up in a world much farther gone into moral decline than the world into which you were born. I have observed that the greatest delusion is to suppose that our children will be devout Christians simply because their parents have been, or that any of them will enter into the Christian faith in any other way than through their parents' deep travail of prayer and faith. But this prayer demands time; time that cannot be given if it is all signed and conscripted and laid on the altar of career ambition. Failure for you at this point would make mere success in your occupation a very pale and washed-out affair, indeed."

Dobson writes, "He helped me realize that it is possible for mothers and fathers to love and revere God while systematically

---

* *Straight Talk* (Word Publishing: Dallas, TX) 1991.

losing their children." He refers to the stories of Eli and Samuel in 1 Samuel 2–4: Eli was too busy with the work of the church to be a leader in his own home. His two boys grew up to be evil young men. Samuel also was a saintly man of God who stood like a tower of spiritual strength throughout his life. He grew up in Eli's home and watched Eli lose his children. Even with that lesson, Samuel proceeded to fail with his family, too! Dobson realized, "If God would not honor Samuel's dedication by guaranteeing the salvation of his children, will he do more for me if I'm too busy to do my homework?"

He discovered that his maternal great-grandfather invested the hour from eleven to twelve each morning in intercessory prayer for his family. However, he was not only asking God to bless his children; he extended his request to generations not yet born! Toward the end of his life, the old man announced that God had made a very unusual promise to him. He was given the assurance that every member of four generations of his family would be Christians, including those yet to be born! Dobson then describes the amazing record of Christian testimony of all of the man's descendants through those four generations. He says it staggers his mind to realize that the prayers of that one man, spoken more than fifty years ago, reach across the generations of time and influence developments in his life today!

But Dobson recognizes he is a member of the fourth generation! It stops with him unless he does his "homework." "A tug of war is being waged for the hearts and minds of every child on earth. There is not enough knowledge in the books, not enough wisdom anywhere on earth, to guarantee the outcome of parenting. There are too many factors beyond our control—too many evil influences that mitigate against the Christian message." Believing that constant prayer is essential, he began to designate one day a week for fasting and prayer specifically devoted to the spiritual welfare of his children.

There is no higher calling on the face of the earth than to lead our children into the faith, and constant, intensive prayer on their behalf is essential to that. If you don't have children or grandchildren, pray for someone else's!

Surely the most important fruit of our lives is the influence we have on other people, especially our children. Now, how do we exert this influence?

How Do We Influence Others?

We all know that "our actions speak louder than our words." Yet we all have inconsistencies between our actions and what we want/intend to do. To have some inconsistency is human; to have gross inconsistency is hypocrisy. Our children, in particular, have a wonderful ability to see the inconsistency and can be bewildered by it—not knowing which message to believe or to follow. However, if we are honest with them, confessing our awareness of our inconsistency and our realization that no one can perfectly live up to his intentions, the children can accept and respect that. They also have their confusion resolved, and they can be a little more self-forgiving when *they* fail to live up to *their* intentions. The implication is that we need to have the same mutual tolerance with the adults with whom we interact.

Recognizing that we can't perfectly model what we want to teach, let us realize that we should teach by words *and* by actions. The way we can try to pass on the things that we have discovered to be good is to write them down (so that they will survive us in the form we want, and can be passed on, referred to, and absorbed) and also to try to model them. Let us first consider what we want to model.

What Do I Want to Model?

There are so many things I would like to model. I could make an endless list of attributes that I would like others to see in me. The list is surely too long to reflect on here. Besides, the most important list for you is the list that you, the reader, want to model. But, to give you an idea, I will pick out just a few things that I most want to convey to others, especially my grandchildren. As I have reflected on this, I would select the following:

- *Authenticity*. I want to be, and want my children and grandchildren to be, authentic: a real person without pretense; genuine; reasonably transparent (you see the real person as he is inside, not some fictional character he would like to be). Of course, everyone needs some privacy of thoughts and feelings, but I would like us to be without false masks.

- *Enthusiasm*. The term enthusiasm comes from the Greek word *enthousiasmos*, which means God-insideness (*en* [in] + *theos* [God]). When we have God inside us we can't help but be enthusiastic. Ralph Waldo Emerson said, "Nothing great was ever achieved without enthusiasm." A person who is enthusiastic has the following characteristics: positive (not negative); optimistic (emphasizing the possibilities, not the limitations); forward looking (benefiting from the past but not burdened by it); wholehearted (not half-hearted); fervent (not phlegmatic); zealous (not apathetic); passionate (not cold or lukewarm); spirited (not lethargic); unstinting (not holding back). We say someone is enthusiastic when we see that she has a zest: for life, for people, for opportunities, for the talents she has, for the work she has to do, etc. When we interact with such a person we can well feel, "Surely, God's Spirit is within this person." How I covet that for my children and grandchildren!

- *Gratitude*. I also want my children and grandchildren to be constantly grateful, constantly aware of what they have to be grateful for. I hope that I am that way and that I can model that for them. I was so thrilled when my grandson Drew, just as he was turning five, offered to say the blessing before our dinner. He proceeded to thank God for a number of things that were true that day: for the opportunity to be vacationing in such a beautiful spot, for the good health we were enjoying, for the opportunity to have Nanny and Papa there with them. I told him how much I appreciated his prayer and asked him where he learned to pray like that. He said, "I learned that from you, Papa." Isn't that thrilling?! It is easy for us to take for granted the blessings we enjoy, but my children and grandchildren will not do that if I can have the influence on them that I want to.

- *Caring.* I am also delighted to see that they are caring people. They care deeply about important issues and other people—especially their loved ones, but also the helpless, those without power or justice. And they are concerned enough to try to do something positive to encourage, nurture, empower, resolve conflicts, etc.

- *Commitment and Faithfulness.* I think we would have many fewer problems if everyone could be truly committed to the principles, people, and institutions that are important in their lives—if they would think about their responsibilities to them; make commitments that they can fulfill, and be faithful to all of their commitments and obligations. In so many cases, these days, people seem to make promises they intend to keep only as long as circumstances favor that or they do a very shoddy or halfhearted job in performing their responsibilities. I am so delighted to see a strong sense of commitment and faithfulness in my children, and so I have an expectation of seeing that in my grandchildren as well.

- *Problem Solving.* I am basically a problem-solver. That can be a problem, because my natural inclination, whenever someone talks to me about a situation, is to go into a problem-solving mode, even when I am not otherwise involved. Sometimes they are not looking for that, but just want someone to listen and react to their own ideas or concerns. But, it has been said, "If we are not part of the solution, we are part of the problem." The world advances because there are people who are not only committed and faithful, but problem-solvers. What a joy it is to feel a part of the solution of things that are troubling other people or impeding progress!

Of course, we can't model what we are not. We talked about being authentic. If I want to model these things, I have to work at having them become a part of *my* being. Furthermore, children and grandchildren can absorb only things to which they have been exposed. I can't model these things if I am not present to my children and grandchildren.

Being Present

By being present, I mean being really involved with, interacting with. I could be in the same house with my children and grandchildren and not be *present* to them.

What are some of the special ways I can be present to them?

- Attending their memorable events and then sharing in the joyful ruminations afterwards. ("Rumination" comes from the Latin word *ruminare*: to chew over. Isn't that an apt word?) These events may be their recitals, athletic events, hospital stays, or other events that are very significant in their lives and create memories they will retain.
- Arranging special excursions with them: to the museum; to the circus; to the mountains.
- Talking to them about the issues that confront them and society. I can watch television or go to the movies with them and then talk about the perplexing or controversial things we both saw and heard. See that they are exposed to the consequences of drugs, smoking, promiscuity, prejudice, hurtful acts, etc., and talk to them about it.
- Create special memorable events. Vacations taken together to some unusual and memorable place can be something they will always remember, along with their memories of you in that context. I find I remember such times much more clearly if I have taken and saved photographs. See that they have a photographic record of the trip. I also love to read over a diary I made on such trips. Write an interest-

ing and crisp record and make sure the kids have a copy in keepable form. A few years ago we rented a beach house and all spent a few days of leisure there: parents, children, and grandchildren. Everyone remembers that with great pleasure. A photograph of us all standing on the porch of that house is prominent in our family room. Last year we all enjoyed a vacation together at the great Christian family camp in the Adirondacks that we enjoyed so much with the children when they were small. Each of us has a copy of the diary I wrote on that trip.

- Affirm and support the noble characteristics in them and their parents.
- Write them letters. Children of any age will delight in letters and often keep them. One woman in my group would send her grandchildren short questions and found that they enjoyed writing down and sending back the answers (e.g., who is currently your best friend and why do you feel that way?) They remember that you were really interested and concerned about something very important to them. It also stimulates them to think about important issues.
- Expose them to the family legacy. My cousin and I recently compiled a family tree and included remembrances of various persons on the tree. We sent that to all the descendants of our grandparents (fourth and fifth generations). They have been so appreciative! The noble characteristics inspire them; the peccadilloes amuse them; the disasters can also teach them.

Some may think that it is reasonable to wait until retirement to compile the legacy you want to provide to your children and grandchildren. Unfortunately, some of us will die before we get to that point. And even if we live to enjoy a good retirement and have ample time, it is much easier if we have anticipated this and have been gradually accumulating the bits and pieces. It is good to have a working draft that you periodically revise.

But what should I try to write down for my children and grandchildren?

What Do I Want to Write Down to Pass On to My Heirs?

I want to pass on to my children my deepest thoughts about life and faith, and also the not-so-deep story of my life and family. They are interested in both. The deep thoughts are contained in *My Handbook* and the not-so-deep story is in *My Memories*. Both are included with other items in *My Personal Museum*. I will tell you about My Memories and My Personal Museum in the next chapter. Let me tell you about My Handbook here.

For quite a few years I have been compiling a handbook that we refer to as the *Bluebook*. (It is a binder that has a blue cover.) My official title for it is *Reminders for an Active Faith*. It serves to collect those things I want to remember in my attempt to be thoughtful about my faith; that I want to put into practice in the midst of an active life; and that I would like to pass on to my children.

This handbook contains the following sections:

1. *A Statement of Faith.* I believe it is important for each of us to write down what we believe about the most important things. So, in this section I first list those things about which I believe we need to be explicit. Then I state what I believe about these things. I further describe the basis for the beliefs I have and the process I have used to build a conviction about them.
2. *Knowing God and His Will for My Life.* This section contains what I have concluded about how I can personally know God as Father; how I can know His general goal or intention for me, as well as how I can know His will for me in a particular situation.
3. *Personal Growth.* I have put down my conclusion that it is maturity toward which we want to grow; the definition of maturity; the process of growth, in general; and the process of growth to maturity, in particular. I have also included

my thoughts on the role of prayer in the growth process and on the process of deterioration (the opposite of growth), which can so easily set in when we are not growing.

4. *Attributes I Strive to Attain.* Subsections on a variety of attributes in which I want to grow and improve. These include Maturity, Balance, Stewardship, Trust & Initiative, Peace & Contentment; Patience & Endurance; Enthusiasm; Gratitude; Discernment; Wonder & Awe; Faithfulness; Fruitfulness; Generosity; Leadership.

5. *Coping with Life's Problems.* Subsections on a variety of life's problems, including coping with the unexplainable; my continued display of un-Christian emotions and reactions (both the external manifestations and the internal emotions and attitudes); suffering and pain; terminal illness; death; other valleys of grief in our lives; the notorious midlife crisis; retirement; and the preoccupation we tend to have with possessions.

6. *Favorites.* Finally, I have a section to include some of my favorite watchwords (e.g., "Live in truth; walk in obedience; act in love"); favorite statements of philosophy (e.g., "To win the race of life: concentrate on the next fifteen feet of the course laid out before you, not on the finish line, nor the crowds, nor even the other runners"); questions I should continually ask myself (e.g., Who are the special people who have been entrusted to my influence, nurture, and interaction this week, and what are the situations/opportunities that are particularly dependent on my attention and action?); some favorite definitions (e.g., PEACE is a contented state that is not the result of avoidance of and escape from issues and trouble, but is the result of confrontation, resolution and reconciliation); favorite Bible verses (e.g., Isa. 12:2–3): "Surely God is my salvation; I will trust and not be afraid. The Lord, the Lord is my Strength and my Song; he has become my salvation. With joy I will draw water from the wells of salvation"); and favorite hymns.

This is a handbook to which I can continually make additions of wisdom that is revealed to me, and one that will convey my thoughts to my children and grandchildren.

I have devoted a lot of space to the issue of fruitfulness and the important fruit, especially that most precious fruit—our children and grandchildren. I am sure we all want to yield good fruit. As we saw earlier, *fruitfulness* is expected of Jesus' disciples and is a major way in which we glorify God. It seems to me that fruit has two important functions:

- First of all, it provides nourishment to others. It is the embodiment of the health and vitality of the plant that bears it.
- Secondly, it contains, buried inside, a seed that, when planted, has the potential to grow and produce other good fruit.

Concentrating on the most important fruit and cultivating my ability to be fruitful is a key aspect of *living intentionally*. I hope that this section, so far, may stimulate you to think about how you can continue to be the best possible influence on your children and what you want to do to accumulate the legacy that you will leave behind you. We leave it behind late in life, but we accumulate that legacy throughout our lives.

Now let us think together for a while about what we believe and how we come to believe it.

The Act of Believing

What we believe makes a big difference in our attitudes and in our behavior. But it is also important how firmly we believe our so-called *beliefs*. Some of us have very strong beliefs, while others have tenuous beliefs. Indeed, *believing* means different things to different people.

1. The cultural definition of believing is "to give credence to." It is simply an intellectual act of not denying. People *believe* all kinds of things until something important depends

on that belief, and then they're not too sure. I heard C. Everett Koop, our former Surgeon General, on the radio one day. He said that millions of Americans do not have any medical insurance. Medical costs are increasing rapidly and an expensive illness can be devastating to those citizens. Some of them work at two or three jobs, but none of their employers provide health coverage. Now, he reported, 70 percent of Americans say they *believe* that we have to do something to provide basic health insurance for these people. However, when asked if they are willing to have their income tax increased by $200 per year to make that possible, the 70 percent drops to 20 percent. Often beliefs are not strong enough to stand up to any significant amount of pressure. Of course there are people who have believed something so strongly that they put up with all sorts of persecution and even went to their deaths rather than deny their beliefs. On the other hand, there are others whose beliefs crumble as soon as someone else gives them the slightest reason to doubt their so-called *beliefs*.

2. The Greek word used most often in the Bible for *believe* (pisteuo) implies more than mere credence. It involves a state of reliance upon, being fully persuaded, and placing one's confidence in what we believe. We would stake a great deal upon its validity; in some cases we would stake our very lives. When thinking about what we believe, we have to ask ourselves, "How much do I believe that? What, if anything, would it take to dissolve that belief?"

3. We find the word *"believe"* often in the Bible. When the apostle John uses the word he makes it clear that believing is not just intellectual, a matter of what's in our minds, but that believing is reflected in behavior. In John 3:36 he says, "He who believes in the Son has eternal life; but he who does not obey the Son shall not see life." John equates believing with obedience. So our behavior is not merely the consequence of what we believe; it is the evidence of what we truly believe. It is contradictory to say we believe one thing and then to act as if we don't.

So to *believe* something can mean merely that we give credence to it and do not deny it, or it can mean that we put our full faith and confidence in it to the point where we will risk something precious based on its validity. But the real test of whether we believe something is whether our behavior reflects that belief.

Believing is not simple. We observe the following things about the act of believing:

- Believing is a deliberate act of will. We usually cannot absolutely prove what we believe. To some degree, we must choose what we will believe, and we have to choose to believe on the basis of inconclusive evidence.
- No matter how strong our belief, there is always some element of doubt. Since we can't prove what we believe, we have to be willing to risk a great deal, in spite of our doubts. We are continually in a state of "I do believe; please help my unbelief" (Mark 9:24).
- Believing has a chicken-and-egg (which comes first?) characteristic: we choose to believe on the basis of partial evidence; as a result of acting on that limited belief we discover additional evidence, which then further strengthens and expands our belief, etc. Thus we may start with a weak belief and it grows stronger as we act upon that belief.

Now, what are the things about which we need to develop convictions, beliefs? What are the things that are so crucial to the way we think and behave that we must take a stand and decide upon the premise that will control our lives?

The Major Issues

Here are a few of the key issues about which I feel I need to establish my belief or unbelief:

1. *The Reality of What We Observe.* Can we rely on the evidence of our senses, or do our senses play tricks on us, and do we create fictions in our minds?

2. *The Existence of Absolute Truth.* Are there things that are true whether I believe them or not? Does my degree of belief influence the *truthfulness* of something?
3. *The Existence of God.* Does God really exist or not, and what can we believe about God?
4. *Evolution.* Are the world and universe evolving spontaneously or according to a plan?
5. *The Purpose of My Life.* Is there any purpose to my life other than to consume the days that have been allotted to me in a manner that is satisfying to myself?
6. *Death.* Is death the end? If not, what then?

Then, if we decide that we will believe in the existence of God, we immediately face a number of subtopics about which we have to establish our belief or unbelief:

7. *The Nature of God.* Is God personal or abstract? Is God present or remote? What are His attributes?
8. *God's Attitude Toward Me.* Does He know me? Does He care about me? Is He angry with me because I don't live in the way He wants me to?
9. *The Person of Jesus.* Did He actually live on earth? Was He man or God? Was He resurrected from the dead? Is He available to me today?
10. *God's Activity Today.* Does He intervene in the world today? If so, how?

Now, why did I even mention item #1: *The Reality of What We Observe. Can we rely on the evidence of our senses or do our senses play tricks on us?* You may think that issue is trivial. However, some of our important beliefs may depend on what we conclude on the basis of our senses. There are people who have failed to believe much of anything because they do not trust our perceptions of what we think we see, hear, and feel, or our conclusions based on those perceptions. So much of what we believe is derived from what we observe that our beliefs cannot be very secure if we can't trust our senses. We realize that our senses *can* play tricks on us and that there are people whose minds construct incredible fantasies. But we believe that, for most of us, multiple exposures affirm the reality of the things we observe. We can sort out, with the help of others, when our senses are playing tricks on us, and we can rely on those things we observe with our senses which are also affirmed by other people.

How about item #2: the *Existence of Absolute Truth. Are there things that are true whether I believe them or not?* Does my degree of belief influence the *truthfulness* of something? I believe there are absolute truths independent of our perception of them and impervious to our attempts to distort or change them. From the earliest known times space, energy, and the laws of physics have existed, whether or not we correctly perceived them. They have not changed; only our understanding of them has changed. We know that we cannot violate the physical laws of the universe (physics). When we try to, we inevitably incur dire consequences. I conclude there are absolute truths and laws in the moral and spiritual realm, just as there are in the physical realm. And I believe we cannot violate the moral laws of the universe without incurring dire consequences. If we really believed there were no absolute truth, there would be no basis for living. Yet some people will accept the immutable laws of physics, while denying that there are absolute moral or spiritual truths.

I believe that there are a lot of parallels between the physical universe and the moral and spiritual universe. Let me name a few:

- *Undreamed of extensions.* We have evidence that the physical realm has dimensions far surpassing our senses: the extension of the physical universe beyond our most powerful telescopes, particles smaller than we can yet detect, electromagnetic waves beyond the visible, inaudible sound, etc. We are continually amazed at new evidence of hitherto undreamed-of extensions beyond what we have previously identified. Would not the same be true of the spiritual realm?

- *Complexity/simplicity.* Another lesson of physical science is that fantastic complexities may be represented in very simple expressions (e.g., the *laws* of physics). Thus, I am not surprised that God's truth is so deep that we never completely penetrate it, but that, as we perceive the truth, we discover its expression to be amazingly clear and simple.

- *Unreached experiences.* There are experiences in the physical realm which we gradually appreciate more and more: richer experiences of music, food, sights. We discover that up till now we have been impoverished. We have not been capable of appreciating the most marvelous realities of life. I have to conclude that there are also experiences available to me in the spiritual realm more profound than what I have already experienced, which will be a delight to my soul.

- *Successive approximations.* In mathematics we can find correct answers by the method of successive approximations: an approximate solution is formulated that has an extra term for the correction that would be necessary to make it complete. That approximate solution is substituted into the equation and a new equation emerges from which we can get an approximation of the needed correction. That process is continued, successively getting closer and closer to the complete answer. We can apply the same technique to other areas. Our conception of spiritual truths has always been incomplete and in fact erroneous in detail. There has been a steady evolution of a truer picture by men of unusual insight who were willing to apply the approximation they had, in a way that sheds insight into the needed correction.

- *Stepwise/discontinuous progress.* Our individual comprehension of the physical universe progresses gradually with small discontinuities. For a while there is no progress, and then suddenly a small breakthrough happens. Shouldn't we expect this to be true also in our understanding of spiritual truth?

- *Role of revelation.* In interpreting our total experience, physical as well as spiritual, revelation plays a part—the special event that illuminates both past and future events.
- *Unique gifts of insight.* Progress in science has depended a lot on persons who were blessed with unusual gifts of insight, way ahead of their time. We might expect also that there would be persons of dedication, blessed with unusual insight, who would make giant leaps of progress in understanding spiritual truth. It behooves us to pay attention to them and what they have discovered.
- *Joy and purpose in discovery/learning.* A scientist has the goal of improving the awareness, for himself and others, of physical and spiritual truth, and in doing whatever he can to improve the perceived content of both for the benefit of mankind. In that he not only finds a purpose, but he also derives great joy. That is true in the spiritual realm as much as in the physical realm. We can find joy and purpose in discovering and learning truth, as well as in helping others to understand it.
- *Necessity of discipline/study/application.* Progress in science comes only to those who discipline themselves, study diligently, and apply the truth they learn to real-life situations. The same is true in the case of spiritual truth.

If we can believe that there are things that are true whether or not we believe them, and that we can trust the reasonings of our minds, based on what we perceive with our senses, then we can go forward and establish what we believe about the other items on our list. But, how do we go about doing that? I believe there is a process for building convictions in which we can have confidence.

The Process for Building Convictions

There are a number of elements in the process:

- *Personal influence:* Our first concepts are absorbed from our parents. We hear what they say and see how they respond and act. That can start us off with very positive, valid concepts, or with negative or distorted concepts. We are also shaped by other persons of authority, such as teachers and pastors.

- *My questions/challenges/investigations*: There is no such thing as good hand-me-down beliefs. My beliefs must be personal ones, forged through the fire of my questioning and doubting, in the crucible of my own experience of life. I must be open to the truth and willing to discard old ideas for better ones as they are revealed to me.

- *Mental integration*: As truths are revealed or confirmed, new ideas tested and absorbed, I must continually integrate them in my mind, consolidating those things of which I am confident and identifying those of which I am uncertain and which require further pursuit.

- *Extrapolation of faith*: As in science, for areas where I am uncertain, I have to adopt a working hypothesis, something I am willing to commit myself to, at least tentatively, and operate as if it were true, observing the consequences of that premise. For instance, as I discover that parts of the Bible are trustworthy, I will act on those parts and trust in the other parts, even if I can't confirm them.

- *Reduction to essentials*: I set aside those issues which are not crucial to my important beliefs, and I do not become distracted by trying to find answers to questions that are not essential.

- *Confirmation by experience*: As I act on my assumptions and working hypotheses, events in my life confirm the reality of the truths and deepen my convictions, or cause me to seek other answers.

Resources for Answers

There are a number of places that we look for answers to our questions in establishing what we believe:

a) the perceptions and reasonings of our own mind;
b) the testimony of history;
c) the testimony of science and the universe;

d) the testimony of others who have lived successfully;
e) the testimony of personal experience; and
f) the testimony of the Spirit.

Let me make some comments about each of these.

a) *The perceptions and reasonings of our own mind*: We have been given our mental faculties for good reason. The thought processes of logical deduction (hypothesis → observation → evaluation → revision) should be used in the moral and spiritual realm as well as in the physical realm. Faith is not an area where we abandon our reason. Our emotions, desires, and prejudices tend to mold our thoughts, and it is an effort to be objective in our reasoning. But we can be objective with the right discipline. My mind has been disciplined by my study of science. That has not only taught me methods of analysis, it has also conditioned me to accept certain concepts that are not obvious and are quite different from what I might naturally expect.

b) *The testimony of history*: The great truths must be consistent throughout history. While many things change in form over the years, there is continuity to the great truths and a framework of permanence. We have to separate in our minds the permanent structure of reality from the variations and changes we experience. So I need to look at the testimony of history. What does the history of the universe and of man tell me when I look beneath the variations of time and form? The essence of God and His workings are not unique to this time and place, and must be consistent over time.

c) *The testimony of science and the universe*: Whatever things are really true will be borne out by our observation of the universe, and we can use some of the lessons we have learned in physical science in our pursuit of truths in the moral and spiritual realm.

d) *The testimony of others*: There are individuals who have gone beyond us in their understanding and application of fundamental truth. This may be due to extraordinary ability, unusual life experiences, or uncommon gifts of insight and revelation. Some are giants of spiritual insight; others have just progressed farther than I have. In physical science and in my quests in the moral and spiritual realm, it is foolish of me not to study their conclusions and the basis for them, even though not blindly accepting them.

e) *The testimony of personal experience*: Life is the laboratory where concepts are put to the test, where conclusions are verified, and where we gain the experience on which to base our progress. Progress requires exposure to risk. It is easier to stay with our present ideas; there is discomfort and stress involved in evolving. Spiritual growth always requires courage. The essence of life is change. If life is not difficult, we are not coping with problems; if we are not coping with problems, we are not growing; if we are not growing, we are not really *living*. So, while I do not court problems, I want to experience life myself, not just vicariously through others, and in so doing grow in my understanding of spiritual truth and in my ability to apply it to everyday life situations, for the benefit of others as well as myself.

f) *The testimony of the Spirit*: The Holy Spirit must intervene in beliefs about God. We may try to believe important things about Jesus and God through force of logical argument. We can reason that a) Jesus made certain claims about himself and about God; b) those claims are confirmed by his resurrection from death; and c) we are forced to believe in his resurrection because nothing else seems to explain the amazing, sudden transformation of the disciples from despair and defeat into conviction and heroic martyrdom. However, no logic is strong enough to make a cast-iron proof or to convince the hardhearted. It is the Holy Spirit who must intervene and convict us of the truth. We need to continually pray for that help from the Holy Spirit.

Jesus realizes that it is harder for us to believe in God and Him than it was for His disciples to do so. They believed because they witnessed the miracles Jesus performed and because they were confronted by the risen Christ (e.g., Thomas in John 20:19–29). As Jesus said then, "Because you have seen Me, have you believed? Blessed are they who do not see, and yet believe."

Jesus did some extraordinary and fantastic things to enable His disciples and us to believe the truth and thereby to have life. Consider the following examples:

- Jesus did many miracles for the express purpose of inducing belief. For example, He fed the multitude with only five loaves and two fish (John 6:1–14) *so they would believe*; He purposely stayed away and let Lazarus die in order that He could raise him from the dead " so that you may believe" (John 11:1–15, esp. v. 15); He said that He did miracles so they would believe (John 10:38).
- Jesus prayed aloud to God in the hearing of people "that they/the world may believe" (John 11:41–42; 17:21).
- Jesus foretold the future (including predicting his crucifixion and Peter's denial), expecting that this was necessary to *convince them to believe* (e.g., John 13:19; Luke 22:33–34).
- Jesus came back and appeared to the disciples, and even let doubting Thomas touch His wounds, in order *that they might believe* (John 20:19–29).

So, coming to believe something involves a fascinating process, and Jesus devoted most of His ministry to helping us to believe crucial things. As I have paid attention to the testimony of people who have broader and deeper spiritual insights than I have, and have applied the perceptions and reasonings of my own mind, incorporating some of the same techniques I have learned as a scientist, and as I have searched for corroboration in history and personal experience, I have gradually accumulated my core beliefs.

My Core Beliefs

For many years I have been convinced that I need to be explicit about my answers to the Major Issues, which we identified earlier, to write down what I believe and why. When our son went to college we attended an orientation session for parents. The Chancellor said that college is a time of exploration, and that we would discover that our children would investigate and try many different things, including attitudes, behaviors, etc. Even though those children usually wound up with similar values and lifestyles to their parents, it was necessary for them to discover the validity of those for themselves and internalize them themselves. So I, too, have found it necessary to examine my own beliefs and be specific about them. I have gradually composed a Statement of Belief, which summarizes the conclusions I have reached as I have searched for answers to the crucial issues. I encourage you to do the same.

We have a number of core beliefs about all of the Major Issues, but each of us has one primary belief that is crucial to all the others and particularly essential for us. For one person, that primary essential belief may be the resurrection of Jesus (if Jesus' resurrection were not true, most of that person's faith would fall apart). Others might respond that the most crucial belief for them is that there is life after death (if that were not so, all else would be different), or that Jesus is both fully human and also fully divine (that He has experienced our suffering and sympathizes with our inadequacies). If I pick out one belief that is primary and essential for me, it is that God does exist and that He is personal, loving and merciful as well as just, and eager to be as close to me as I will let Him. I see the story of the Prodigal Son (Luke 15:11–32) as the crucial picture of God: He allows us to choose freely, to suffer the consequences of our choices, and waits patiently for us to come to our senses and return to the love He wants to shower upon us as we repent of the errors of our ways. That, for me, is the *Good News* of the Bible.

Everyone puts his or her faith in something. For some it is because they need something stable and dependable in the constant change and chaos they experience in this world; for others it is because they need something to provide support during the troubles they have in this world; for others it is because they need something to give them a hope that will transcend the despair that is often engendered by the circumstances of this world. Yes, everyone puts his or her faith in something, but that something had better be reliable. There are a number of persons or things that can be the object of our faith:

- Some put all their faith in themselves: their abilities, their integrity, their financial assets, etc.
- Almost everyone finds that faith in themselves is insufficient and that they need faith in someone beyond themselves. They may put this faith in their spouse, or a parent, a really wise and trustworthy person they know, the leader of a cult, a political leader, or some other person who will give them stability, support, a reason for living and working.
- Then when they find that no person is entirely dependable or sufficient, they may put their faith in institutions: the government, the law, the Church, etc.
- But institutions also disappoint us, for, after all, they too consist of individuals. Even when we learned that we couldn't trust the U.S. government, we thought we could rely on the big respected corporations. Then they disillusioned us by departing from their traditional standards. Sometimes it is not until a person has been disappointed by people and institutions that he puts his faith in a transcendent God—a supernatural being who is not of this world. That God is different for various people: Jehovah, Allah, Buddha, Brahman. Christians and Jews put their faith in God of the Bible and find therein the answer to many of life's essentials. Those who cannot believe in God or who have a distorted view of God, which makes him seem a

tyrant, or disinterested, or absent, seem doomed to hopelessness and despair once their confidence in persons, institutions, and societies is disillusioned. It has been said that every man was created with an empty space in his spirit, which is designed to be occupied by God, and that he is not complete until he allows God to fill that space, and, indeed, that he is continuously frustrated if he tries to let something else fill that space.

- Those who place their faith in God also find

    a) an explanation for life, a reason for their being (we are rational beings and it is hard to believe that there is no purpose to our lives other than to flame briefly and then flicker out); and

    b) a source of spiritual nourishment (we have facilities and professionals to help us exercise, grow, and heal physically; we have facilities and professionals to help us exercise, grow, and heal mentally; it is in our temples and churches where we find the facilities and professionals to help us exercise, grow, and heal spiritually). It has been reported that more and more people are flocking to the new *Club Meds for the Soul* in recognition of this need.

I hope that by this time you are very aware of the importance of your own individual *prevailing attitudes* and *core beliefs*. I also hope you will try to write them down explicitly. In the next chapter we will go on to talk about the role of our personal and family history as a key aspect of the person we are.

Synopsis

- Our traits and behaviors, which can be observed by others, are really an outward manifestation of our *prevailing attitudes* and of our *core beliefs*.

- The adjective *prevailing* has three connotations, related to strength, frequency, and scope. A prevailing attitude is the attitude that seems to have the most influence on our behavior. A prevailing attitude is the one that is most noticeable and that we observe most frequently. A prevailing attitude is the mental set that seems to permeate so many of our actions, feelings, and thoughts.
- Our *core* beliefs are those beliefs which are keys to the way we live, central to our being, at the root of our attitudes.
- We have to be careful that our prevailing attitude is not one of *backlash*. Backlash is an unusually high state of rebellion against all movements and institutions in our culture. It is a product of unsettled feelings due to change, disillusionment, and fear. I realize that I have to be careful that my prevailing attitude is one that is worthy and purposeful, and not one of reaction.
- When we think of the fruit of our lives, we realize that nothing really lasts except for our influence on other people (especially our children) and the quality of the story we write with our lives.
- We need to be specific about the attributes we desire for our children, and find ways to model those attributes. We can model those attributes only if we are truly *present* in the lives of our children. There are a variety of ways in which we can be present to our children.
- Other devices for identifying and passing on our deepest thoughts about life as well as the things which have been important in our lives, include a personal handbook, a compendium of memories, and a personal museum.
- What we believe makes a big difference in our attitudes and in our behavior. But it is also important how firmly we believe our so-called *beliefs*. Some of us have very strong beliefs, while others have tenuous beliefs.
- Believing is a deliberate act of will. We usually cannot absolutely prove what we believe. To some degree, we must

choose what we will believe, and we have to choose to believe on the basis of inconclusive evidence. No matter how strong our belief, there is always some element of doubt. Since we can't prove what we believe, we have to be willing to risk a great deal, in spite of our doubts. Believing has a chicken-and-egg (which comes first?) characteristic: we choose to believe on the basis of partial evidence; as a result of acting on that limited belief we discover additional evidence, which then further strengthens and expands our belief, etc. Thus we may start with a weak belief that grows stronger as we act upon that belief.

- There are a number of vital issues about which we have to decide what we are going to believe, and there is a process for building convictions about those issues.

- Everyone puts his or her faith in something. Some put all their faith in themselves: their abilities, their integrity, their financial assets, etc. Almost everyone finds that faith in themselves is insufficient and that they need faith in someone beyond themselves. They may put this faith in their spouse, or a parent, a really wise and trustworthy person they know, the leader of a cult, a political leader, or some other person who will give them stability, support, a reason for living and working. Then when they find that no person is entirely dependable or sufficient, they may put their faith in institutions: the government, the law, the Church, etc. But institutions also disappoint us, for, after all, they too consist of individuals. Sometimes it is not until a person has been disappointed by people and institutions that he puts his faith in a transcendent God—a supernatural being who is not of this world. It has been said that every man was created with an empty space in his spirit which is designed to be occupied by God, that he is not complete until he allows God to fill that space, and, indeed, that he is continuously frustrated if he tries to let something else fill that space.

Personal Reflection

- Can you identify a prevailing attitude that seems to lie behind many of your actions, feelings, and thoughts?
- Then, can you identify a core belief that seems to account for that attitude?
- To what extent do you think you have been infected with a *backlash* attitude?
- How conscious are you of your legacy (other than property!)–both what has been handed down to you and what you want to hand down to others?
- What do you consider the important fruits of your life? What seems to you to be the most important and why?
- At this point in your life, with what kind of fruitfulness are you particularly concerned? (See categories on page 247–248) What specific fruit of this kind?
- How are you currently trying to nurture that particular fruit?
- How do you feel about your fruitfulness in this area? (E.g., Good—my actions seem to be highly conducive to producing the fruit I want; or Chagrined—my desired fruit is not getting enough nourishment; or Dismayed—I find that I have been busily nourishing the wrong fruit.)
- Is there important fruit that you desire from your life eventually, that may shrivel on the vine because you are undernourishing it now (perhaps you have put it off, planning to get to it later, but later will never come)?
- Do you feel it is important for you to be explicit about the ways in which you want to influence your children, grandchildren, and close associates?
- What could you do to help achieve that influence?
- What attributes do you most hope for in your children and grandchildren?
- What children are prime in your life right now (e.g., your own children, your grandchildren, those of a friend or relative)? What prayers by you would be most appropriate on their behalf?

- What actions could you take that might facilitate those prayers coming true?
- Have you written down a summary of your essential beliefs? Do you think it is important for a person to do that? What is accomplished by doing that? What are the hazards of not doing it?

Points I Want to Come Back To

Later, when I have more time, I want to think more about the following sections, questions, or ideas associated with this chapter:

_____

_____

_____

_____

_____

_____

_____

_____

_____

CHAPTER 14

Personal History

I am a product of my personal history. If I want to understand myself, I have to recognize the influence that my personal history has had on what I am today and what I will or can become in the future.

This chapter could be subtitled, "Gaining a Perspective on the Progress of My Life." There are two important words in this subtitle: *Progress* and *Perspective*.

Progress, as a word, has two connotations: a) forward advancement, an unfolding; and b) development and improvement. Our life unfolds as we advance along the path (including the forks and dislocations). In the process, we are broadened by our experiences so that we have more knowledge and ability to cope. At the same time, we think we become more abundant persons, with greater depth of personality and of character. Thus, we hope the unfolding of our history also involves gradual growth and improvement. We make progress!

Do you feel that you are a better person today than you were ten years ago? Wiser? Better able to cope? more understanding of yourself and others? With a better sense of what is truly important and valuable? In some ways we would all like to keep our youthful qualities, but one of the real blessings of growing older is this enrichment of our lives as we *progress* through our history.

We could merely view the progress of our lives as a chronology of events. That chronology might make an interesting story, but it would not have any real utility. To profit from a review of our progress, we need to also *interpret* those events. The events of our past have helped to shape us into the people we are and also strongly influence our future. So we want to do more than chronicle the events; we want to put those events into *perspective*.

Perspective is a combination of the Latin words *specere*, meaning to look, and *per*, meaning through, thoroughly, throughout, completely, overall. It refers to the overall "big picture." It implies comprehending or depicting the various parts of the big picture with respect to their relative position, relative magnitude, relative distance. It can refer to a diagram on paper or to a mental image. When we look at our history in perspective, we not only see the events of our lives in chronological sequence, but we have a proper sense of their relative importance and the connections between them.

It is as we gain a *perspective* on the *progress* of our lives that our story can be helpful to us (as we try to shape our future) and also helpful to other people.

Gaining a Perspective

There are several things that stimulated me to try to get a perspective on the progress of my life:

1. When I confronted various forks in my life, I felt the need to get my whole situation in perspective and to arrive at a better understanding of the person I am and what I really want out of life.
2. When I confronted my various midlife crises, I also knew I had to get a perspective on my life.

3. When I began to think of what I wanted to leave to my children and grandchildren, I felt the need to look at my life in perspective and decide what was really important.

4. When I decided that I wanted to live more intentionally, I began to do the analysis that I felt was necessary for me to understand myself and to chart my course. I found that I had to ask myself the questions that are implicit in seeing my life in perspective.

5. I have been in groups with younger men and found that they wanted to look at life in perspective and ask questions like these of older men:

- Is the world really worse today, or is it just my perception because of the manipulation of the news by the media?
- Are you really more at peace than I am, and, if so, why?
- How did you balance your life with the competing pressures of job, family, community service, etc.?
- How do you deal with failures and frustrations?
- How did you go about making the difficult choices in your life, at the forks in the road?
- How do you face the fact that you are approaching the end of your life?
- What makes a marriage successful?
- How can one prepare for a gracious retirement?
- How does one inculcate values and stimulate a spiritual life in children?
- How does a man cope with the disappointment of having his child turn his back on him and on everything that he has tried to teach the child?
- Were higher moral values really prevalent in your younger years? How can we reverse the decline in moral values?
- Does greater clarity come with aging, and can you help me understand some of the things that presently confuse me?

- I gained a real appreciation for what has already happened in my life, how I have grown, the way God has led me, and the people and events He has beneficially caused to intervene in my life, and I found a reason to rejoice!
- It gave me a context for discussing the important aspects of my life with other men, to our great mutual enlightenment and benefit, and I found companionship!
- It enabled me to make some peace with troublesome aspects of my life as I saw them in proportion alongside similar aspects of other men's lives, and I gained increased serenity!
- I gained increased appreciation for my parents and their role in shaping me, as well as increased appreciation for the many other events and persons who helped to shape me.
- I developed an increased interest in history, biography, and how other men's stories shed light on my own.
- It helped me to see what possibilities exist for me and what preparations I need to make in order to realize those possibilities.
- It stimulated me to make an adjustment in my personal priorities and in the way I try to live my life.

So I have found it extremely worthwhile to study myself and to try to see my life in perspective. I also find that other men and women have found it very worthwhile to do the same thing when they have been prompted to do it.

Perhaps if I tell you a little of my own history, you will see some parallels to your own and will be stimulated to reflect on your life in a similar fashion.

Looking at Our History

I found it helpful to look at my history in chapters corresponding to the thirteen-year eras that I defined in chapter 2: childhood, youth, etc.

Recollections of My Childhood

It is hard to recollect much detail about our childhood. However, while we cannot really remember the details about some things, we can see evidences of them in our later life, such as the nurturing love of our mothers; our introduction to the wonders of discovery and joy; our exposure to a sense of pride and of shame; becoming aware of the distinctions of sex, race, and class; etc.

Some of my specific recollections from my childhood include

- Passing a bottle of cream around a circle in kindergarten, taking turns shaking it until it turned to butter and then sharing that on crackers.
- The excitement of the fourth of July, and being able to set off firecrackers in the street all by myself.
- Lying in my bed on Christmas Eve and "hearing" the snow fall outside, punctuated occasionally by sleigh bells.
- The rumble of the coal as it flowed down the chute from the truck into the bin in our basement.
- The dog on our street that bit me three different times.
- Family vacations at the seashore, especially crabbing in the Manasquan Inlet.
- The time I hit my sister in the head with a sledge-hammer while pounding in tent stakes, and being exiled to my room with the shades pulled down, not knowing how she was doing.
- The pride of watching my Uncle George tip his drum sticks to me as he paraded by with the police band in the Thanksgiving Parade.
- The book of poems that my mother gave me and that I still have (minus its covers).
- Moving from one house, school, town to a completely different set.

It is much easier to remember specific events of my youth than those of my childhood. And it seems to me that the events of my youth had more effect on me. However, I realize that the events of my childhood, like the nurturing of my mother and father, set the foundation for my whole life. Unfortunately, some men and some women spend a lifetime trying to overcome the unhealthy foundation that was established for their lives during that era.

My Youth Era

I have found that the youth era has a particularly significant effect in shaping our personality and character, and strongly influences the future course of our lives. In order to gain a perspective on this period, I decided I should try to correlate my own personal experiences with what was happening in society and my environment. I therefore made a time line, as in Fig. 14-1. You might want to do the same, so let me illustrate my own, by way of example.

Fig. 14-1 is a timeline that shows my ages thirteen to twenty-six and the corresponding years from June 1938 to June 1951. (I was born in June 1925.) I put some of the key events of my personal experience on the left alongside the timeline, and some of the key things happening on the world scene at that time on the right.

Considering first the right side, we see, first of all, that in 1938, when I turned thirteen, the United States was still in the grip of the Depression. Unemployment was 20 percent and the minimum wage was forty cents an hour. That sounds low, but actually the value of money has gone down by a factor of ten since 1938, so that corresponds to four dollars in present terms. World War II started with the invasion of Poland in September 1939 (when I was fourteen), Pearl Harbor was December 7, 1941 (I was sixteen), and the war lasted until August 1945 (twenty). I have included the dates of the Marshall Plan, the Berlin Airlift, and the beginning of the Korean War.

I also included a few technology dates to give you a feel for what an ancient society I was born into. In my early youth we relied on the radio. After the war TV began to be available and in 1947 a ten-inch black-and-white TV was becoming popular. These were built with big vacuum tubes; the transistor wasn't invented until 1948. The first color TV broadcast was in 1951. The Haloid Corporation began investing in xerography in 1947 after IBM and

Fig 14.1 My Youth Era

PERSONAL EXPERIENCE					WORLD SCENE	
Relatives	Education	Military			Military	Social

Relatives	Education	Military	age	date	Military	Social
Jackie Drowned 7/5/38			13	6/38		Depression 20% unemployed
			14	6/39		
			15	6/40	WW II	
	High School		16	6/41		
			17	6/42	Pearl Harbor	
		N.J.S.G.	18	6/43		
			19	6/44	WW II	
		Navy Seabees o.s.	20	6/45		
Met Jean 9/46			21	6/46		Cigs ' Cancer Xerography
	Rutgers		22	6/47	Marshall Plan	10 in. B/W TV
			23	6/48	Berlin Airlift	Transistor Invented
Married Jean 6/18/49	BS		24	6/49		
			25	6/50		First Color TV Broadcast
Mother Died 7/16/51			26	6/51	Korean War	

others turned the inventor away. It was at the end of 1946 that lung cancer was first related to the smoking of cigarettes. Before that everyone smoked, especially during the war. I didn't stop smoking until 1959.

Well, now let's look at the events of my personal life during that era. The era began with the drowning of my brother and ended with the death of my mother. These events taught me about the suddenness with which we may be deprived of people very close to us.

My mid-teens were colored by the effects of the Depression and the ominous, worldwide threat of German militarism. My high school years began at the same time as WWII. In my senior year I was in the New Jersey State Guard (N.J.S.G. on the chart). The National Guard had gone to war, so a new State Guard was established and we would spend our evenings in the Armory, learning how to be soldiers and how to handle weapons and combat. After high school I went to war and spent three years in the Seabees, almost all of it overseas (O.S. on the chart), particularly in the South Sea islands, including the invasion of the Mariana Islands with the Marines.

Studs Terkel has written a book about WWII called *The Good War*. Obviously the war was not good, but many people who survived it look back and feel that those were some of the best years of their lives. That is primarily because we were all pulling together with a common purpose, and everyone felt important and heroic. After the frustration of the Depression, we had a clear-cut enemy we could fight and defeat.

The Seabee motto was *Can Do*. We did the difficult immediately, and the impossible took a little longer. Each battalion contained specialists in every construction trade and every type of construction equipment, including huge earthmoving machines. We built the airfields that the B-29s used for their raids on Japan, including the atomic bombs and the firebombing that preceded them. It was a time of accomplishment and victory, even though it involved pain and hardship. While I was overseas my father wrote me a letter every day, for almost three years.

When the war was over, we came back to a grateful nation that provided us with the GI Bill so we could get a college education. All the GIs were anxious to reclaim the world and build the careers and lives we had been missing out on, so the diligence on campus was terrific. It was a time of intensity, vigor, and dedication to getting the job done without a lot of fooling around.

I met my wife, Jean, when I went back to college, and we were married in 1949 when we received our bachelor's degrees. Since I was a major in physics, I really needed a Ph.D. education. So Jean worked in the university library in order to supplement the money I received for teaching part-time. We lived in temporary housing for veterans on the outskirts of the university campus, and our rent was sixty dollars a month. Altogether we lived on $2,950 a year. We budgeted eighteen dollars a week for food and a dollar a week for entertainment. How things have changed!

Some of the other experiences of my youth included

- Going away from home and living with other young men: Boy Scout camp in the summer and camping trips with other young men during the winter; fraternity life at college; going off with other men to "boot camp" and the war.
- Part-time employment: shoveling snow with my hometown road crew to clear sidewalks at intersections that had been piled high by the plows; a newspaper delivery route on my bicycle in the frigid early morning; delivering fresh farm eggs from house to house; loading railroad freight cars.
- Responsibility for younger children: I can remember taking a Sunday School class to a ball game in New York on the ferry and subway (how could those parents have entrusted them to me for that?!); being a patrol leader in Boy Scouts; being a leader at a YMCA camp.
- Leading a team: High School Youth Fellowship; the high school track team; my college fraternity.
- Gaining experience in the arts and letters: the lead in the high school junior play; learning to play an instrument for the high school band and orchestra; writing articles for the

3. My father also taught me fiscal prudence that has stayed with me to this day. This was no doubt stimulated by the Depression, but my father taught me to pay as you go—if we couldn't pay for it, we couldn't afford it. My father never borrowed for anything except his house mortgage. Savings came off the top, not from whatever is left, because usually nothing is left. It is only because of those savings that we can live comfortably in retirement today. He taught me the value of financial planning and accounting. I have account books on my closet shelf that record every dollar Jean and I have spent in our fifty years of marriage. He also taught me the value of replacement funding. I have replacement accounts, in which I accumulate money to replace the cars, the curtains, the lawn mower, and everything. This may seem overly conservative, but that's what I learned from my dad and I need that in order to feel that my life is in order. Other people would be more comfortable with a freer approach to the organization of their lives.

4. From the Seabees I learned "Can Do": do the difficult now and take a little longer for the impossible; teamwork can work wonders; be alert to all the opportunities, and things will work out if you persevere in the midst of adversity.

5. From the period after the war, I learned to be vigorous, industrious, and optimistic.

There is no doubt in my mind that the experiences of my youth have shaped my subsequent life.

We can recall the events of other eras in a similar way. We can then compile the events of the different eras into a total history or time line. I have not included all that detail. The youth era is particularly important and illustrates the procedure.

Now why have I related all that? Is it because I want you to know so much about Andrew Eschenfelder? No! It is because I hope you will develop an interest in looking at your own life in a similar time perspective. Your chart will be different, but mine has some typical ingredients. In youth we have lost some grandparents; some traumatic things have happened in the family; but we don't yet know what's in store in terms of the evolution of our careers, our children, or our grandchildren. As striving adults we are harried by the rigors of our career; we are coping with teenagers and anticipating the costs of their college and their leaving home; our parents are aging and we are anticipating a shift in our parenting concerns to them in our midlife instead of our children, who will be going out on their own.

In each era we can look forward as well as backward. As we look forward it is good to talk to others who have already passed through the eras we are approaching, in order to gain from their experience. As we look back, we should be able to see some things we could share with younger men and women that would be helpful to them. In appendix B there is a worksheet on which you can summarize your reflections on the most joyful and exhilarating times of your life and those times when your life was a struggle.

Looking Back

As we look back on our history, we can get a good perspective on the various peaks and valleys of our lives. At the same time, it is good to get several other categories of things in perspective: losses, gains, and "modern miracles."

COUNTING OUR LOSSES

As we look at our time lines and the component eras, we are struck by the losses we have suffered. Some of the losses are cataclysmic (e.g., loss of a parent or child); other losses we may tend to overlook (e.g., death of a pet, loss of certain friends when we or they moved away, loss of a cherished keepsake). Our losses have more of an impact on us than perhaps we realize. And we are profoundly affected by the way in which our families taught us to handle losses. A participant in one of my women's groups recited a story of a man who, as a boy, found his dog dead on the front lawn. His father told him not to cry and to pick the dog right up because they were going right to the dump to dispose of the carcass. Even as the grown man told the story thirty years later, he broke into sobs! A family trauma has differing impact on the various family members. A loss that may have seemed trivial to your parents, may have been devastating to you.

Another member of that women's group suggested drawing a time line and marking the various losses we can remember on that time line. She extended from the time line a bar whose length was proportional to the impact of each loss. That provides a graphic way to view our many losses in perspective.

REALIZING OUR GAINS

Along with our losses, we recognize that we also have realized significant gains. Like the losses, some of the gains may have been bonanzas; others we might tend to overlook. When we look at the gains, sometimes we see that they are directly related to some of our losses. For instance, some loss we have suffered may have opened the door to a wonderful and extraordinary relationship with some other person. Or, a delightful new living environment (climate, friends, opportunity) might flow out of the disappointing necessity to leave another environment we had really enjoyed. As an example, when our family was transferred to California and lost the proximity of our relatives, the summer vacation places we so loved, etc., we never dreamed we would find California so delightful that we would turn down the opportunity to return to New York.

One approach to putting our gains into perspective would be to note them on the same time line as the losses, and extend bars off the time line in the direction opposite to the *loss* bars, with the length of the bar proportional to the delights that have flowed from the event.

LETTING GO

We tend to avoid *losses* because they hurt. But we have also realized that sometimes a loss is necessary. If we think even more carefully about it, we may conclude that some additional losses are desirable. We tend to hold on to things beyond their useful life. And some of the things we hold on to may so consume our time and energies, or clutter up our lives, that we can't find room for the exciting new things that are waiting to be born.

We remember the scripture that says, "Unless a kernel of wheat falls to the ground and dies, it remains only a single seed. But if it dies, it produces many seeds" (John 12:23). The man who tries to hold on to some part of his life may lose even more than that part, while the man who gets rid of that part and plants it in the earth may see it blossom into new fruit.

We resist letting go of too many things that need to die (old friendships that have lost their authenticity, an image of ourselves we want to cling to, old habits and practices). Let us try to identify the dead parts of our lives that we can let go and open the way for the new. Make space for what's coming!

MODERN MIRACLES

As I have gained a perspective on my gains and losses, both major and minor, I have realized that some have been so ultimately beneficial and so improbable that I have been stimulated to call them modern miracles. We sometimes tend to think that miracles only happen in other times and in other places. But I have a list of things that have happened in my life, which I have compiled into a record of my *modern miracles*. I have over two dozen entries in that record.

Just one example is God's wonderful provision for us when my stepmother died. We suddenly learned that she was terminally ill with liver cancer. She did not yet know that, and we were faced with the prospect of going back to New Jersey, telling her of her fate, caring for her during her final days, arranging the funeral, and then breaking up the home that she had shared with my dad before he died one year earlier. We had never done any of those things before and didn't know how to go about it. It would be a long story, but that story is a record of miraculous happenings that allowed everything to get done when it needed to be done and produced an experience that we look back on with gratitude and rejoicing, rather than with horror and pain.

Just a few of the ingredients were the fact that she lived long enough to get done what she wanted to and yet short enough that she did not suffer long; the way that she died peacefully at a time when we were at her side; the many, many people who appeared to smooth our path (a visiting nurse who provided gracious care and advice, helpful neighbors, bankers, car mechanics, movers, a lawyer, the real estate people who sold the house, our "Wednesday Man" who came and relieved us of all the residue of the home that relatives didn't want, the old car holding up just as long as we needed it before collapsing, the phone calls from California that sustained our spirits,) etc. So many things just happened at the exact moment they were needed, and so many potential problems evaporated. We felt we were in God's hands, that He had it all planned out and that we just went along with His plan. It seemed too wonderful to be chance.

Cultural Impact

There are types of events and experiences that are common to almost all lives, no matter where lived, nor in what human generation. Others depend very much on place and time. I have reflected on how the experiences of my parents, my wife, and my children differed from my own, because they grew up in a different place or time. The experiences we have of the various types depend on the local culture we grow up in, and also on the mores and events of the world scene (variations of place and generation).

a) *Variations of place.* Some of us grow up on the farm (as did my wife), some of us in suburbs (as did I and my children), some in the big cities. For some it may be a pleasant place that sweeps us up and shapes us in very positive ways; for others it may be an ugly place with all sorts of hazards which threaten to drag us down. Certainly the local culture in which we grow up has a lot of influence on how we are shaped, sometimes in spite of the influence of parents and teachers. It also makes a difference if we grow up in different cultural regions of this country or another.

b) *Variations of generation.* Certainly, while the categories of events and experiences that shape us can be common in the lives of people in different generations, the specifics will be quite different. In fact, I realize that I grew up in quite different cultural circumstances from my parents and my children, even though we grew up in the same geographical area. Let us reflect some on these differences.

Variations of Generation

There are differences in the threats that exist to our lives and also in other elements of the prevailing style of life.

THREATS TO OUR LIVES

- *Military threats.* Almost every generation has had to deal with a military threat to their very existence. When I was a young man the world was torn up by the Germans and the Japanese, and we were all subject to military service and potential death or maiming. We also had to go for long periods of service away from familiar people and circumstances. When my father was a young man it was the great catastrophe of World War I. For my grandfather it was the Spanish-American War, and for my great-grandfather, the Civil War. After WWII we thought we would have an indefinite period of peace, but it wasn't long before there was a major threat from our WW II allies, the Russians. From 1950 to 1953 many young men were involved in the Korean War.

  In 1957 the Soviet Union successfully flew the first space vehicle, Sputnik, and caused alarm in the United States because of this evidence of their missile capability. By 1961 we were building air raid shelters in our basements against possible radioactive fallout, and the world came to the brink of nuclear war with the Cuban Missile Crisis in 1962. When my children were six and eight they were learning how to dive under their desks in school for shelter and how to protect themselves from radiation. Then when my son reached high school age, we had the long Vietnam conflict, which sucked up young men from 1964 to 1975. With the breakup of the Soviet Union in 1991, the greatest threat to peace seems to have disappeared, but Desert Storm shows that our youth are still exposed to military hazards as we try to help the United Nations police the world.

- *Health threats.* When my father was a young man, there was the terrible flu epidemic of 1918. In my youth the great hazards were tuberculosis and polio. Every summer there were friends who would come down with paralysis, and we hesitated to go to the local swimming places. That persisted even after we were married and the young son of one of our good friends caught polio. Thank God for Jonas Salk, who invented the polio vaccine and eliminated that threat. But in more recent years we have been much more aware of what seems like increased threat from cancer and heart disease, and now, most recently, the onslaught of AIDS.

- *Criminal threats.* This is one threat that seems to have gotten much worse lately. Of course, there was a lot of lawlessness on the frontier, and many young men died from that. And there were the gang wars of the 1920s, which took a lot of lives. But for my early years there was an amazing lack of criminal threat. People would leave their doors unlocked and never expect a robbery or assault. We never read of assaults on the street. In more recent times, especially with the advent of drugs, risks of robbery and assault have become pandemic. Now we also see the sharp rise in acts of terrorism, which can afflict large groups of innocent people (such as the bombing of the World Trade Center in 1994 and the gassing of the Tokyo subway in 1995). Terrorists have much greater potential for evil with the advent of high technology.

These classes of threats persist for all generations, but they differ in magnitude and particular characteristics. Besides changes in these threats, there have been changes in other dimensions of our lifestyle.

LIFESTYLE

- *Communication.* When I was a boy we were not very aware of things that were happening far from home. We did receive an evening newspaper, but that was concerned mostly with the local scene. There was no television, and the news broadcasts were infrequent on the radio. The big change in news broadcasting came with World War II. In the days of my youth, the major exposure to international news was via the newsreel that was shown in conjunction with the feature film at the local cinema. Now we are continually bombarded with news from all over the world, and in many cases, we observe it *live*, just as it is happening. In addition to TV and our local newspapers, we have many news magazines that come into the home weekly. The result is that we are shaped by the worldwide culture and events more than ever before. A large portion of that is catastrophe oriented. We are very familiar with droughts in Africa, floods in China, earthquakes, fires, uprisings, and terrorist events. We see whatever demonstrations, protests, and sufferings exist, and perhaps have a much greater sense of the tentativeness of life and health.
- *Peer pressure.* Also, when I was in high school, the biggest sins were smoking and a little drinking. I was completely unaware of any drugs. We knew that there were a couple of kids in school involved in sexual escapades, but they had a bad name. Our peer pressure was to avoid such things and we were, for the most part, not tempted. What a difference for the young people of today. They suffer tremendous peer pressure to succumb to all forms of destructive behavior.

- *Environment.* In my youth, the only environmental hazards we were aware of were the freaks of nature: hurricanes, tornadoes, an occasional earthquake in some far-off place. We were not aware of any pollution problems; most of us would not have known what such a thing was. Automobile traffic was very light, and we were unaware of any auto emission hazards. We sunbathed with enthusiasm and ate whatever we fancied. We looked forward to setting off our own fireworks on July 4. Now we are very aware that there is something wrong with almost all of the things we are inclined to do or ingest.
- *Stability.* Certainly there was war. There was occasional crime. But, for the most part, our situation was quite stable. We had a very high regard for our public servants and institutions. We felt that the government could fix almost anything that was wrong if they decided to do that. We also felt that God would not only bless us and our country, but that he would also protect us from harm. Now there is just as broad a conviction that government is helpless to solve anything and that many of our public and private servants in government, banking, law, etc., are inept, if not crooked. Young people today live in a much more unstable world.
- *Opportunity.* We felt that we had wonderful opportunities: to get an education, a decent job, improve ourselves, obtain a home, and participate in the American Dream. Even if we didn't have money, we had the hope of those things. I worked toward my college education, received substantial scholarship aid, and finally was supported through my education by the GI Bill after the war. Young people today are seeing the American Dream as just a dream, and doubting their ability to participate in that.
- *Economic pressure.* All of this adds up to a lot more pressure on wage earners these days. Usually, both mother and father have to work; even during the Depression my mother was able to spend her time nurturing the children although my father worked two jobs. To compete today, most people

have to work very long hours. My father worked five and a half days a week, but he didn't work much beyond forty-eight hours a week. He was able to be present to us when he was not at work, and did not feel, as far as I know, the terrible pressure of time that we feel today. Of course, there was much less to do: we didn't have TV to consume us; we had few opportunities to participate in or attend sports; we didn't go to shows or out to dinner much. Our young people have a wonderful breadth of opportunities, but it is almost overwhelming. On the other hand, one of the reasons we can enjoy so many of these opportunities today is the tremendous increase in convenience: convenience foods, labor and time-saving equipment, speed of communication and transportation, accessibility to services.

Yes, there have been tremendous changes in our culture, and it is surely true that my children and grandchildren experience a very different impact from culture from the one I experienced, just as my experience was very different from that of my parents.

The Cultural Pendulum

Some of the things in the current culture appear to be swinging to an extreme. For instance, have the threats to our children grown so great that we are beginning to smother them in the name of protection? Are employees being driven to such excesses of working hours and intensity, because of competition, that their personal health and that of their families is being threatened (if you don't do it, someone else will, and you will be left behind)? Have we become so imbued with the notion that there is something wrong with almost all of the things we are inclined to do or ingest that we deprive ourselves of some of the pleasures of living? As the pendulum swings to extremes, pressure builds for correctives. Even now we can see the measures being taken to increase public safety, limit access to guns, put away repeat offenders, lay on cumbersome environmental controls, apply what some people would call censorship of media and art.

299

the flow and when to swim upstream, and courageous in pursuing the objectives we set for ourselves.

Benefits for My Children

As I gain a *perspective* on my life, and reflect on the way that events have shaped me, a couple of questions come to mind:

- Are there certain kinds of events that have such a profound effect on our lives that we would like to ensure that our children and grandchildren either experience them or avoid them?
- Would our children benefit from knowing more about our family history and its influence on us?
- Are there good ways to communicate these to our children?

I am sure that the answer to the first question is yes. I have already cited many of the events that I feel had a beneficial effect on me. I am sure you can do the same. Your events may be different in the particulars, but similar in type and effect. We can help to provide beneficial experiences for our children and grandchildren, and also help them to avoid the debilitating ones.

I would include in the good experiences the kinds listed on page 287. I realize how important it was that I was encouraged in the early days to be a part of collaborative teams; to accept my first leadership roles; to seek and successfully perform wage-earning, part-time jobs; to learn to play a musical instrument and discover the joy of making music with others; etc. Later, how important it was that Benjamin Ward got me up in front of the math class to "teach" the lesson to my classmates; that Bob Foster pushed me into participating in leading worship services (first just by reading the Scripture, then a short prayer, eventually giving the lesson); that Lloyd Hunter made me get up in front of other young scientists and talk about the direction our research should go. All of these required someone else being alert to the opportunities and pushing me a little to take advantage of them.

My grandson, Drew, was elected in the fourth grade to the student council in his grade school, as activities director. He had to decide to go for it, then make posters advocating his election, and finally, scariest of all, give a campaign speech in assembly. I think he was surprised that he was elected. It has been a wonderful *occasion* to point out to him that many voted for him because they had observed his team spirit on his baseball and soccer teams; because he had been friendly and cooperative with others; because he had voiced his opinions before, and they were convinced he would have good ideas and was not overly presumptuous. We talked about how he could involve some of the other candidates in helping him lead some of the activities—they had already demonstrated their interest and ability. We also helped him to recognize lessons for the future: people whom you help today may later turn out to be instrumental in helping you accomplish important future objectives; people notice and remember your enthusiasm, cooperation, leadership, and commitment; it is often surprising what you can accomplish if you take a chance and do your best; future opportunities build on the opportunities you accept today; etc. I would not have thought that Drew would be interested in being a leader or would take to "politics." I am grateful to the person who introduced him to that opportunity and encouraged him to pursue it. He followed up, in the fifth grade, by running for and being elected president of his class. He is on a roll. Maybe some day he will be President of the country! Whatever he does, I am sure he learned important life lessons during that experience.

I want to help all of my grandchildren to benefit from the kinds of experiences that were so beneficial to me. I also want to pass on other things that have been important to me. I already told you about my *Bluebook* in the previous chapter. I have also told you how my cousin and I have passed on information about members of our family tree to all of the great-great-grandchildren of Andrew and Emma Eschenfelder. But what about other aspects of our family history?

Passing It On

I have found that my children are very interested in the facts and recollections of my early life and that of our forebears. They have given me two workbooks that are formatted with blank sections to provide a convenient and organized way to write down the key aspects of my personal history. One is called *My Memories—A Written Record of My Life and Times to Hand Down to My Family*, published by the Metropolitan Museum of Art (ISBN 0-87099-388-7). The other is called *Grandpa's Story–A Keepsake and Memories Album for Grandchildren*, published by WinCraft, Inc., Winona, Minnesota. I would certainly appreciate having such a workbook filled in by my father, mother, grandfather, etc. I don't believe we are vain in believing that our children and grandchildren would like such from us.

The following outline is my own adaptation of the one used in the workbook *My Memories*, cited above.

I. MY FAMILY

1. My birth (date, place of birth; photos; other circumstances).
2. My family tree (a brief description of the generations and branches of the family).
3. My parents (their identities, personalities, occupations/hobbies, griefs, and deaths).
4. My grandparents (their identities, personalities, etc.).
5. My sister and brother.
6. Favorite aunts, uncles, and cousins.
7. Family traditions.

II. GROWING UP

1. Life at home (towns in which I lived, what our houses were like, neighbors).
2. Family holidays and vacations (how we celebrated, where we went, and special memories).

3. Recollections from my adolescence (ages 12–18) (jobs, events, sports, friends, etc.).

III. Recollections from My Young Adulthood (18–27)

1. Graduation from high school.
2. College.
3. Military service: what/where/when in my youth.
4. Dating and romance: first date, what was popular in music, dance, clothes, where/how I met the person I married, etc.
5. Engagement, wedding, and our early married life.
6. Employment.

IV. Recollections from the Days When I Was Employed Fulltime (27–56)

1. Where we lived.
2. Vacations.
3. Special times with the children.
4. Career experiences.
5. Other noteworthy events.

V. My "Retirement" Years (56–)

1. Mode of living.
2. Improvements in our home.
3. Our activity in the Saratoga Federated Church.
4. Participation in other community endeavors.
5. *Living Intentionally* book and study groups.
6. Golf.
7. Family weddings.
8. Cruises and trips.

VI. Other Reflections on My Life

1. Influential people (remembrances about people who most influenced me and the ways that they affected my life).
2. Modern miracles (those happenings in my life which were so important, beneficial, and timely that I can't believe they occurred merely by chance).
3. Alternate paths (suppose I had taken the alternate path at my forks?).
4. The effect of World War II (an example of how something horrendous can result in substantial benefit).
5. Investments (lessons to be learned from attempts to "get ahead" financially).

Of course, all of these things are not necessary in the memoirs you would compile about your own life (it is meant to give ideas). You may also think of other important categories I neglected. I am convinced that time spent on this type of project will be appreciated by our descendants and will help to communicate the things that are important to us.

My Personal Museum

As I thought about communicating my memories, it occurred to me that there are other things I would like to tell my children and grandchildren about, and also look over myself every once in a while. So it occurred to me that we should all draw up plans for a *Personal Museum*, which displays things that are very significant in our own personal history. This museum would have bookshelves for key books (like, for me, in addition to my *Bluebook* and *My Memories*, my high school and college yearbooks, the electronic technology textbook I wrote, my souvenir book about the 67th Seabees in which I served from 1943 to 1946, etc.); a photo gallery for favorite pictures (such as a picture of me and my family sitting outside our little cabin on the shore of Lake Winnepesaukee, a picture of our extended family at Camp of the Woods, and pictures of our children and grandchildren at younger ages); a library for scrapbooks of other key documents (like birth certificate, diplomas, most treasured letters, etc.); a catalogue containing chronologies of cars, residences, vacations, education, career, etc.; a file of CDs for favorite sounds (both music, like my favorite drum corps pieces, or recordings of the Canadian Brass, and also other sounds, like the water lapping on the rocks at Camp of the Woods); my golf trophies and framed card from the first time I scored less than 80; and, finally, other memorabilia standing around the room (like the experimental setup for the research I did for my Ph.D.)

It is fun to speculate on what should be included in such a museum, to gather and look again at those items that can still be found. If you construct such a museum, either actually or conceptually, I'll bet you, your children, and your grandchildren will be delighted and enlightened as to what it says about you.

Appreciating Our History

It is good to gain a perspective on our own personal history. It helps us to understand why we are the persons we are. It helps us to better understand the personalities of other people, especially our parents, and perhaps our children. It can even lead to an increased desire for reconciliation where there has been estrangement. The cyclical nature of the generations can give us hope for the future when we are overwhelmed by the "strangeness" that younger people exhibit. Preparing some notes on our history can also be very interesting and illuminating to our children and grandchildren. In addition, it is wonderful in our older years to review and celebrate the history that has been ours. When Jean and I celebrated our anniversary the other night, we spent our time reflecting on our situation on other anniversaries. Because we have had so many, we concentrated on five-year anniversaries. Of course, we can't remember all the details, but before we went out I referred to our notes and refreshed my memory. I was able to do that because I have kept a simple chart that notes, for each year, what house we occupied, the vacations we took, the employment and specific assignments that occupied us, the cars we owned, the stages of our children at that time, and our particular interests. It is easy

culture is cyclical, and we need not expect our society to suffer an irreversible moral decline.

- The prevailing culture does strongly influence the attitudes and behavior of people. The more we think about it, the more we realize that the variety of factors that are key ingredients in our lives is indeed diverse and complex. In some cases we may be shaped in very positive ways as we are swept up in the tide; in other cases we may have to fight against the prevailing tide in order to become the person we want to be. In any event, we need to be discerning to separate the good influences from the bad, thoughtful in deciding when to go with the flow and when to swim upstream, and courageous in pursuing the objectives we set for ourselves.

- It is good to gain a perspective on our own personal history. It helps us to understand why we are the persons we are. It helps us to better understand the personalities of other people, especially of our parents, and perhaps our children. It can even lead to an increased desire for reconciliation where there has been estrangement. Preparing some notes on our history can also be very interesting and illuminating to our children and grandchildren. In addition, it is wonderful in our older years to review and celebrate the history that has been ours. The cyclical nature of the generations can give us hope for the future when we are overwhelmed by the "strangeness" of younger people.

- Some of the ways to facilitate an appreciation of our history, and to communicate important aspects of it to our children and grandchildren, include compilation of a *Bluebook*, *Memoirs*, and a *Personal Museum*.

Personal Reflection

- Make a list of some of the specific things you remember from your childhood and your youth. It might help to sepa-

310

rate them into two categories: those that you think had a very positive effect on you and those which might have had a negative impact.

- Use the worksheet in appendix B to list some of the high points (peaks) of your life and some of the hard times (valleys).
- Do you feel that you are captive to some aspect of your family history or to your own previous behavior patterns? Please elaborate: to what are you captive, and in what way?
- How have you tried to escape from this captivity and with what success?
- As you think over the total scope of your life so far, what are some of the items you would include in your Museum, to commemorate both the high points and the low points?
- What lessons have you learned from your own personal history that might be instructive or helpful for your children or grandchildren as they face the problems and opportunities of their own lives?
- Does this presentation help you to understand the lives and personalities of your parents any better? Does it give you any different perspective on what your children will likely encounter?
- In what ways do you think the pattern of your own life so far parallels the pattern experienced by most people, and in what important ways is your pattern unique?

Points I Want to Come Back To

Later, when I have more time, I want to think more about the following sections, questions, or ideas associated with this chapter:

_____

_____

_____

_____

_____

_____

_____

_____

Epilogue

I hope your thoughts have been stimulated by this book, and that you now see your life in a clearer, undistorted perspective. I hope you feel better equipped to decide your forks, cope with your dislocations, and take advantage of your occasions. I also hope that you have recorded the key thoughts, reactions and convictions you have had while reading this book. That recording may have been in a journal, or by highlighting on the pages, or by writing in the margins. Don't forget to go back to the points you may have listed at the end of each chapter as ones you wanted to revisit. And don't forget to review the worksheets you used in the appendix. I hope that your journal or your notes in this book turn out to be an important resource for you, and that some day in the future you will look back on this as a turning point in your life. I wish you the very best in your determination to *live intentionally*, to be a good *steward* of the life opportunity you have been given, that you may become much more satisfied with your life and confident that you are producing the kind of fruit you desire, especially for the benefit of your children, grandchildren, and other people who can be blessed by your life.

We have been given the great gifts of memory and imagination so that we can *live intentionally*. Go for it!

Appendix A

Small Group Study

A particularly fruitful way of using this book is as the text for a small group study. This material has been tested in groups of men and in groups of women. Those who have participated in such groups have felt that they received a much greater benefit from their time together than from studying alone. This is because of what they learned about the issues from the other participants and also because of the close relationships they established with each other. The purpose of this appendix is to provide some guidance for successfully running such small groups, based on our experience.

Organizing the Small Group

1. *Leadership.* An essential ingredient is a good leader who can stimulate the members to interact and can keep the discussion interesting and on track. We have found that our best leaders are people who have already participated in one of these groups. It is interesting that both men and

women find it very valuable to participate in a second and even third group, using the same material. Each group offers a different complexion and new, important insights. Almost anyone who sincerely desires to facilitate a small group and understands the essential ingredients can usually do a creditable job. The leader should be someone who can be present for almost all of the sessions. It is good to have an assistant leader who takes over when the leader must be absent, or who takes over occasionally just to gain experience to later lead another group.

2. *Membership.* Obviously, it is important to pick a group of members who will be compatible and have some things in common. There is not much difference between a group of men and a group of women. Both men and women are acutely interested in making the most of their life opportunity, and both hunger to learn what others may have discovered that will help them to do that. Modern notions suggest that women are eager to share their feelings, while men are more concerned with not revealing any weaknesses. This would suggest that it might be harder to get a group of men to interact intimately. However, we found that effective sharing and bonding depends mostly on the compatibility of the people involved, not whether they are men or women. Both groups will open up to each other once they have decided to trust each other. Interacting over this material quickly builds a sense of trust and comradeship that facilitates meaningful sharing. We have found at least as much variation in attitudes, personality, etc. within a group of men or within a group of women as between men and women.

3. *Size of the Group.* The optimum group to work with this material is six to twelve. There are some advantages to having more than this, especially to get a broader range of points of view and to ascertain whether certain things are com-

mon to many people. We have worked with a group of twelve, enjoying that kind of diversity. However, this material really sparks questions in the minds of men that they want to discuss with the others, and the only way to have enough time for that with a larger group is to extend the sessions. With a group of six to eight, significant personal interchange can occur in meetings that do not last more than ninety minutes nor take more than twelve to fifteen weeks. In addition, busy men inevitably miss an occasional session and, when that happens, with six to eight you still have a reasonable group. Actually groups as small as five (including the leader) have been very fruitful. This is because everyone realizes the importance of participating, and there is less opportunity to hangback–and also because there is more time to go into greater depth. In this case, however, we met on an average of once every two weeks, picking the weeks when not more than one person would be missing.

4. *Recruitment.* There is nothing as effective as a personal invitation. Very often, pastors will know of men or women who are ready for such an experience. An invitation from the leader or another member can be enticing. Interest can be stimulated by posing the following questions to potential participants (obviously, for women's groups the gender would be changed):

- Do you know what it is about yourself and your circumstances that you really would like to change?
- Do you feel that you can take control of your life, or do you feel too much like a helpless victim of your history, your circumstances, the hectic pace of our culture?
- Are you aware that the problems you face in living your life closely parallel the problems that other men face? And that the same principles can be used in facing those problems even though your circumstances may be quite different?

- Do you realize that you can benefit enormously by comparing notes on these problems with other men in a confidential, trusting environment?

Then, if these questions strike a responsive chord, the participants can be told who the leader will be, and invited to call him/her to learn more details and explore the possibilities.

Conduct of the Small Group Interaction

1. *Participants' agreement.* We have found it good to have an agreement that spells out what the group agrees to do together. This includes the commitment that each person makes to the group in terms of participation, preparation, and confidentiality. A suggested agreement is included at the end of this appendix.

2. *Conversational agenda.* It is good to have a conversational agenda prepared by the leader for each meeting, which allocates the time in the meeting between particular activities and describes the things that need to be said. Generally, it is recommended that there be one topic for sharing for each meeting that takes up most of the time, preceded by some opening remarks and concluded with some closing activities, including handing out the worksheet for the next meeting, evaluation of the session, and prayer.

3. *Topics for sharing.* A prep sheet is given to each group member to use in preparation for discussing the topic for Sharing. Some sample prep sheets are included in appendix B. B1 or B2 is most appropriate for the introductory session. Other such sheets can easily be made up by the leader, in anticipation of future sessions, using some of the questions listed at the end of each chapter or questions stimulated in the leader's own mind in reaction to reading the text. We have found that a very important topic for sharing is the one on our aspirations, in conjunction with chapter 10. We have to know our aspirations, the things we hope will

happen, in order to decide what are the most important next steps in our lives. Our members have sometimes taken several sessions to talk about this topic.

4. *Allocation of time*:

a) A minimum total time is twelve sessions, spaced one per week, and they probably should be held to not more than ninety minutes per session. Twelve sessions will not allow discussion of section 3 of the text. For that, fifteen sessions are needed. Some of our groups have become so interested in particular topics that they have decided to extend the number of sessions, even spending four sessions on one chapter.

b) In each session, it is recommended that the majority of time (seventy five out of the ninety minute total) be spent on discussing the topic for sharing for which the participants have prepared using the prep sheets. Before that, members may want to comment on their reactions to other aspects of the text they have read, or share their reflections on the previous session.

c) We have found it good to have evaluation forms to get feedback from the men so as to be able to improve the sessions. This could be done by distributing an evaluation form periodically during the sequence of sessions. The form should include such questions as

- Can you think of ways in which we could improve the fruitfulness of these sessions?
- Has the group been discussing the issues of most concern to you?
- Can you think of other questions for sharing that you would like to ask other participants?
- Do you feel that everyone, including yourself, participates in the discussion?
- What did you like best about the sessions, and what adverse reactions have you had?

After the session the leader(s) can review the comments on such forms and discover how to make the sessions more interesting and useful as the series is in progress.

5. *Discussion of the Topic for Sharing:*

   a) It is a good idea to vary the approach to the discussion from session to session.
   b) It is good to finish the discussion with a question that is oriented toward ways for each man to use the material and discussion to advantage in the future. This responds to the major interest of men in ways to improve their lives, and concludes the session on a positive note.
   c) It is essential to find a way to have each man make some verbal contribution to each session. They need to feel a significant part of the group, and usually like the fact that they have contributed. No one wants to be strictly an observer/absorber.
   d) It is good to leave adequate time for meditation after a question or thought. That is, allow each person to quietly think about the question or thought long enough for it to penetrate and to have an effect on them. We sometimes think that if someone doesn't answer right away, he doesn't have anything he wants to say, and we go on to the next thought or question. Indeed, group members may have something very important to say if we give them a little more breathing room, give their response a longer incubation period. Don't be afraid of a period of silence while members think about their response and until each has made his response.

6. *Vulnerability.* No one can candidly discuss these issues without feeling exposed to potential criticism, ridicule, etc. Members must be convinced that they can trust the group and that being vulnerable is important to gaining the most benefit from the sessions. It is therefore essential that the

leader model this attitude and be transparent and vulnerable early on as an example.

7. *Prior to the First Meeting.* Prior to the first meeting, it is good to send each perticipant a letter that contains the following:

a) A copy of the proposed participants' agreement, making it clear that there will be an opportunity at the first meeting to affirm or change this agreement, but that it is important that all have a common understanding of what to expect.

b) A copy of the prep sheet for the first meeting, making it clear that a) Prep Sheets for the topic for sharing are not handed in and that group members should be candid in writing their thoughts on them while preparing for the session; and b) more should be written on the sheet than could possibly be discussed in the meeting, and that each person will select and edit what she discusses with the group.

c) A listing of the participants, their addresses, and phone numbers, with an encouragement that the participants have been selected on the basis that they share enough in common that they can build excellent personal relationships and mutually profit from sharing the sessions together.

d) An encouragement to obtain a blank journal before the first meeting, to be used to write down and preserve thoughts and responses as the member is reading the text and participating in the meetings.

Referral

In the process of these sessions, individuals (men or women) may get in touch with issues in their lives that they have not thought about before, some of which can be quite painful. It is good to be able to offer additional private discussion and to have a pastor or counselor identified who is eager to help them work through these issues.

THE PARTICIPANTS' AGREEMENT

The following is a suggested text:

(The purpose of this agreement is to clarify what the group intends to do together. This includes the commitment that each member makes to the group in terms of participation, preparation, and confidentiality.)

1) *Our Objectives*. We are committing ourselves to participation in these sessions and to preparation for these sessions in order to achieve the following objectives:

   a) As individuals to reflect on various aspects of our personal lives:

      - to realize what things are most important to us in the living of our lives;
      - to identify particular changes we want to make in the way we live our lives; and
      - to discover how to accomplish these new directions intentionally.

   b) As a group of men to discern some important lessons from each other's lives.
   c) To build some strong personal relationships and experience the joy of fellowship.

2) *Our Sessions Together*. We anticipate having 14 sessions with each other. The sessions will be limited to ninety minutes and we will start and adjourn promptly at the scheduled times. After a first introductory session, the remaining sessions will involve a discussion of some aspect of each of the chapters

of the text *Living Intentionally*, by Andrew H. Eschenfelder. For each session a topic for sharing will be selected. Each week a preparation sheet will be distributed for the next session's topic for sharing. This prep sheet will contain a few simple questions to facilitate our preparation for the discussion. These sheets are private and will not be turned in, so we expect to be perfectly candid in noting our responses that the questions stimulate. Then we can select from that written response what we will share with the group.

3) *Our Participation*. We intend to participate as fully as possible in order to derive the full benefits of the sessions for ourselves and the other participants. That means that each one needs to be bold to speak up. At the same time we each need to husband our words so that all have time to participate. We realize that it will be necessary for each member to miss an occasional session because we all have some important other obligations. However, we all agree to make these sessions a very high priority and will attempt to be present and prepared for each one of them. When we can't be present we will still prepare for them as if we were going to be present.

4) *Our Preparation*. Before each session we will read the appropriate chapter of the text and prepare the preparation sheet for the selected topic for discussion. We realize we can't think through our answers to all of the personal application questions at the end of each chapter, because that would take too much time in the week we have between sessions. However, we will read them and note the ones we would like to return to when we have more time.

5) *Confidentiality*. We want to be candid and learn from each other, but we believe that each individual has some things that are best kept private and not shared with the whole group. Furthermore, we will keep in confidence the personal stories that *are* shared. We may talk to our spouses about the way that the session was conducted, the benefits that are being gained and some general conclusions we reach, but we will not relate other member's personal stories.

Appendix B

WORKSHEET B-1

Peaks and Valleys of My Life

1) What have been some of the most joyful and exhilarating times of my life?

2) What have been some of the most traumatic times of my life?

3) Identify some of the other times when my life was a struggle.

4) What are some of the continuing joys of my life?

Worksheet B-2

Session 1: Influential People and Events

PREPARATION: Please read section 1, *Living Intentionally*, and answer the following questions in preparation for our group discussion:

1) Name several persons who have strongly influenced the shape of your life or of your person:

2) Identify some events that have had a significant impact on who you are as a person or how your life has gone:

3) For one or two of the persons you named in 1), above, identify the specific way in which you and/or your life were shaped by that person:

4) For one of the events you named in 2), above, identify the specific way in which you and/or your life were shaped by that event:

A reality: As we proceed down the course of our lives, we are shaped by the people with whom we associate and by the events we encounter/experience/endure.

WORKSHEET B-3

Session 2: The Path of a Person's Life

PREPARATION: In future sessions we will talk about ways of handling forks, dislocations, and other elements common to any person's life, as well as steps we might take to make our life more pleasurable, satisfying, and productive. Let's reflect briefly on our past experience with some of these elements.

1) What are some of the decisions you have had to make in your life so far, where, if you had decided otherwise, your life might have been quite a different story? Are you satisfied with the way you went about making those decisions?

2) What are some of the times in your life so far when your situation was suddenly and irrevocably changed due to some drastic happening (e.g., death of a loved one, accident, job loss, etc.)? Do you feel you were reasonably prepared for such events? Do you see things you could have done ahead of time that would have equipped you to handle those events better?

3) Can you identify a time in your life when you were at your wits' end—there was no way to go and the problems were insurmountable? Was God there when you called on him, or was he absent, as in Psalm 77?

4) What changes have you intentionally made in your life situation as a result of thoughtfully analyzing what would make your life more pleasurable, satisfying, and productive?

NOTE: Either we modify our circumstances to be more compatible with our tastes, or we have to adapt ourselves to our circumstances.

Worksheet B-4

Coping with Previous Forks in My Path

1) Name a fork that is already behind you which may have yielded the most significant insight about dealing with forks:

2) With respect to this fork, list some of the factors that complicated your decision:

3) To what extent were the following factors involved in the issue? (rate each fator on a scale of 0–5, and include comments):

____finances
____family
____ego
____moral/ethical/principles
____personal goals and convenience

4) To what extent did this fork imply

____changes in family circumstances
____changes in close personal relationships
____changes in your personal behavior/attitudes

5) How did you go about making the decision you did?

6) Who did you have available to help you? Who or what influenced you most?

7) In retrospect, what did you learn about the process by which you think a person should face a major fork? What recipe would you prescribe?

WORKSHEET B-5

Coping with Future Forks: The Future Decisions of Our Lives

1) Name the fork you are facing right now or the one that will likely confront you in the near future:

2) What are the most crucial issues in that fork? What complicates it?

3) What things discussed in the chapter most obviously apply to that situation?

4) Who do you have to help you consider this fork, and how do you think you might involve him/her?

5) What are your present thoughts as to how you should evaluate the alternatives and go about reaching a decision in this fork? How does the material in this chapter of the text apply to this specific case?

6) Which of the *Observations about Forks* (pp. 6–13) seems most important for you to remember?

7) Which of the *Guidelines for Facing Forks* (pp. 6–16) seems most important for you to remember?

WORKSHEET B-6

MY AGE:								
MY ERA:	CHILD	YOUTH	YOUNG ADULT	RISING ADULT	MIDLIFE	ELDER	OLD AGE	

TIME PERSPECTIVE FOR

NOTES

M=Date married
C=Date finished college
R=Date of "retirement"
$=Family trauma

ACTUAL YEAR

My Timeline for One Era

PERSONAL EXPERIENCE				WORLD SCENE	
Relatives	Education	Employment		Political	Social

age   date

Worksheet B-8

Our Aspirations

Please study chapter 10 in preparation for this session.

1) What things in chapter 10 would you most like to discuss in the group?

2) What are some aspirations you have, i.e., the things you hope will happen? Identify some of your aspirations in each of the following categories and estimate how realistic they are.

a) Your personal nature—what you want to be: attributes in which you want to grow and improve; your physical fitness (exercise, dieting, etc.); your emotional harmony (being more content, etc.); your patterns of thought and behavior (e.g., living more intentionally); your spiritual maturity.

b) Your relationships: perhaps with your spouse; with your children or grandchildren; with your parents or grandparents; with your business associates, your good friends and confidants, your neighbors, your siblings or other family members.

c) Your family prosperity: financial security (perhaps involving budgeting, insurance, wills, investments, etc.); your physical home (obtaining one; repairing or protecting the one you have, etc.); your family happiness and serenity.

d) Your personal accomplishments—what you want to do: perhaps things you want to make, to write, to complete; perhaps places you want to visit or experiences you want to have.

e) Your lifestyle and environment: the way you spend your time/energy; the environment in which you dwell, work, play.

3. What are some of your primary constraints that limit what you could do (responsibilities you must carry out, people you depend on, skills you lack, financial obligations, etc.)?

4. Can you think of some compromises you could consider or have considered that could help these aspirations become reality?

Appendix C

Complementary Attributes Needing Balance

1. *Trust vs. initiative*: To some degree we need to relax and trust God to work things out; to some degree He expects us to use our initiative to do what we can. Either too much self-reliance or too little personal effort is wrong. I continually struggle with this and probably err on the side of trying to be too self-reliant.

2. *Justice vs. mercy*: Justice implies getting what we deserve. Fortunately God is merciful and instead of giving us what we deserve, not only forgives our shortcomings but even puts them out of His mind. On the other hand, occasionally He lets us suffer the consequences of our actions and attitudes because that is what we need. We too should be merciful to others, forgiving and forgetting, but there are times when we should let others face the consequences of their actions when that is important to their growth.

3. *Questioning vs. accepting*: To have the strength of our convictions we need to have doubts, raise questions, and reach conclusions. God respected Thomas' doubting, and He promises to give us answers if we honestly seek answers.

On the other hand, there are some areas where we can never absolutely determine answers or change circumstances, and we just have to make up our minds to accept that and go forward, at peace with our acceptances.

4. *Security vs. risk-taking*: Growth involves risk, so that if we emphasize security too strongly we miss out on the joy of growth and the excitement of crossing new horizons. On the other hand we all need a fundamental amount of security in our lives. Thus this balance must be sought in our personal relations and in our business life.

5. *Simplicity vs. complexity*: Too much simplicity can lead to boredom. We need some variety in our life. I think life should be like a gem with many facets. When one facet is dormant, another may be fruitful. But each facet is unpredictable; what happens when they erupt together? We need to remember that everything is more complex than it appears; everything takes more time than we think. Therefore, if we go in too many directions we may get consumed and have no time for relationships, study, meditation, play, etc. So we need a continual effort to simplify our lives if they are too complex, but to sustain enough complexity to make them rich.

6. *Sensitivity vs. Callousness*: It is through our senses that we perceive the world around us and become a part of it. It is also through our senses that we experience the pleasures of our existence. So we want to be sensitive to people, to things, to situations. Often it is the nuances that are most meaningful; the perception of nuances requires sensitivity. However, there are times when we need to develop a few calluses, so that we are not overly sensitive to the particular idiosyncracies of certain people or situations. Hypersensitivity can drive us crazy.

7. *Pride vs. Humility*: No one likes a prideful person. We know that the strength, talents, and opportunities we have are mostly gifts and not things we have earned ourselves. We want, therefore, to preserve a proper level of humility, grate-

ful for our blessings and ready to defer to others as appropriate. However, to slough off a compliment that is deserved is to slap the considerate grantor in the face. Even to say, "It was not I, but God did it through me" is arrogant. Humility is not denying every good thing about ourselves; it is appropriate to acknowledge what we have done that is worthy. It is not easy to preserve a balanced humility, while accepting justifiable appreciation.

8. *Scheduled vs. Freewheeling*: Some of us are so heavily scheduled and organized in all of our activities, even recreation, that we miss the blessing of spontaneity. We need to make an effort to have time where we just fly by the seat of our pants and enjoy spontaneity. On the other hand, some of us plan and organize so little that our lives are a jumble, and we are limited in the things we can enjoy because we are so inefficient in the use of our time and energy.

9. *Interaction vs. solitude*: We spend so much of our lives interacting with events and other persons that there is hardly any time for communing with God or meditating about the important issues of life. An effort is necessary to ensure a regular period of solitude. Obviously a healthy diet of interaction is also necessary.

10. *Privacy vs. openness*: We recognize the virtue of being open to each other, but there are some things which should be kept private. There are some things about ourselves that other people just can't handle and shouldn't be expected to. However, if we are private about everything, we stifle intimacy and the benefits of relationship. Total openness and total privacy are destructive.

11. *Contentment vs. dissatisfaction*: Like Paul, we need to learn to have a basic contentment with the circumstances of our lives; yet we also need to be dissatisfied with the status quo to the point where we will actively work to improve it.

12. *Nurturing vs. being nurtured*: Some people are so busy nurturing others that they wither from lack of feeding of themselves; others are so busy seeking to be nurtured that they

never feed anyone else. The Dead Sea is dead in spite of having fresh water input, because it has no outlet. We need to balance input/output; nurturing and being nurtured.

13. *Self-orientation vs. other orientation*: Most of us are too oriented toward ourselves and not enough toward the well-being of others. I know I am. But, on the other hand, it would also be destructive to be so oriented to others as to neglect the protection of our own health and sanity. Even though I have to worry more about moving more toward others than about moving too far that way, I need to be sure to maintain a healthy balance between orientation toward self and toward others.

14. *Talking vs. listening*: This is another area where reciprocity is very important. There is always a danger of doing too much talking and not enough listening; but on the other hand, there is also the danger of not speaking up and making the contribution we are capable of.

15. *Feeling vs. thinking*: Some people are so emotional that they are irrational; some people are rational machines and miss the joy of emotions. For each of us, there is a time to think soberly and keep our feelings under close control, and there are other times to stop thinking and to go with the flow, enjoying the emotional content of the experience. Our relations with other individuals will also suffer unless there is a balance between our thoughtfulness and our emotional reactions.

16. *Sacrificing for the future vs. enjoying life today*: The need for a balance here would seem to be self-evident, but it is surprising how often we can get out of balance in this area. Some people always, and perhaps we all sometimes, work so hard for the future that we fail to enjoy the life which God has given us today. Each day is a blessing unto itself, and we should not squander them, since we do not know how many days we will have. On the other hand, it is possible to be so into enjoying our present life that we fail to contribute to progress or the evolution of the future. We

may spend some days exclusively working for the future and other days exclusively enjoying the present. Or each day may have some element of each, even though some days be more heavily weighted one way or the other.

17. *Work vs. play*: All work exhausts the mind and the body; all play erodes the refreshment in play and prevents growth. When growth stops, decay sets in.

18. *Functional vs. aesthetic*: Some items are enjoyed because they are so practical And perform so beautifully the function for which they were designed. Other items may have no practical utility at all but are enjoyed strictly because they are beautiful. The designers of modern appliances try to make them highly functional and aethetically pleasing at the same time. We, ourselves, need to have a balance between being practical and being aesthetic; between spending our time on practical activities and on those that please our aesthetic senses, such as music, art, and literature.

Some of these pairs are easier than others to keep in balance. My favorite metaphor is that life is like driving a chariot pulled by multiple pairs of spirited horses. Each pair represents two complementary attributes which must be kept in careful balance. Unless the reins are carefully managed, one or the other of the pair may become too dominant and pull life's chariot off the intended and desired course, with chaotic results.

Appendix D

Growing in an Attribute

In chapter 11, we realized that one of the things that we might decide we want to do, in order to find more satisfaction in our lives, is to gradually work to improve in one of our attributes. We recognized that this is a very difficult endeavor and must be undertaken with a certain amount of personal effort in collaboration with prayer and the work of the Holy Spirit.

I would like to give a few more details of my attempt to discover how I could improve in my patience, as an example that might be helpful to readers who also want to work on one of their attributes.

Growing in Patience

I observed certain things about myself, which I interpreted as a lack of patience. These included:

1. Speeding through life without sufficiently enjoying the riches of the moment. This included being so preoccupied with achieving some goal or finishing some job that I didn't sufficiently enjoy the process of getting there.
2. Being frustrated with delays, traffic, meetings, interruptions, other people's slow conversation, red herrings that divert my path, etc.

3. Jumping to conclusions without taking the time to sufficiently gather more information or to explore other points of view.
4. Being intolerant of other people's shortcomings and impatient with their rate of progress.
5. Doubting God because I don't see Him meeting the urgent needs I see around me in the way I would expect Him to or in the timing I expect.

I could undoubtedly enumerate more, but these were sufficient to indict me.

I didn't like these things about myself and, in addition, I realized this kind of impatience is potentially destructive to my health and potentially destructive to my relationships. So I wanted to grow/improve in patience.

When thinking about an attribute I usually do two things right at the beginning: see how the dictionary defines it and see what the Bible says about it. My *Oxford Universal Dictionary* describes three aspects of patience:

1. the suffering or enduring of pain, trouble, evil, etc., with calmness and composure;
2. forbearance under provocation of any kind; especially, bearing with others, their faults, limitations, etc.;
3. the calm abiding of the issue of time, processes, and etc.

My symptoms were clearly symptoms of impatience.

Webster's Dictionary says: "Patience implies the bearing of suffering, provocation, delay, tediousness, etc., with *calmness* and *self-control*." I could really resonate with that. It isn't only bearing suffering, but also provocation, delays, tediousness, etc. Those are my problems. I don't well tolerate delays, tediousness, other provocations. But the definition of patience doesn't imply that these things don't irritate us, just that we bear them with calmness and self-control.

In order to learn more about what the Bible has to say about patience, I first referred to my biblical dictionary.* There too I learned that Patience is intertwined with endurance, forbearance,

---

* *An Expository Dictionary of New Testament Words*, W. E. Vine (Fleming H. Revell Co.) 1940.

and steadfastness. I didn't find an explicit reference to the third aspect described in the dictionary: the calm abiding of the issue of time, processes, etc. This one seems very important to me, perhaps because I am impatient in that sense. To me it means making the most of the present, without being so preoccupied with the future or conclusions that the fullness of the present is lost.

My Bible dictionary taught me that there are two different words used in the Greek text of the Bible to convey the different aspects of patience:

1. *makrothumia*, which is a quality of heart with respect to *people*, variously translated as patience, forbearance, long-suffering; and
2. *hypomone*, which is a quality of heart with respect to *trials/events*, variously translated as patience, endurance, steadfastness, and perseverance.

That reference also lists numerous particular places in the Bible where these words are used.

Next I went to my concordance.* This also lists the particular places these words are used in the New Testament in a way that I can find the ones that are used in a particular context. I found patience on page 434; endurance on page 169; forbearance, page 209; steadfastness, page 553; perseverance, page 441.

From these I learned that:

1. Patience is an essential characteristic of love (1 Cor 13:4). If I truly love others, then I will be patient with them. In order to cultivate patience with people, I have to try to love them as God loves them.
2. Patience is a necessary ingredient in Christian life (James 5:7–11). If I want to live a Christian life, then I need to try to be more patient with people and situations.

---

* *An Analytical Concordance to the Revised Standard Version of the New Testament*, Clinton Morrison (The Westminster Press: Philadelphia, PA) 1979, ISBN 0-664-20773-1.

2. Increasing my expectation of problems and delays, so that I would be less frustrated by them.
3. Trying to be satisfied with the imperfect, settling for 80 percent.
4. Have a goal of each day putting off till tomorrow something that could be done today;
5. Lowering my expectations with respect to what others will do.
6. Saying "no" to some invitations to take on tasks or responsibilities.
7. Starting 10 minutes early to get to any destination.
8. Playing favorite music in my car so I don't view time in the car as wasted time.

In addition, I need to:

1. Keep reminding myself of God's long-suffering in His patience with me as he allows me to be myself and to keep on making mistakes. Remembering His graciousness helps motivate me to be more patient and tolerant of the differences or disappointments with other people.
2. Keep rereading the biblical injunctions, and also the examples of the patience and endurance of the great biblical personalities. This biblical food is intended to fuel my growth.
3. Repeatedly pray for a graceful discipline (to change my pace, etc.) and for a disciplined grace (to enjoy doing it and seeing the beauty of it).

One thing I found to be helpful was to consider each opportunity to exhibit patience as an opportunity to make a gift to Christ. It is one thing if I try to be patient in a given situation because I ought to. It is different if my attitude is as follows:

1. I love Christ for all that He is: my savior, my guide, pure, compassionate, etc.
2. I want to give gifts to him in gratitude.

3. Each day I can identify multiple gifts for Him. Jesus said,

- "If you love Me, keep My commandments."
- "If you love Me, love your neighbor."
- "If you love your neighbor, you will be more patient with him."

4. So every time I am tempted to be impatient, I can say, "Jesus, this is hard, but I am going to back off, bear with this person or situation, as a gift to you."

While I was preparing these comments on my computer, the stupid machine went kaput! I was ready to blow up, but instead I was able to say, "Lord, instead of blowing my cool, I will try to face this provocation with calm and control, as a gift to you. Thank you for being patient with me and for loving me." Then I went back and patiently reconstructed an hour's work. That wasn't sufficient. The Lord tested me by allowing it to happen again!

Of course, I didn't miraculously become a patient man. But this approach has helped me to become a little more patient with people and with events, and also has helped me to endure. Even as I grow more patient, I am aware of my impatience. We all slip backwards as we try to go forward, and we find that as much as we desire to exhibit the better attribute, the old nature keeps reasserting itself. Even Paul suffered from that. He said:

> For that which I am doing, I do not understand; for I am not practicing what I would like to do, but am doing the very thing I hate. . . . The wishing is present in me, but the doing of the good is not. For the good that I wish, I do not do; but I practice the very evil that I do not wish. . . . I joyfully concur with the law of God in my inner man, but I see a different law in the members of my body, waging war against the law of my mind, and making me a prisoner of the law of sin which is in my members. (Rom. 7:15–23)

May God give you patience even as you strive to grow in a desired attribute.

Index

A

adapting   48
allergies   122
anticipating events   22; 39; 45
Armor of God   152-158
aspirations   189-192; app.B8
attitudes   21-22; 243-247
attributes   210-212; 251-254; app C; app D

B

backlash   246
beliefs   243; 258; 269-271
believing   258-269
Bluebook   256-257

C

change, process of   212-215; app D
changes of season   27; 31
chaos   20
children, benefiting   248-258; 302-304
Coffin, H. S.   125
constraints   194
control   19
creative stewardship   54-60
cultural impact   294-301
Cunningham, R. B.   54

D

dislocations
    types of 26; 34; 115-116; 120; 141
    author's dislocation 111-113
    preparing for 117-119
    nature of 121-124
    coping with 128-135
Dobson, J. C. 249
doubt 149-151

E

Engelson, A. L. 4
eras 28; 283; 284-290
essentials 195
events of our lives 26; 40-44

F

fear 149-151
forks
    types of 26; 30; 79
    evaluating past forks 92; app B4
    author's fork 84-91
    Jesus' fork 93-95
    coping with 95-97; 101-107; app B5
    observations about 97-101
fruit 248-251

G

generations 295-301
Givens 47; 188
goals 60; 189
Golden Rule 198
Gray, John 230
group studies 12-13; app A

H

handbook 256-257
hindrances 147
history, our own personal 180-183; 283-294
Holmes, O. W. 11

I

inclinations 192
interactive maze 37

Isaiah 12:2-3   128-129; 158-162
issues, crucial   260-263

J

Johnson, Stanley M.   3; 67; 160; 164; 214

L

limitations   194
Living Intentionally
   what is it?   8; 38; 49
   why do it?   63-68
   why so called?   49
   can I do it?   68
loss of mate   130
losses   291

M

Martians/Venusians   230-235
meditation   165-169
memoirs   256-257; 304-306
miracles   293
Moody, R. A., Jr.   217
museum   306

N

Nouwen, H. J. M.   166

O

occasions
   types of   27; 34; 173-175
   importance of   175
   observations about   176-180

P

patience   213; app D
perception types   238
personality types   228-239
perspective   278-282
Piattelli-Palmarini   99
Pipher, M.   173
planning
   current situation   204-205
   changes desired   206-207

questions for   208-210; 216
prayer   165-169
preferences   192
present, being   254
progress   277
purpose of my life   50-54

R

remaining in Christ   163-168
resources   142-147
Reviving Ophelia   173
River of Live   18

S

scars   121
self-worth   196-197
sensory types   235-237
SHAPE   225
skills   194
small group studies   12-13; app A
social types   237
stewardship   54-62
Strauss, W. & Howe, N.   301
suffering & pain   124-128

T

temperaments   228-230
thinking straight   147-149
time-line   180-183; 286; app B6; app B7

V

values   192

W

wells of salvation   158-163
Wilcox, Ellen   10
worksheets   app B

Y

Yount, D.   168

To order additional copies of

Living
Intentionally

send $16.99 plus $3.95 shipping and handling to

Books, Etc.
PO Box 4888
Seattle, WA 98104

or have your credit card ready and call

(800) 917-BOOK